FAIR AS THE MOON

Fair as the Moon
Mary, Purest of Creatures

FAIR AS THE MOON

MARY, PUREST OF CREATURES

By

FATHER M. OLIVER, O. C.S.O.

MOUNT ST. JOSEPH ROS CRÉ

THIRD IMPRESSION

THE NEWMAN PRESS
Westminster, Maryland

First Printed, December 1949.
Second Impression, January 1950.
Third Impression, July 1952.

Nihil Obstat :

FR. M. DOMINICUS NOLAN, O. CIST. R. } *Censores.*
FR. M. IOANNES MORSON, O. CIST. R.

Imprimatur :

FR. M. CAMILLUS CLAFFEY, O. CIST. R.

Abbas.

Nihil Obstat ;

EDUARDUS GALLEN,
Censor Theol. Deput

Imprimi Potest :

✠ IOANNES CAROLUS,
Archiep Dublinen,
Hiberniæ Primas

Dublini, die 2° *Decembris, anno* 1949.

Made in the Republic of Ireland.

To
MOTHER BRIGID
AND TO
MARGARET AND BETA
THIS BOOK
IS GRATEFULLY DEDICATED
BY THE AUTHOR

CONTENTS

vii

PREFACE

THAT A child should think lovingly about its mother needs no apology. If, moreover, he goes so far as to write down his thoughts for her honour and his own pleasure, it still remains absolutely his own business. But if he claims that what he has written holds an interest for others also, then may he be fairly asked to substantiate this claim. The author makes just this claim for his thoughts on the best of mothers and this preface is his attempt to justify what to many may well appear an unwarranted assumption.

In the beautiful and most touching discourse of Christ after His Last Supper, the Divine Master promised the Holy Ghost to His apostles. "But the Paraclete, the Holy Ghost whom the Father will send in My name, He will teach you all things, and bring all things to your mind, whatsoever I shall have said to you" (St. John xiv, 26). The apostolic age saw the perfect fulfilment of that Divine promise. What the Church through Pope or Council has done ever since is to declare the content of revelation, not to add thereto.

This truth has a special application to the development of devotion to Mary from the earliest times. Let it be remembered that when the greatest and grandest things are said about her they are no new things. They are, if you will, a clearer expression of the old abiding truth.

Almost from the beginning Mary has been the object of reverent and loving enquiry, issuing, of course, in a deepening volume of praise.

Perhaps it is particularly in relation to her that it may be said that no one ever says anything worthy about her to-day which has not been far better said yesterday by the very Fathers of the Church. Why, then, do we keep on gilding the lily? Above all why does the present writer dare to add his voice to the divine symphony and further claim that he is sounding a note that is new, in the theme which is so old?

Despite the richness and abundance of literature on Mary a

want was felt by some souls. Amongst these latter may be
counted the great saint of modern times, St. Thérèse of the Child
Jesus. She complained that certain sermons and books on Our
Lady so exalted her that she would appear to be utterly inimit-
able by ordinary humans. Such sermons in particular reaped
an abundant harvest of exclamations from their audience, but
nothing more. The greatness of Mary sometimes tempts writers
and preachers to forget her humanity. This was a danger which
threatened to obscure even the sacred humanity of Christ Himself. But He checked that impulse at its very inception. And
when it rose again in the early heresy of the Docetae, He smote
it again through His Living Church. Let us watch it in its first
beginning. " Now whilst they were speaking these things, Jesus
stood in the midst of them, and said to them: Peace be to
you, it is I, fear not. But they being troubled and frighted,
supposed that they saw a spirit. And He said to them: Why
are you troubled, and why do thoughts arise in your hearts?
See My hands and feet, that it is I myself, handle, and see,
for a spirit hath not flesh and bones, as you see Me to have.
And when He had said this, He shewed them His hands and
feet. But while they yet believed not, and wondered for joy,
He said: Have you here anything to eat? And they offered
Him a piece of a broiled fish, and a honeycomb. And when
He had eaten before them, taking the remains, He gave to
them " (St. Luke xxiv, 36-43).

. These inspired words filled the author of this book with joy.
For they emboldened him to contemplate Mary, not in the
clouds, but living her life amongst ordinary men and women.
He has tried to do for Mary what the Divine Master found it
necessary to do for Himself, and in the very same way. For
he has endeavoured to present a virgin who has flesh and blood
and bones, a virgin who eats and sleeps and talks. For in all
truth Mary did all those things.

We know that prophetic vision has seen Our Lady crowned
with stars and with the moon beneath her feet. But the fact
is that over the period of a life which tradition holds to have
been full of years, Mary had the moon and the stars high above
her very human head in that holy land where she once lived
as countless others lived before and after her.

A word now as to the method employed. The author has
only a horror for fairy-tales woven around God's holy ones.
They do not need them and still less does their Queen. He

will keep within the limits of the most legitimate deductions
from Mary's office and endowments. It will be in the field
of the practical results of her immaculate conception that he
will find and display the rarest treasures of beauty and dignity,
and above all of Mary's kinship with human kind. Let the
reader look for this in these pages, certainly not for profound
learning. As already expressed, spiritual and intellectual giants
have written about God's mother. But she is the mother of
the present writer too. May he not write about her with his
own love and in his own way?

FR. M. O., O. C.S.O.

November 21, 1949.

Feast of the Presentation of Our Lady,
Cistercian Abbey of Mount St. Joseph,
Ros Cré.

FAIR AS THE MOON

CHAPTER I

THE HUMILITY OF HIS HANDMAID

WE have already stated it as our object to begin at the beginning. What then was the beginning of the Blessed Virgin? The answer is as true for each one of us as for her, and it is that Mary began by being "Nothing." We are told by the Holy Spirit, using St. John as His instrument, that "In the beginning was the Word and the Word was with God, and the Word was God" (St. John i, 1). See there is no mention of Mary, because in that ineffable beginning of which St. John speaks, only God is, in the sovereign loneliness of His Divine Essence and in the company and fruitfulness of the Divine Trinity. Mary is not. No creature as yet is, no angel, no man, nothing at all. The shoreless, fathomless abyss of utter nothingness still holds, as it were, in its dark depths all creatures, and Mary, too, with them all. Over these formless waters the Spirit of God has not yet walked.

What a beginning! And it is Mary's. And she eternally exults in that primal truth "Because He hath regarded the humility of His handmaid."

We would invite all our poor separated Brethren who object to the honour we Catholics pay to Mary to join with us in this fundamental meditation on Mary's beginning. For their teachers will never say less in favour of Mary than we gladly say about her primal origin. For what can be less than nothing? And that is how Mary began. We are dealing now with the one capital limitation in Mary, a limitation involving no fault because it is simply inherent in her very being as in the being of us all. We mean her "Creaturehood."

By that one fact an impassable gulf is raised between Mary and God. God is. Mary, in her origin, is not. All is expressed by saying that Mary is always a creature. No prerogative, no endowment, no eulogy, thought, said or written can alter that fact of creaturehood, and all such praise must ever be interpreted in the light of it.

Let us dig deep the foundations of this Tower of David, deep into the very abyss of utter nothingness. For strange as it may appear, we are thereby establishing all the reality and loveliness that will be. And here again we ask the earnest attention of those to whom Mary's glory, as we Catholics see it, is a scandal.

By emphasising the nothingness from which Mary was drawn we concentrate attention on Him who did actually draw her forth into being—and what being! Tell us this, dear protesters against Mary, since she was originally nothing, surely what she is to be lies neither with you nor me, not indeed with Luther or Calvin, not even with St. Bernard or St. Alphonsus Maria Liguori, not even with Mary herself but solely with her Creator. It is into His Blessed Eyes we must look if we are to see the plan of her being. For He is the planner. And from His very nature as God, if we retain the Christian concept of the Deity we are forced to deduce certain facts about Mary, as about us all. One of the first of these facts will give us the material for the next chapter. And by one of these delightful paradoxes, in which Christianity abounds, it will be seen to apparently contradict the basic statement with which we began. For we said, nay, we shouted, that Mary began by being nothing. Now we must realise that there is a very real sense in which Mary always was. Because God is by nature immutable it follows that if He creates anything in time He must have designed that creature's existence in eternity and from eternity. He said as much to the Prophet Jeremias: " I have loved thee with an everlasting love." Mary is a reality. She exists. Therefore she has always existed in the Divine Mind, as planned, as designed. It can no longer be imputed against Mary if that Divine Plan involved for her being incomparable grandeur. Nor can it be urged against Catholics as a fault that seeing God's plain plan for Mary they not only accept it, but are even glad of it, are exultant even. Can we oppose the Spirit which spoke through her, coupling her essential nothingness with God's plan for her and the natural sequel, the approbation of all other creatures? Hear her own words. " Because He hath regarded the humility of His handmaid, for behold from henceforth all generations shall call me blessed " (St. Luke, i, 48).

CHAPTER II

HAVING gazed into that abyss of nothingness from which all creatures, including Mary, were drawn, let us now turn our eyes to an abyss of quite another kind, even to that infinite ocean of all that is, to the source of all being, to the Great Creator, blessed for ever more.

Through Revelation God has deigned to tell us all that is necessary for us to know of His Divine nature and attributes. With adoring reverence let us now reflect on that Divine nature. God alone is, in the fullest sense of the weighty term, no creature has any existence apart from God. God has existence in Himself, and from Himself. He subsists. He is very existence, very being. He alone is necessary and self-sufficient. While being One in Essence He is Three in Persons. Even before He is Creator, He is Father, God the Father, the First Person of the Adorable Trinity. He is the Beginning without any beginning, the Principle without any principle. He is infinite. God is Intellect, and God is Will. By an ineffable and immanent act of the Divine intelligence God knows Himself. That is to say, He perfectly and adequately comprehends His own divine perfections in their totality. To use the language borrowed from human mental operations God thinks a thought perfectly embodying His own infinite perfections, and He utters an ineffable word perfectly expressing His thought. But human analogy must now be corrected. For God's utterance of His Thought must not be considered as externating It, as when we externate our thoughts by giving verbal expression to them. The activity of the Blessed Trinity is immanent. Moreover, while our verbal expression by no means gives external reality to our thoughts, the Father's utterance begets a Word, who is a Person, One with the Father, and coequal with Him. "In the beginning was the Word, and the Word was with God, and the Word was God" (St. John i, 1). God is also Will. And beholding His Divine Word, adequately expressing all His own

3

Divine Perfections, God the Father loves the Word with all the love of His Godhead, and the Word returns that love in the same infinite measure. But this very mutual love of Father and Son is a subsistent person, even the Holy Ghost, proceeding from the Father and Son by spiration, as the theologians express it. This, then, is the revealed doctrine of the Most Adorable Trinity. We see that God is, that moreover there is in Him infinite unity and yet infinite fruitfulness in the divine flowering of the Three Persons. We see that God by His very Nature is both subsistent and self-sufficing. But He is also infinite Goodness. And as Goodness is diffusive of itself, God quite freely determines to create, that is, to draw out of nothing beings upon whom His own pulsating life shall pour in torrents of actuality and well-being, creatures who will glorify His adorable attributes.

CHAPTER III

THE fiat is said. And behold God surrounded by myriads of His first creatures. These are spiritual substances, endowed with intelligence and will. But it was not God's design to people Heaven with beautiful statuary. These are living, thinking beings and, above all, they are free. Our centuries of time have robbed many a word of its native meaning. And freedom is such a pilfered concept. But here, in the first flush of the angelic creation, free will demands no analysis. It is obvious. These new creatures, in all the fresh exultancy of their new-found being, are free, gloriously free to look into their Creator's Eyes and read therein both their own origin and His plan for them. Could a creature demand more, or a Creator less? What did they see? We can only surmise. But this much is certain, that, as all their good began through Him, so its permanence must be bound up with His Will, which, indeed, is Himself. Will being accept its being, the mode of its being willed by the infinitely loving Creator? Will these pure spirits, untrammelled by flesh, find any room for yea and nay in their choice? Was God taking or imposing a risk when He created such a noble freedom for so delightful a destiny? To-day, men say they are puzzled by many things, by the permissive Will of God, by the uneven distribution of wealth . . . but sin they seem to understand well. It is so understandable!

No, a million times no. The spirit of truth has thrown out the challenge. "Who can understand sin?" In the angels above all who can understand the hideous defect drawn out of their own flawless being, whereby some, even many, would not choose the blessed Will of their Creator? Now is there added to the Divine harmonies of the Deity the jubilant hosannahs of the angel choirs. And in the very ears of God are heard also the blasphemies of the damned. Hell has begun.

Before we turn to the creation of the human race a word may be opportune touching the swift and immediate punishment of

5

the rebel angels. We saw that those spiritual substances were endowed with intelligence and free will. Now, the proper object of intelligence is truth and that of the will is good. The latter is a blind faculty and must be instructed by the intelligence. In the case of the angels, their probation very likely precluded the full light of truth shining upon their intelligence, yet perfectly true it was, if dimmed to allow of meritorious choice. Their wills were offered true good. And these wills were made to embrace the good when thus presented. Their vision was not distorted by any external illusion or corrupted by any miasma of a perverted sense. In spite of all this some of them made the great refusal. Moreover, such pure spirits could not waver in their decision. When they chose they chose wholly, they chose for ever. This is quite relevant to our purpose, for it shows up the tremendous gift of free will with the equally tremendous responsibilities involved. We see that God will respect this gift of His even if it be abused with consequences of eternal tragedy. Also, we will not be likely to take things for granted when another free human creature will be offered God's Plan and will say : " Behold the handmaid of the Lord. Be it done unto me according to Thy Word."

The creation of the angels did not exhaust either the Divine omnipotence or His infinite goodness. This latter will now flow over a new race of beings who in their composition will be a " little less than the angels," sharing, indeed, their spiritual nature, but enclosed in bodies framed from no celestial star dust, but from the slime of the newly-created earth. As we are hurrying on to our real objective, we would say but a word in passing about the doctrine of evolution. It would be well for all Catholics to realise that for children of the Church evolution may be considered only in relation to the human body and not at all in relation to the immortal soul which forms that body. It is the soul which makes man what he is, and the soul is the direct creation of God. We have God's word for that. There is at least room for intermediate processes in the revealed fact that man's body was fashioned from earth's slime. And our modern scientists have right here and now— we are writing in the late winter of 1947—delivered what may be fairly regarded as the *coup de grâce* to old father ape. For they have now discovered remains of an undoubted " man " who predates the apes by millions of years.

The first in order of the inspired books tells us in sober

language the origin of our race. Perhaps we have never read the account with the reverence, awe, gratitude and exultation which it deserves. For we forget that it is a Divine record of an act of God, an act which both explains how we began and why we continue. We are familiar with the sequence. God created Adam, and then Eve. And once more He will no more people earth with statues than heaven. So our first parents are free to choose all that God has planned for them. Moreover, although corporeal spirits, unlike their elder brothers, the angels, they are endowed with a perfect intellect pointing infallibly to truth, and a flawless will ready to embrace the good when it is pointed out by the intellect. This time we are not left to surmise the nature of the trial. The Divine word has told us as much about it as is necessary. To their free will was offered by the great Creator every variety of fruit-bearing tree, with just one reserve. After all, it is a very modest thing for the Creator to have but one reserve.

We know what happened. But before we leave the Garden of Eden with our banished parents we will consider one point which is too often ignored. Unbelievers scoff at a simple apple involving such tragic issues. And there are not a few Catholics who would really prefer if revelation had pointed to a graver misdemeanour. But what actually happened in that beautiful paradise of earth? There is a theological school which would hold that in any case God would become Man. What we are now going to say must not be thought to be just that. But this much is certain: our first parents in deciding to sin decided thereby that when the Word of God should come to His own, it should be as a Man of Sorrows. How our radical selfishness prevents us from seeing things from God's point of view! And that is the reason why so few people read all this into the momentous drama in the primeval garden. But let us remember what we have already said about the Divine nature. God is. He is an Eternal now. It is only for us creatures of a day that the scroll called Time must be unrolled page by page. And how little of the script is even glimpsed by the individual! It is quite otherwise with God. He sees all now. And for this reason we may say with truth that Eden became the very vestibule of a hall which would be Pilate's. Up, up from the distant future stands clear the vision of One Who is accused. Our first parents were the wretched leaders in that later hellish chorus: " Crucify Him, crucify

Him." Truly, the disordered appetites of these two anticipated
the mob that would be. We too, were there. Far more truly
and with more terrible and more university significance was
that affront implicit in the rebellion of our first parents than
ever in Jewish mouths. "His blood be upon us and on our
children." Yes, the great refusal has again been made, this
time for us, too. Oh, dark had become that first morning
of creation, and the gloom of night has settled on the earth.
But see, oh, can it be, is that a ray of purest light which has
defied the dark? It is, even so. Behold the sweet shining of
the star of the morn!

CHAPTER IV

OUR LADY OF EDEN

WHEN God's creative fiat went forth and the spirit of God moved over the initial chaos, darkness fled before the created light. Movement after movement of the Divine generosity issued in order, verdure, beauty and in living souls. Then came the catastrophe. God's gifts are without repentance and the sun still shone. But it was as if the true light of its light had been extinguished. Still sang the birds, but their primal song was not there with its exultant note. They were dirgers now. The luxuriant beauty of foliage and flower was but the sickly parasitic clinging to mouldering coffins and to dead men's bones. But it was above all in the souls of the first pair that the sun had set. In a word, death had come. Not yet in very deed, but its shadow was over all. The calm beauty of innocent creation had given place to a dark, turbulent sea. And yet, as we have already said, that dark, far-spreading ocean was not without its silver-trimmed horizon. Far, far off a dawn was already heralded by Divine prophecy. In order to realise even a little the darkness that was, and to appraise even now the effulgent light of which the first glimmerings were already visible, we must examine the tragic happenings in the first Eden. God had but one plan for the angels. He had no second one of reparation. Their dowry was complete in that keen, penetrating intelligence, in that mighty will which could love or hate for ever. They saw what they saw. They chose. It is all over. Harmonies of legion choirs resound. Eternal blasphemies also rise to the ear of God. It is so now. It will ever be so.

Not so did God deal with His creatures of clay. And yet He might have done so. It is true that our first parents were not pure spirits. But what is the intended deduction, that their choice was impeded? A thousand times no! Theirs, too, was a flawless intelligence, working through media, it is true, yet perfectly endowed to extract truth from all presented

9

objects. Their wills, too, were swift and strong, and at least potentially unerring. Not as yet were the mists arising from a corrupt sensibility. Far be it from us to carp at our first mother. But we want to appreciate our second one. And so we will calmly examine what Eve really did. We will see what the great God has said about the matter. " And the Lord God took man, and put him into the paradise of pleasure, to dress it, and to keep it. And He commanded him, saying: 'Of every tree of paradise thou shalt eat, but of the tree of knowledge of good and evil thou shalt not eat. For in what day soever thou shalt eat of it, thou shalt die the death.' And the Lord God said: ' It is not good for man to be alone, let us make him a help like unto himself ' " (Genesis, Chapter ii, verses 15-18). Then follows the description of the creation of Eve.

Let us return for a moment to the angels. For, alas, they returned to us! Could there be a more cogent proof of the implacable hatred of the fallen angels for God and for all that pertains to God than their intervention in human affairs, and especially their first intervention?

" Now the serpent was more subtle than any of the beasts of the earth, which the Lord God had made. And he said to the woman . . ." (Genesis iii, 1). Here we must go slowly. For we are apt to lose a lot of the significance of an event which has never ceased to affect the world and each one of us—save only one.

Snakes have never spoken to sober human beings since snakes or humans began. It was no serpent of earth that addressed Eve, but the spiritual intelligence which used the serpent as his mouthpiece. Now, in the first ecstasy of their new being we may well believe that our first parents were prepared for anything. In themselves they had experienced and were still experiencing the exultant effects of the creative fiat, and they saw it likewise at work in all the objects which surrounded them. They had not yet reached that blasé attitude to creation's wonders which makes moderns yawn at it all, aye, and question the Creator's rights and power. It cannot be; it must not be, were phrases completely foreign to their vocabulary.

But we must not confuse this fresh and wholesome reaction to creation with stupidity. Our first parents were children in the highest, noblest sense, but they were far from being childish. And

Eve must have known by a flash of illuminating intuition that there was something here at least calculated to arouse a salutary and defensive doubt. Let us here yield to the impulse to bridge the centuries between. We see a second Eve. And no serpent speaks to her, but a resplendent archangel. And this Eve's reaction? "Who having heard was troubled at his saying, and thought with herself what manner of salutation this should be" (St. Luke, i, 29). O Eve, our first mother, why did you not yield to the warnings of your peerless intelligence?

Whatever trust characterised Eve in her first innocence and which would have prepared her for a voice proceeding even from a serpent, the very next word should have brought the conversation to a close. "Why hath God commanded you that you should not eat of every tree of paradise?" (Genesis iii, 1). We are here brought to the very kernel of all that was wrong with the world then or now, and that is the inexplicable and execrable fact of sin. Here at least nothing has changed in a world where almost everything else has altered. For in its essence sin is to-day what it so clearly was in the angels and what the Divine Word shows it to be in our first parents. For what is it but the abuse of creaturehood in its very essence? Let us analyse it here. For if our modern world is characterised by any outstanding vice, rather than by just every possible one, it is its loss of the sense of sin. The ancient Greeks knew how to sin, but they were saturated with a very wholesome sense of sin's sinfulness. Hybris, they called it, and their dramas are always woven around the theme of sin and sin's punishment. But our age has even a new vocabulary from which the very word sin is deleted. Men are no longer dubbed immoral, but merely amoral. A pretty piece of philology surely, insinuating that when a man owns to no code he can violate none. But sin is a fact. And sin is what God sees it to be. In the first Divine record of creation we see the monstrous thing developing before our eyes. Let us face up to it. Sin, as we have said, is the violation of creaturehood. It will take many forms, but it is always that at bottom. For what does it mean to be a creature? Things stand in various relations to men, and men one to another, but in all the world of created things there is no relation similar to that which exists between the Creator and His creatures. There was nothing. And now there is something or someone. The Creator has wholly made the creature by a mere act of will. He creates mind with all its modes, all its powers and its limitations. There is a point against which the insufferable pride of men has ever thrown itself in impotent rage, namely, the limitations inevitable in the creature. He has made the faculties and their proper objects, the senses and all the wide range of their actions. Moreover, having brought all into being, He must conserve it in being at every moment by a continued fiat. To whom can the creature go for information concerning its new being if not to its Author? Where can it get an adequate concept of being or good or truth if not from the Creator of all the being, goodness and truth which it possesses? Will the creature bandy words with its Creator? Will it cry out "Why" to any of His Wills? A reverent " how " is possible as when another later on will ask " How shall this be done . . . ?" (St. Luke i,34). And so when Eve heard the audacious question hurled at the Divine Will she should have turned away immediately from the tempter. By speaking he had shown himself to be no mere harmless serpent of earth, but the Fallen One, and by asking a justification of the Divine command he had discarded the mask completely. Alas, Eve continued the fatal conversation. Already the venom of the abominable viper was infecting her. For listen to the turn she gives the Divine threat. " But of the fruit of the tree which is in the midst of paradise, God hath commanded us that we should not eat, and that we should not touch it, lest perhaps we die" (Gen. iii, 3). No, Eve, that it not what God said. In Him there is no yea and nay, no " perhaps." " For in what day soever thou shalt eat of it, thou shalt die the death" (Gen. ii, 17).

Later on, and many centuries later, that same malevolent intelligence will bandy texts of Scripture with Scripture's Author. And he will be discomfited by true texts, true in their application and true in their content. Here poor Eve is the progenitor of all those who, consciously or unconsciously, receive the devil's interpretation of verses quoted falsely by the liar from the beginning.

Those there are who wonder why God permitted the devil so to tempt our first parents. We will be content to answer just this, there were absolutely no odds weighted against them in the conflict. For the devil had one weapon only and that a negative one, namely, a lie. He was forced to betray himself at every move, first by speaking through a creature of its own nature calculated to keep even unfallen Eve at just a civil distance, and secondly, by contradicting the Creator's Word, he gave Eve the sufficient cue towards the breaking off of the conversation.

Now the devil grows bolder. Although we tremble to say it, he gives the lie to God. " And the serpent said to the woman : ' No, you shall not die the death. For God doth know that, in what day soever you shall eat thereof, your eyes shall be opened and you shall be as gods, knowing good and evil ' " (Gen. iii, 4, 5). We have said that the sin of the angels is unknown to us in its precise nature. But theological opinion believes it to have been one of proud desire to be equal to God. May we not take a clue from the very name of the great arch-angel who led the hosts of loyal angels, Michael, that is, who is like to God?

At any rate, we may well read an echo of Lucifer's fall in those audacious words to Eve : " You shall be as gods." There is an old saying : " Fool me once, more shame you, fool me twice, more shame me."

Here in the very dawn of creation we find Satan's technique revealed to us. And he has not been able to add anything to it except the fresh forms with which experience and each succeeding age enables him to camouflage it.

First of all, he can never make any suggestion to us without in some way disturbing the soul into vigilance. The speaking serpent should have at least performed that office for our highly endowed first mother.

Then he questions God's prescriptions. He hurls his eternal " why " against the blessed Creator.

The question has assumed different forms with the lapse of time, but it is ever the same impious revolt of the creature. Why has God created souls when He knew they would be lost eternally? Why does He permit temptation? Why does He permit evil? And a thousand other interrogations of the Creator by the puny creature. And even now we do not read a lesson into Eve's folly. We listen, we try to answer, to apologise for God, to soften down His dogmas. Hell, oh yes, but . . . the Church, well, you see . . . the Pope, oh, I am not an out and out Papist—all an echo of Eve's softening down of the direct Word of God—" lest perhaps we die." In all the centuries which have passed we have sad realisation of the significance of Eve's " perhaps."

" And the woman saw that the tree was good to eat, and fair

to the eyes, and delightful to behold and she took of the fruit thereof, and did eat, and gave to her husband who did eat" (Gen. iii, 6).

These are the most tragedy-fraught lines ever penned. The impious crescendo of creature-rebellion has reached its swelling climax. First of all, a creature's voice is listened to instead of God. This is too constant. Then it was the serpent who was believed, other voices there will be from the first heresiarchs right down to our moderns. And all of them with adherents.

Next the senses, God's creatures too, are enrolled against Him. " And the woman saw . . ." all the excellencies of creatures put into them by God alone now become baits for rebellion, " good to eat and fair to the eyes and delightful to behold." See the warping of judgment, the poisoning of the actual data furnished by the senses. For the tree was not good to eat— the senses had never said that.

And what was the devil's contribution to all this attractive presentation? Nothing, save a lie.

Our age has witnessed the harnessing of atomic energy and Japan has tasted the dead sea fruit of scientific achievement. We are even promised bigger and better explosions later on. But when our first parents sinned the devil expected there and then the atomic resolution of the universe which would have cried finis to it all. And why would he not expect it? Here was sin. Here was that thing which had already happened in heaven and which was being already punished by eternal banishment from God and woeful torment of penal fires.

Why was this new world still existing? Why were Adam and Eve still there in the garden instead of with him in the inferno?

We, too, should ask these questions. For we were there. Our destiny, too, was at stake. And as far as could be seen our destiny was eternally wrecked. When the angels sinned they found themselves on the moment involved in the punishment of their rebellion. God had no further parley with them. Surely it must have whetted that diabolical envy of the human race to harbour the suspicion that God had a plan of mercy for them as well as of justice. And that suspicion became a certainty when, to his unutterable rage and confusion, he heard the Voice: " And the Lord God called Adam, and said to him : ' Where art thou?'" It is characteristic of merely human eloquence to cover poverty of thought with an abundance of words, to express very little truth in very involved language.

How different it is with the Word of God. See what a complete picture of innocence, integrity and happiness is limned for us by the single verse: " And they were both naked, to wit, Adam and his wife, and were not ashamed " (Gen. ii, 25). We are not told how long this state of affairs lasted. It seems as if such time data so necessary to the learned discourses of modern scientific historians did not appear necessary to the Eternal God when He deigned to tell us truths necessary for our salvation. But the end of innocence is very clearly indicated and in words just as sparing and significant withal. " And the eyes of them both were opened. And when they perceived themselves to be naked, they sewed together fig-leaves and made themselves aprons " (Gen. iii, 7). In case we would have missed the connection of cause and effect, God said to Adam: " And who hath told thee that thou wast naked, but that thou hast eaten of the tree whereof I commanded thee that thou shouldst not eat?" (Gen. iii, 11). We have said that creation is not an event which happened, but one which happens. These inspired words tell us of what God has done and is now doing. Alas, how near to the first sin is our present experience. Every son of Adam, with one exception, tastes to the full the present horror of that first opening of eyes to a nature denuded of its original endowments.

Let us now hear what God says to that fallen intelligence clothed in the serpent's form. And the Lord God said to the serpent: " Because thou hast done this thing, thou art cursed among all cattle, and beasts of the earth. Upon thy breast shalt thou go, and earth shalt thou eat all the days of thy life . . . I will put enmities between thee and the woman and thy seed and her seed, and she shall crush thy head, and thou shalt lie in wait for her heel " (Gen. iii, 14, 15). Who is this mysterious woman of whom God thus speaks? Who is He Who will be her seed? And how strange that a woman alone, without any mention of a man, should be accredited with seed? Not Eve, certainly, for she had just concluded a pact with death and hell. She was indeed the potential enemy of the serpent, but now she is seared with his slime. Not any seed of hers and Adam's for now that seed is corrupted in its very source. In one generation she will bring forth a murderer, the progenitor of countless others.

No indeed, we know who this blessed woman is and we know her Divine Seed.

It is as if even the great God cannot wholly conceal the ineffable secret of His mercy.

Already He mentions her, giving to our first parents that light of hope which sustained them, and later the Twelve Tribes, until the dawn came and the Morning Star brought forth the Sun of Justice. O, Our Lady of Eden, already at the very time and in the very place of our calamity, we salute thee!

And once more we invite all those to whom our praise of Mary is distasteful. Come, now, you who claim to reverence the Book. Tell us who is the first to mention her? Who is the first to outline her magnificent rôle in the eternal enmity between light and darkness, between good and evil? In a word, who is the first to be devoted to the fair creature, the masterpiece of His mercy and His love through whom and through whom alone the one and only Mediator was to come?

Cease, then, your cavillings, ignorant when not criminal! Join with the great Creator, join with the Church of Christ, join with each and every humblest of Catholic believers and salute with us the Bright Star of Morn. Our Lady of Eden, we salute thee. Pray for us, poor banished children of Eve.

CHAPTER V

THE DIVINE PLAN

WHILE our first parents are fleeing from the Garden of Delights, affrighted by God's just punishment, yet consoled by the promise of future mercy, let us, in reverence and awe and yet with love, gaze into the ever placid depths of the Three in One. For placid they are, without the slightest ruffle on that infinite Ocean of Peace. It will be in His own light that we, too, shall behold light, for in our faith He has enabled us to see Him as He is, though now in a dark manner.

All the operations of the Most Adorable Trinity are immanent. The ineffable begetting, the Divine Filiation, the Processions of the Third Person and the Circuminession of the Persons, all are immanent. Now, creation has taken place out of an act of infinite love, and for the first time creatures exist outside of God, though utterly dependent on Him. In Him they live, and are, yet they are not God. The peaceful depths of the Deity remain undisturbed. A new attribute of God has been brought into play by the Fall, both angelic and human. It is no new attribute in so far as it is God Himself under a certain aspect, and God always is apart from aspects. But it is new inasmuch as it had no proper object until creatures furnished that proper object. We refer to His justice.

Now God's justice operates according to the Divine Plan for this or that creature. For the angels He had one plan. In human language we can put it something like this: A strong illumination was to flood an equally strong will with light, urging a choice of God and His Will. This illumination was not to be a series of lights waxing and waning, but one strong, flawless beam. Nor was the will to be vacillating and dubious, but immediate, certain, eternal.

All the odds were for a correct choice and an eternal felicity. Some of the angelic beings acted against the clear light, refused God instead of choosing Him. Now Divine justice comes into play and, withdrawing the scorned light, leaves the perverted wills in their eternal disorder. That is the history of hell's commencement.

In the case of our first parents and the human race, God has a second plan, one of justice to be sure, but one also of reparation. The Fall has taken place. Let us see what is taking place in the Blessed Trinity. Eternally the Father begets His Word, eternally the Holy Ghost proceeds from the Father and Son. And God's first plan—we speak in human-wise—for the human race is shattered by the sin of our first parents. Then His second plan comes into operation. In the silent depths of the Godhead an ineffable counsel of the Divine Persons may be imagined to take place. It did take place, but not as human counsels with discussion, objection and decision.

The Word sees the outraged majesty of His Eternal Father and, with a movement which is one with His Godhead, offers Himself as Repairer of the Divine Honour, and thereby Saviour of humankind: " Behold, I come." The Father, in His great love for the world, delivers His Only-begotten for its redemption while the Holy Ghost, by His Divine Operation, accomplishes the Mystery in time.

But what are the details of this Divine Plan of Reparation? Once more God Himself has left us in no doubt.

The Second Person of the Most Adorable Trinity, the Only-begotten of the Father, will become man. That is to say He will assume a human nature while remaining forever in the bosom of the Eternal Father, and this human nature will be hypostatically united to the Divine Person. But where will the Word get His human nature? Will it be created from nothing? Will the Second Person descend from the clouds already clothed in this garb of flesh and blood, woven by even angel fingers? No, that will not be God's plan. His Word will become flesh by being born of a woman, bone of her bone, flesh of her flesh. Without any father on earth He will be His mother's Son more truly than any son of any earthly mother.

And it was the first divulgings of this sweet, Divine secret that fell on our first parents' ears when they heard God menacing the serpent with the woman who was yet to be.

CHAPTER VI

DECET, ERGO

"Wishful thinking" is a phrase which apparently our current age has coined. And it stands for base coinage in the mint of reality. Nevertheless, there is one sphere wherein it has always been admitted as a quite legitimate and laudable practice. That sphere is none other than what may be called speculative theology. Here "wishful thinking" is a traditional practice, but it is shorn of all caprice and unreality with which it is necessarily associated in things quite profane. The process has its objective and its rules. It may be explained someway like this. We reverently review the actual content of Divine Revelation as we know it here and now. Already we are aware of certain things which God has done. He has revealed them Himself. Quite legitimately, therefore, we may deduce other things which God is likely to have done. After all, by revelation God has to a certain extent revealed His mind, His attitude to things, His point of view, so to speak. We also employ those radical and wholesome instincts which God Himself has implanted in all human nature. These instincts give us a very fair idea of what ought to be done under certain circumstances. In other words, they are signposts to congruity.

When we engage in "wishful thinking" in this theological way we possess a tremendous advantage. We have as one factor God Himself, who has, to say the least of it, a much nicer mind than His creatures for the congruities; secondly, He is absolutely able to realise every congruous programme. Now, theologians do not claim too much for this process. It does not of itself create a dogma. But it often prepares the Christian conscience for an actual Dogma which is in the content of revelation, though as yet undefined.

And a very big element inducing a final authoritative definition is always this universal Christian consensus. It is right here and now paving the way, we trust, for the definition of Our Lady's Corporal Assumption. But we must not go too fast. We are still in the wrecked Garden of Eden, and we are going to employ this method of wishful thinking. Of course we know the end of the story already. But we can still have the thrill of seeing how right and proper that beautiful ending is. So let us start. We will first ask a question. Just how much does God the Father love His Only Begotten Son? Only God could adequately answer that question. For it asks the length and depth and profundity of the Divine Life itself. And God the Father will fashion a worthy mother for this Son of His love. Nay. The Word will create His own mother, for He and the Father are one. That is to say, He alone will have the unique power of choosing His Own Mother and making her so. As all the Divine operations are common to the Three Persons, the Holy Ghost will create this woman. And this time His Light will suffer no reverse, as in the creation of Eve. There never was darkness, there never would be darkness in this lightsome being.

What, then, will God do? Will He look out over the sin-wrecked human race and, choosing one already involved in the hideous deprivation, restore her to justice and then raise her to the Divine motherhood? Let us soberly examine what this would involve. On the moment that Adam became a partner in his wife's guilt, he and she and all their future progeny became, at least juridically, and, indeed, in fact, infected with that ugly deformation which we call sin. In our first parents it was actual sin, in their offspring it was original sin. This latter, while not involving personal guilt, did entail all the deformity which followed in the wake of the first transgression. Now we must at least try to realise what sin means in the eyes of God.

We humans have many loves and hates. One of our modern wise men has such an abhorrence of corruption vermin that he cannot imagine any really nice God would create such. The fact is that God has done so. Therefore, it would seem that God sees nothing hateful in these little beasties. Others there are who would have left rats out of the scheme of things. God has decidedly included them. And we could go on like this for a long time. But God hates sin. Hates it with all the omnipotence of His Godhead, hates it eternally. It must therefore be very hateful intrinsically. Even we can come to a better realisation of its odious nature by honest meditation. If we reflect upon creaturehood and the dependence it necessarily involves we come to see even in a dim way how malicious it is for the creature to defy its Great Creator. We go a step further and grasp the ingratitude of sin when we face up to the fact that the creature insults by sin the infinite gratuitous love which has brought it into being. Perhaps the most convincing proof is one which we have suggested already in our very first pages, namely, that sin derives its greatest horror in the Divine eyes from its effects in time on the Word made Flesh, that is, on God Himself. In light inaccessible it is hard for us to understand how sin can reach out at God. But even to the dullest mind the fact is painfully plain in a God Man agonising on a cross. Sin killed God, when, by taking passible flesh, God put Himself into the reach of sin.

Need we again ask if it is likely that God will choose a mother for His Son from that "massa Damnata," that ferment of utter damnation that was the human race when its first parents had spurned Their Patrimony?

How will this woman be endowed by nature and grace who is to be the most real Mother of the Word Incarnate? Let us think out all that is involved in this concept of Motherhood. The Word is to become Flesh without the co-operation of any earthly father to be sure, but nevertheless completely after the manner of any other child of woman. That is to say, He will be enclosed in a human womb for nine months and during that time will receive from His Mother all that any infant receives from his mother. The least sequel to this wonderful fact will be that the mother of God will be a perfect woman even physically. It was not for nothing that later on the Spirit of Truth will inspire His Evangelist to record the blessing invoked on the womb that bore Christ and the breasts that gave Him suck. We stress this fact because it constitutes one of the bed-rocks upon which must be based reverence for womanhood with all that the terms involve of spirit and of flesh. The old pagandom degraded womankind because it had forgotten her divine origin. The new heresy also forgets. It either denies all rights to the weaker sex, or it bases these falsely. Women betray their own sex in this. Is not the feminist effort to-day directed towards the imitation of man—a sad insult to themselves, as if mankind represented the total idea, even physically. The fact is that woman is a Divine idea. And when we say woman we mean woman in all the fulness of her total being and in all the limitations thereof. Not only did God create woman, but He made an authentic woman of His mother.

This most intimate union between mother and Child such as the Incarnation involves shows up another truth. It is this: God is Truth. Nothing is so foreign to His nature as make-believe. And His Incarnation will be a kind of Divine exposure of all human relations to Himself, such as they were before He became Man. For instance, big business generally forgets God. In the persons of Bethlehem's inn-keepers it will slam its doors in His Human Face. The Jewish people had fallen away from Yahweh. They will reject Christ. And so on. Now think what must have been the actual relation to God of that unique being who would possess Him Incarnate in her womb, who would bring Him forth, suckle Him at her breasts, and, in a word, mother Him voluntarily, consciously and perfectly over all those years when He willed to need a Mother as much, as if not more, than any child of earth.

We think we have done enough wishful thinking. We will turn now to God Himself for information touching His own mother.

But we will have this fruit from our ponderings, that we cannot be surprised at any privilege of grace or nature which we shall find conferred upon her who was to be the worthy mother of God.

CHAPTER VII

WOMAN IN THE DIVINE MIND

WE have said that womanhood is a Divine idea. That is a type of truth which, at first presentation, seems over-bold, until one realises how utterly true it must be. Even a casual survey of the chaos of thought and—of course—of action, which characterises modern life convinces one that mankind was never so desperately in need of immutable standards as in our time-crisis. For all the old wholesome values are called in question, and that in every sphere. A learned and most orthodox Catholic litterateur made quite recently a rather pathetic defence of those artists whose creations seem not only meaningless, but mad. What he said in effect was that those modern artists no longer find conventional standards of anything. Consequently, since objects have become so fluid in connotation, obviously media of representation must follow suit. So that these young, muddled mystics must not be chided if they can represent the concept " pretty girl " only by two or more heads one on top of another!

Perhaps there is a viewpoint here. But if we must sympathise with those modern mariners who sail uncharted seas, may we not boldly say that the seas are charted, that the standards are there, and that in all vital things values have remained unchanged, because chalked up by the great Creator Himself. Since their apologist ventured to suggest the theme of a " pretty girl," we will now enlarge on woman as God meant her to be. And when she conforms to His idea she will be found to be pretty, too, nay, incomparably lovely.

Our Lord Himself suggests to us the proper way in which to assess values, and it is precisely the way which we propose to follow now. When He was asked a question touching the ever-fashionable problem of sex relationships, He answered by referring back to God's plan in creation : " Have ye not read that He who made man from the beginning made them male and female?" (St. Mark, xix, 4). Woman, then, is God's creation. She represents an idea in the Divine Mind. One of

23

the first and most obvious conclusions from this is that woman
is a very good idea. Despite its obvious nature, this truth has
not always found full acceptance by the darkened and corrupt
human mind. Certainly, the Church of God, perfectly mirroring the Creator's mind, has kept untarnished this true concept
of womanhood.

We will now consult the Divine Word itself. When God
decided to create Eve he gave formal expression to man's innate
need, not only of company, but of congenial company.

" And the Lord God said, it is not good for man to be alone "
(Gen. ii, 18). At the very start, therefore, God Himself asserts
that man is not sufficient to himself. Wherever women occupied
a too subordinate position it was because this verse of Genesis
was overlooked. We have stressed " congenial " company, for
God Himself underlined it. He did not bring to Adam any
irrational animal to keep him amused, and that proves that the
person He will bring must never be regarded as such. What a
vista opens before us of woman as man's creature, crudely once,
in a supposedly refined manner to-day, yet always reprobated
by the very primal charters of our existence. " Let us make
him a help like unto himself " (Gen. ii, 18). Here God stamps
woman-nature with that divinely imposed obligation of helping
which must ever bless by its realisation or curse by its frustration.
No woman, be she mother or maid, be she woman of the world
or cloistered virgin, can escape her destiny to be the helpmate
of man. In fact, some of the greatest woman benefactors of
humanity were those who renounced one family to mother the
world, while a greater catastrophe can hardly be conceived
than the selfishness of a woman battening on the very vitals
of a good man, and wrecking for him the life that now is, if
not also the future one.

See how the great Creator underlines woman's vocation to help
man. When he has brought before Adam all the beasts of the
earth and all the fowls of the air, the pathetic, if Divine, refrain
again is sounded, " but for Adam there was not found a helper
like himself " (Gen. ii, 20).

Then follows the Divine account of Eve's creation. And
when He brought her to Adam, the latter said : " This, now, is
bone of my bone and flesh of my flesh, she shall be called woman,
because she was taken out of man. Wherefore a man shall leave
father and mother, and shall cleave to his wife, and they shall
be two in one flesh " (Gen. ii, 23, 24). Divine words these and

full of mysterious significance. As a doctor of the Church remarks, these words of Adam do not tally with an ordinary and complete sleep. Rather are they the words of one to whom vision was vouchsafed. And had we any doubt about it, our doubts would be shattered when we find the Incarnate God defining holy matrimony in terms of this ecstatic utterance of the awakened Adam (St. Mark, xix, 4-6).

In God's plan the first woman and prototype of all woman was a virgin. She was given to Adam as wife it is true, but historically, the virginal state preceded the married state. No concept, therefore, of womanhood is true which does not honour both, and exemplify both in practice.

Such is God's plan for woman. And there can be no doubt that when the woman of prophecy appears she will come up fully to the Divine expectations.

CHAPTER VIII

THE WOMEN IN BETWEEN

As we have already said, woman and womanhood are Divine concepts. Eve fell short of the Divine plan, but that plan was to find its fullest completion in that woman of prophecy whose radiance is already refracted from the future on to Eden's doleful garden. From that moment until prophecy became fulfilment, womanhood has been represented by two very distinct types. The first may be said to consist of the seed of Eve in so far as Eve was a sinner. The second and more consoling category is composed of those who approximated more to the people subsequently chosen by God to preserve and transmit His Divine Revelation. We say almost exclusively because, as God's grace is coextensive with His own omnipotence, there may have been worthy women even outside the chosen people. But we do not know of them. It does not seem to be without significance that the history of the deluge is introduced by repeated references to the daughters of men. In Genesis, chapter vi, verse 2, we read: "The sons of God seeing the daughters of men, that they were fair, took to themselves wives of all which they chose." Who were these " daughters of men " and why are they so designated? Commentators state that they were the race of Cain, an ungodly race, whereas the " sons of God " were those stemming from the pious and godly Seth and Enos.

Already we notice the development of sin's primal deordination, for, although God made Eve surpassing fair, it was the Divine Will and not a creature such as mere physical beauty which drew Adam to her. Now, it is plainly insinuated in the Sacred Text that men had already accustomed themselves to follow blind desire without any reference to the Creator. The result was that these women were far from helpmates to their husbands or the race. They provoked and brought about God's first mass punishment, the deluge. The first worthy woman next mentioned in Scripture was Sarai, the wife of Abram.

"The name of Abram's wife was Sarai" (Gen. xi, 29). In almost the next verse the Holy Spirit tells us that "Sarai was barren and had no children" (Gen. xi, 30). Here attention is drawn to another aspect of woman's vocation in God's plan for her. She is to be supremely fruitful. However, this fruitfulness cannot be confined to the bearing of children in the corporal sense alone. Because God the Lord and Giver of life seems to show Himself very jealous on this point. Very often He does not give this fruit to the womb. And yet His ordinance stands. It is quite clear, therefore, that woman as such must always produce abundant fruit of virtue even if physical motherhood be denied her. Moreover, there will be women who will voluntarily choose physical barrenness in order to secure and multiply spiritual fruitage. And when the woman of prophecy appears, by choosing virginity she will be found fruitful even in her womb of the only Child absolutely necessary to this earth. We are told both of the fidelity of Sarai and, incidentally, of her beauty of person in the subterfuge adopted by Abram in order to secure his life at the hands of those whose admiration for Sarai might prove a menace to the latter. This good woman was sufficiently near God's first plan not to willingly allow her beauty to be a snare. If women would but be faithful to their Divine vocation God would make Himself their protector and vindicator. "But the Lord scourged Pharao and his house with most grievous stripes for Sarai, Abram's wife" (Gen. xii). To return to the barrenness of Sarai, we see that it was made the very subject of that Divine promise to which Abram gave such wholehearted belief that it could be written of him by the very finger of God: "Abram believed God, and it was reputed to him unto justice" (Gen. xv, 6). For Abram had drawn the Divine attention to his childless condition and for answer God had shown him the eastern sky, powdered with the stars of night. "Look up to heaven, and number the stars, if thou canst." And He said to him: "So shall thy seed be" (Gen. xv, 5). If very often God continues to withhold the blessing of parental fruitfulness, often, too, He shows His goodness and His omnipotence in just this very matter. And so we find Him promising a son to the hitherto barren Sarai. Later on, when Abraham entertained the three angels, this promise was repeated. We notice that God had waited until there was no merely human possibility of progeny for the aged pair. How is it that when God has time and again revealed this Divine characteristic, as we may call it, men still set bounds to the Divine power and cry: "It cannot be?" When Abraham sojourned in Gerara he employed the same pious ruse in order to safeguard his life from corrupt men. This time it was the King Abimelech who sent for the beautiful sister of the sojourner. But once more God intervenes and we see in the most palpable form God's love for married chastity and His abomination of its profanation. He actually imposed barrenness on all the women of Abimelech's household because of their master's mistake. But at the prayer of Abraham it was removed. Sarai, according to the Divine promise, bore a son, Isaac.

In this short résumé of Sarai's life we see how fully she exemplifies the Divine command given to the first woman to be the helpmate of her husband. She accompanied him wherever he went, followed his advice even when it led to most serious complications. Yet God had always intervened. Her very barrenness became the indication of the Divine omnipotence. And when she died she left behind her a son in whom all the nations of the earth are ever blessed.

In this pageant of women, truly fair because truly godly, we next meet Rebecca, the wife of Isaac.

If sin, in its essence, is to abuse one's creaturehood, that is to act in defiance of God's rights over us, so also much of our stumbling in life's road is due to our forgetfulness of what God is likely to do for the living and thinking works of His hands. The ancient Patriarchs were too near to their origins to be forgetful on this point. And so we find Abraham sending his servant to choose a wife for Isaac from his own country and kindred. Moreover, he is assured that such a choice will be the direct object of Divine Providence. Why are we sketching the lives of those remarkable women who form, as it were, the maids of honour of the woman who is to come? It is to show by each successive exemplar how God's plan for perfect womanhood is always constant. It is to restore to us the truth so lost sight of in our days that woman is God's creation, and that she stands or falls by her conformity to the Divine Plan for her. That, moreover, by her essential vocation, she raises many with her or involves many in her own destruction.

Since God Himself has bound up such mighty issues in the proper conception of womanhood, can we be surprised that she may, she must, consider herself the special object of His Providence in her acts and in her alliances, most especially in that most sacred alliance with one man which was the very setting of her creation? At any rate, the plain testimony of Holy Writ shows us that it is so. See the beautiful, trusting prayer of Abraham's servant: "O Lord, the God of my master, Abraham, meet me to-day, I beseech Thee, and shew kindness to my master, Abraham. Behold I stand nigh the spring of water, and the daughters of the inhabitants of this city will come out to draw water. Now, therefore, the maid to whom I shall say: 'Let down the pitcher that I may drink,' and she shall answer: 'Drink, and I will give thy camels drink also.' Let it be the same whom Thou hast provided for Thy servant, Isaac. And by this I shall understand that Thou hast shewn kindness to my master" (Gen. xxx, 6, 12, 2, 14).

Does not this seem laying down conditions for God? Yet these words are inspired by the Holy Ghost, and on closer examination we see that the servant asks God for such a woman as may be true to the Divine model—a true helpmate. And so far is God from rejecting the apparently audacious prayer that "He had not yet ended these words, within himself, and behold Rebecca came out . . ." (Gen. xxiv, 15).

All this is more than significant when we consider the choosing of another woman, this time in view of the very Motherhood of God.

Upon what other qualities does the Divine favour rest? "An exceedingly comely maid, and a most beautiful virgin, and not known to man" (Gen. xxiv, 16). Here is the picture of fair womanhood beautifully limned. Beauty of person, rising from beauty of soul and chaste integrity, a virgin in very deed. Yet all these most amiable qualities are in view of human espousals. There will be others. But we must tarry yet awhile.

Everything worked out according to the servant's prayer, causing him to break forth in jubilant thanksgiving: " Blessed be the Lord God of my master, Abraham, who hath not taken away His mercy and truth from my master, and hath brought me the straight way into the house of my master's brother" (Gen. xxiv, 27). It would have little availed if Divine Providence had merely arranged the external circumstances of this desired troth, had that same Providence not also prepared the hearts involved to acquiesce in the Divine Will. God had

made Eve perfect. Yet she failed. It will be the preparation
of His omnipotence, His wisdom and His love which will
always secure the " Behold the handmaid of the Lord." And
they said: " Let us call the maid and ask her will." And they
called her, and when she was come they asked: " Wilt thou
go with this man?" She said: " I will go " (Gen. xxiv, 57,
58). O blessed docility to God's Will! O fiat with such
salutary consequences for the human race! And often this
decision lies with a woman. Once it lay with The Woman!
And we are redeemed. We have stressed the constant features
of God's plan for womanhood.

Surely the lesson oft repeated by the Great God must be
for our learning. Despite all God's providential arrangements
for the union of Isaac and Rebecca He will leave no doubt
as to Who is the ultimate Master of life. He had promised
Abraham that his seed should be as the stars of heaven. God
is faithful, and He gave fruitfulness to Sarai's womb. Even
when Abraham was faced with the sacrifice of Isaac his faith
staggered not. For God could raise up from the dead. Now,
Isaac married Rebecca and lo she is found barren. But the
Divine arm is not shortened. " And Isaac besought the Lord
for his wife because she was barren, and He heard him and
made Rebecca to conceive " (Gen. xxv, 21). Esau and Jacob were
the fruit of that miraculous conception.

When we first met Rebecca she bore a pitcher on her
shoulder. From this we see that she was no stranger to
domestic toil. Her character in this respect is further expressed
by her preference for Jacob, " a plain man," as contrasted with
the more rollicking Esau, who " became a skilful hunter and
a husbandman " (Gen. xxv, 27). It is obvious that the exigencies of the chase left in Esau little time or appetite for the
simple service of home life. We know how this very simple
matter issued in Esau's loss of his first birthright. Let those who
dare cavil at this mysterious barter remember only that as
creatures we cannot evade the awfulness of our destiny. And
unless we develop the habit of putting first things first we, too,
may rate a mess of pottage against eternal life. We are again
reminded of the seed of the sinful Eve by the words of Holy
Writ touching the wives of Esau: " And Esau married Judith,
the daughter of Beeri the Hethite, and Basemath, the daughter
of Elon, of the same place.

" And they both offended the mind of Isaac and Rebecca "

(Gen. xxvi, 35, 35). We are next told how Rebecca contrived to secure for Jacob the blessing, or first birthright which Esau had really surrendered to the latter for the mess of pottage.

We will not dare to add words to a discussion upon which the great St. Augustine has written. For simple minds here are the facts. By right of temporal priority—and how temporal it was—Esau had a right to the first blessing of his dying father. As in all cases of sin where God inflicts punishment, culpability is measured by knowledge. Now Esau knew well how fraught with Divine issues this first birthright was. And he voluntarily sold it to allay his corporal hunger—verily an epitome of all sin. Of course the aged Isaac was not privy to this negotiation and he would have blessed Esau. It was the maternal and we may call it wifely intervention of Rebecca which procured for Jacob the birthright duly purchased from his brother.

Rebecca's love for Jacob counsels the latter to flee to Haran, to her brother Laban. For so great is Esau's anger that he designed his death. Like a golden thread in the life of this splendid woman is that love whereby she was such a perfect helpmate to her husband, and to her son Jacob, the Lord's elect. Once more we see that the continuance of the Divine blessings is made consonant on Jacob's choosing a worthy spouse. " And Rebecca said to Isaac, I am weary of my life because of the daughters of Heth. If Jacob takes a wife of the stock of this land, I choose not to live "; and again, " and Isaac called Jacob, and blessed him, and charged him saying, take not a wife of the stock of Chanaan " (Gen. xxvii, 46, and xxviii, 1).

Almost as a final testimony to the perfection with which Rebecca fulfilled her Divine vocation as helpmate to her husband are the words which tell of her last resting place by his side: " There was Isaac buried with Rebecca, his wife " (Gen. xlix, 31).

The Book of Judith presents to our view another woman whose virtues illustrate the Divine Plan for her sex.

She was a widow, and a widow indeed. For, on the death of her husband, Manasses, she made it quite clear that her heart would never again be engaged by man. In her case, too, we see that beauty is a gift from God and is not in itself a cause for apprehension. The Word of God assures us that Judith " was

exceedingly beautiful " (Judith viii, 7). And by placing this
eulogy in close connection with the record of her penances and
fasts wishes, no doubt, to indicate cause and effect. All daughters
of Eve have ambitioned beauty. But it seems to belong to those
of our generation to place all their hope in exterior embellish-
ments which are so far from achieving their purpose that they
only accentuate the lack of charm. Judith was also very rich
and yet her heart was not captured by earthly possessions. Had
it been so, her very widowhood would not have been creditable.
Even her reputation as it existed in the mouths of others was
based wholly upon her piety. " And she was greatly renowned
among all, because she feared the Lord very much " (Judith
viii, 8).

Wherever womankind departs from the Divine standard she
immediately becomes degraded. Have we not quite accepted the
slogan of the " weaker " sex, no longer confining the epithet to
physical structure but even to gifts of soul and mind? Judith
was not moulded on these decadent standards. For she is full of
concern for her country's plight and has no hesitation in mixing
herself in the counsels of war. She heard that Ozias meditated
surrender and saw in this attitude an insult to the God of Israel.
" And who are you that tempt the Lord?" (Judith viii, 11).
Her speech, as recorded in Judith, chapter viii, 10-27, is a
masterpiece of faith, humility and unswerving trust. In our
chaotic times the advice of Judith might well be meditated on
and reduced to action by those who are oppressed on every side
by modern Assyrians. Well was it for Ozias and his counsellors
that God inspired them to give ear to this holy woman. Without yielding to elation at the effect of her words Judith
emphasised the need of prayer for the furthering of her design
and, having secured this weapon alone, undertook the work
wherefor the armies had proved inadequate.

To ensure her success what does she do? There is more
penance and more prayer. The prayer of Judith (Judith ix, 2-19)
is also a model for our sad times. As the primal vocation of a
creature is good creaturehood, we see this prayer shot through
with the truest avowal of God's omnipotence and man's nothingness. " For Thy power, O Lord, is not in a multitude, nor is
Thy pleasure in the strength of horses, nor from the beginning
have the proud been acceptable to Thee, but the prayer of the
humble and the meek always pleased Thee " (Judith ix, 16).

But Judith is always a woman. And it is by the due exercise

of her womanly gifts that she will both honour God and deliver her people. This is a cardinal point, because only too many women consider the peak of fame accessible to those alone who ape men most nearly. See Judith's preparation for her encounter with Holofernes—who is always a man. "And she washed her, and anointed herself with the best ointment, and plaited the hair of her head, and put a bonnet upon her head, and clothed herself with the garments of her gladness and put sandals on her feet, and took her bracelets, and lilies and earlets, and rings, and adorned herself with all her ornaments (Judith x. 3). Did ever a woman of the most modern salon lay her wardrobe under contribution so? God designed woman to be attractive, and see what Judith's efforts earn from Him! "And the Lord also gave her more beauty, because all this dressing up did not proceed from sensuality, but from virtue. And therefore the Lord increased this her beauty, so that she appeared to all men's eyes incomparably lovely" (Judith x, 4). It is not our purpose to give details of the divinely inspired actions which finally cost Holofernes his head. The triumphant speech of the returned Judith is in keeping with all that went before. "Praise ye the Lord, our God, who hath not forsaken them that hope in Him" (Judith xiii, 17).

Surely is she a type of that other woman who is to come. Of Judith the Holy Spirit said, "The God of Israel, to whom thou gavest testimony, that He revengeth Himself of His enemies, He hath cut off the head of all the unbelievers this night by my hand" (Judith xiii, 37). While of that other woman, the Church, bride of the same Spirit, cries out, "Thou alone hast destroyed all heresies in the whole world."

Finally, we will turn our regard to that noble woman, who so well rose to the heights of her vocation that she was the help-mate, and indeed the saviour not of one man alone, but of all her people, namely, the royal Esther.

The Book of Esther introduces us first to Vasthi, wife of Assuerus and sharer of his throne. The latter made a great feast and at a certain stage in it desired the presence of the queen "with the crown set upon her head, to shew her beauty to all the people and the princes. For she was exceedingly beautiful" (Esther i, 11). When we remember that the true author of this book is the Holy Spirit we can hardly refrain from turning our thoughts to the first woman created by the Great King of all. Truly regal were her endowments and

D

destiny and God wished Eve to serve as an exemplar to those of her own sex who would come after her, as well as to all mankind. But as it was written of Vasthi, so was it also tragically true of Eve. " But she refused . . ." (Esther i, 12).

In the decree of punishment it was stated " that Vasthi come in no more to the king, but another that is better than her be made queen in her place " (Esther i, 19). Now Esther was the niece of Mardochai, a Jew who had been amongst the captives King Nabuchodonosor of Babylon had brought from Jerusalem.

Of Esther, too, it was written that she " was exceeding fair and beautiful." She was also among the young women chosen according to the edict for the good pleasure of the great king. And when Assuerus saw her, the chances of the other damsels faded to nought.

In the beginning, acting on the advice of Mardochai she did not divulge her people or country. When Esther in her turn was brought to the king " he loved her more than all the women. And she had favour and kindness before him above all the women. And he set the royal crown on her head, and made her queen instead of Vasthi " (Esther ii, 17). The Holy Spirit underlines a trait in Esther's character, her docility to her uncle, Mardochai. For as yet, in conformity with his instructions, she had kept her race and people secret, " and she did all things in the same manner as she was wont at that time when he brought her up, a little one " (ii, 20). We are then told, incidentally, how Mardochai had been instrumental in crushing a plot against the king's life. This, too, he did through the agency of Esther, " And it was put in the histories, and recorded in the chronicles before the king " (Esther ii, 23).

Then enters the villain of the piece—one Aman, who seems to have curried favour with Assuerus. We read, " and all the king's servants that were at the doors of the palace bent their knees and worshipped Aman. For so the emperor had commanded them. Only Mardochai did not bend his knee nor worship him " (Esther iii, 2). Aman becomes infuriated with this one man who will not honour him, and his fury is directed against all the people of Mardochai, the Jewish race.

Using his great influence with Assuerus he pointed out the damage done to the royal interests by this one people who refuse to be absorbed, or observe unconditionally the royal ordinances. He begged for a mandate for their destruction and added force to his arguments by an offer of ten thousand talents to the royal treasurer. Assuerus had sufficient dignity to refuse the proffered bribe but he gave Aman licence to deal with the Jews as he wished. Aman lost no time. Immediately royal letters were speeding in every direction appointing a given day for the mass destruction of the Jewish people.

When Mardochai heard of this design he gave expression to his anguish by stationing himself in sackcloth and ashes right at the very gate of the royal palace. When Esther was told of this she sent to enquire of Mardochai the reason of his strange behaviour. He told the messenger the facts, and instructed him to admonish Esther to " go into the king and to entreat him for her people " (Esther iv, 8). Esther responded by reminding Mardochai of the prevailing law that any one who dared to come into the king's inner court, without being summoned, should be put to death forthwith unless the king should hold out the golden sceptre to such a one in token of clemency. But Mardochai's only reply was to stress the urgency of the matter, warning Esther that her own fate would not be other than that of her race and suggesting that her very position was given her by Providence as a source of salvation for her and for the Jews.

Then Esther demanded the united prayers of all the Jews in Susan. She also asked that these prayers should be strengthened by a fast of three days and three nights, in which she and her handmaids would join. Having thus secured the good favour of God she promised to go into the king, unsummoned, and risk the forfeiture of her life.

So Esther approached the king, " and when he saw Esther the queen standing, she pleased his eyes, and he held out towards her the golden sceptre which he held in his hand. And she drew near, and kissed the top of his sceptre. And the king said to her, what wilt thou, Queen Esther? What is thy request? If thou shouldst even ask one half of the kingdom, it shall be given thee " (Esther v, 2, 3). However, Esther's request was a lesser one, merely an invitation to the king, and the wily Aman, to a banquet prepared by her. The king signified his immediate assent and sent for Aman. After the first banquet, Esther merely repeated her invitation for a similar entertainment on the following day. Aman was elated. But his good spirits were damped by the continued refusal of Mardochai to pay him honour. He recounted to his family the greatness of his present attainments, the wonderful invitation of Esther twice repeated, but he admitted, " and whereas I have all these things—I think I have nothing, so long as I see Mardochai the Jew sitting before the king's gate " (Esther v, 13). The charitable solution proposed by his wife and friends was the immediate preparation of a scaffold on which to hang Mardochai. Aman needed no further instigation, " and he commanded a high gibbet to be prepared " (Esther v, 14).

To put it in a human way, now God shows His hand. And His instrument is nothing more than a dose of insomnia for Assuerus. " That night the king passed without sleep. And he commanded the histories and chronicles of former times to be brought him " (Esther vi, 1). In the course of the reading, Mardochai's discovery of the treasonable plot on the king's life was mentioned. Whereupon Assuerus asking what reward had been meted out to Mardochai, found that he had received none. At this crucial moment Aman approaches and his mission is none other than to procure the royal mandate for Mardochai's hanging. When Assuerus heard of his presence he ordered him to come to him. Then he asked Aman a strange question: " What ought to be done to the man whom the king is desirous to honour?" (Esther xi, 6). Trapped by his own insensate love of self Aman thought the question could have reference only to himself and he replied: " The man whom the king desireth to honour, ought to be clothed with the king's apparel, and to be set upon the horse that the king rideth upon, and to have the royal crown upon his head. And let the first of the king's princes and nobles hold his horse. And going through the streets of the city, proclaim before him and say, thus shall he be honoured, whom the king hath a mind to honour " (Esther xi, 7-9). What was his discomfiture when Assuerus ordered him to do all this for Mardochai the Jew? This was punishment for his proud irritation. But the end was not yet. That very evening another invitation is issued to Aman in the queen's name, to the banquet which she had prepared.

At this banquet too, the king invited Esther to make her petition. This time she openly pleaded for her people, and added: " We have an enemy, whose cruelty redoundeth upon the king " (Esther vii, 4). Upon Assuerus asking the identity of this enemy Esther replied: " It is this Aman that is our adversary and most wicked enemy " (Esther vii, 6). The culmination of the royal anger was the hanging of Aman on the gibbet prepared by him for Mardochai.

We gave to this chapter the title of " The Women in Between." Our reason for this was because womanhood is God's creation and God's ideal stands. We saw how Holy Writ in describing the creation of Eve gives a very clear indication of what womanhood means in the Divine Plan. But the ideal is scarcely presented when it is shattered before our eyes in the sin of our first mother. That might have been all the glimpse we might have got of the Divine ideal had God's mercy not decreed the restoration of the race, through a God-Man " made under the law, made from a woman." This woman who is to give us the Saviour is the ideal which Eve had failed to achieve. In view of her, all womanhood is again raised up, and the approximation of any woman to her is the measure of her womanhood.

Even in the old law women there were who in many ways did achieve some approximation to her. We have just studied four such, namely, Sara, Rebecca, Judith and Esther. In creating these noble types and making them the very subject of the Divine Word we are convinced that God had always before His Divine eyes the perfect woman towards whom each of these approximated in certain ways. Therefore the study of their virtues, especially of the typical feminine virtues leads us to expect what we shall actually find when the woman of prophecy enters into history.

We have not hesitated to give Esther's history in some detail. For in view of what the woman will be, this woman is almost the most finished shadowing-forth of her. In fact there are times when the shadow seems to take on the very substance of reality and we see before our eyes certain facts which will be again visible though on a more divine scale in God's chosen woman of predilection. For instance, Esther is not only a help-mate to one, but a very saviour of her people. And she achieved her power for good through a remarkable privilege. For as we saw there was a general law forbidding approach to the great king prior to his personal summons.

Esther disregarded this royal ordinance and so her plea for her people might have had as only result death for herself as for them. But it was not so. And most touching is the scene wherein Assuerus assures Esther that she does not come under this law. " Thou shalt not die for this law is not made for thee, but for all others " (Esther xv, 13). Who can read these words without immediately thinking of another woman who saved her race by giving flesh and blood to the Saviour, a woman who by a singular privilege was removed absolutely from that corruption of death which fell upon all others save her?

CHAPTER IX

OF DAVID'S ROYAL LINE

WHEN we read the works of St. Teresa of Avila her reference to God as His Majesty has for our ears a peculiar ring. A little reflection, however, assures us that the title was never so well placed. What claim can earthly royalty urge on our respect, if not merely the culture associated with a family long privileged, an ancient name which from time immemorial has borne the crown? But what if the culture proves itself to be lacking, and how can time alone heap up honour? But God is King by every right. Moreover, human kingship can claim to be hallowed if it acknowledges the Divine Majesty as the first source of its authoritative pre-eminence. On this score there was once a royal line which owed its very origin to God's election. The story of that origin is told in the eighth chapter of the first Book of Kings. And it is an origin which ennobles kingship and humbles it at the same time. For we see the great God protesting against the appointment of any human king in the great theocratic family of the chosen people. We are told that the sons of Samuel did not walk in the just ways of their father. "Then all the ancients of Israel being assembled, came to Samuel to Ramatha. And they said to him, "Behold thou art old, and thy sons walk not in thy ways. Make us a king, to judge us, as all nations have" (Kings xiii, 45).

God expressed His disfavour at this request: "For they have not rejected thee, but Me that I should not reign over them" (Kings xiii, 7). However, He bade Samuel to accede to their request and finally Saul was anointed as first king over Israel. The great significance of his anointing was that it set God's seal on the regal line.

In Saul's tragic career we are brought face to face with something which happened in creation's very dawn, namely, a vessel of election choosing freely to be a vessel of wrath. Even in our stumbling human way we may arrive at the conclusion that if ever God attached the salvation of the human race to the

39

fidelity of a human will, that human will must be fenced in and preserved by very special privileges from playing us false.

Scarcely is Saul anointed as king than he, too, plays false to his great dignity and responsibilities. He is immediately rejected from the kingship and in his stead Samuel, by Divine command, anoints David, the son of Isai the Bethlehemite, as king. David will give abundant proof of his weak corruptibility but always he will remain a man after God's own heart, and the royal line will persevere. It is from this royal line that will come the woman who will bring forth the Saviour.

CHAPTER X

THE PARENTS OF OUR LADY

AT first sight it would appear that we can know little or nothing about the parents of Our Lady. Tradition does not do much more than give us their names, Joachim and Anne. But would we be better off if we could enclose those names between precise dates, if we could localise these lives, if we had evidence of what they said or what they did? Such, it is true, is the information which history gives of its characters. But is it very fruitful information after all? What does it really tell us of the historical person; does it enable us to assess his mind and soul? It is only in the measure that it does this that it is valuable information. Perhaps on deeper consideration we will find that we have a fact concerning Joachim and Anne which does precisely enable us to unlock at least some of the rare treasures of their souls and personalities. It is indeed the salient fact about them and it is that they were the parents of Our Lady.

It is only too well known that parents exercise a unique rôle in the making or marring of their children. How could it be otherwise? For many years, when even the physical well-being of the child is in their hands, parents exercise the most stupendous formative influence. Is it any wonder then that normally we find that God bestows very highly endowed parents on those whom He calls to exceptional heights of sanctity? It is not that God loves less those children whom He has not so favoured. God's plan is always perfect, but free will has its play and so we find God's initial designs too often frustrated, and at best, delayed in fulfilment. But high sanctity is certainly helped by the loving nurture of good parents, and Divine Providence generally sees to it that the parents are worthy of their predestined progeny. The two sides of the matter are abundantly illustrated. Of the mother of Victor Hugo it is said that when making arrangements for his initial schooling she did not wish daily Mass to be obligatory on her darling. On the other hand, a biographer of St. John Bosco begins his book with the significant words: "In the beginning was the mother." For Don Bosco's mother warned her son when the holy oils of priesthood were still moist on his hands that if ever he became a rich priest her door was shut upon him. From this one example we may judge the nature of the saint's early and constant training in true values. We can scarcely find a more touching and a more convincing proof of the influence which may be exercised by parents than in the household of St. Teresa of the Child Jesus. But now let us bring it home to ourselves that we are dealing with the parents to whom God entrusted the immaculate flower which was destined to bear the Divine fruitage of His only-begotten Son. What immense graces must not have entered into the predestination of this chosen pair?

It is quite obvious that for a period which represents the most formative of life the child almost wholly depends upon its parents for its physical, mental and moral moulding. There is soft wax ready to be impressed, and there are hands which can and must give the impression. The vital question is, therefore, what sort of hands are these?

Experience assures us that children may all through life bear physical blemishes due to ignorant supervision during the plastic period. And the mental and moral effects may be more disastrous and more lasting still. On the other hand, as the child is father to the man, it would be difficult to estimate how much of health and strength, how much of genius, and how much of sanctity had its foundations laid in early parental training. The question which confronts us here is just how much we may expect from Divine Providence in the early setting of a child's life. It is true that in general God will leave free play to free will and created agencies. Eternal salvation is God's destiny for each and every soul. And we can be certain that God will make even mistakes minister to this glorious end if His grace be duly accepted and followed. But for some souls God has a special predestination covering not only ultimate salvation but a very special rôle in this life, fraught perhaps with eternal consequences for countless others. Might we not expect in such cases a special exhibition of Providence, preventing even more than healing grace? When we examine the lives of the great saints we find that it is precisely so. And in the very forefront of these choice graces has almost inevitably been a very chosen parental milieu. Now let us ask ourselves what kind of a child was entrusted to Joachim and Anne, what her destiny was, and what graces we may presume this destiny involved for the moulders of her infant years, for her parents.

We are often too prone to forget the very practical consequences of the Immaculate Conception. These consequences are in the physical and mental no less than in the moral sphere. At the moment we will be content to say that the infant bestowed by God on Joachim and Anne was, to say the least of it, the most perfect child ever born to human parents, and that physically, mentally and morally. We consider that the very words we have used exclude that other child who will have no father on earth.

Original sin is the root cause of all human defects in every order. And so, by her singular privilege of exemption, Mary was totally free from both the cause of these defects and the defects themselves. In the purely physical order this already means that the child of Joachim and Anne was in a most unique and perfect sense, a perfect child. But this immunity from physical defects did not mean that the child could not suffer from insalubrious circumstances. Heat and cold, hunger and thirst and the like could wreak their full external effects on Mary as on all human beings. Consequently her parents were by no means exempt from the duty of constant and wise care over her physical well-being from her very conception. And it is because it was God's positive will that Mary should bring perfect health to her unique motherhood that this intelligent and constant care of her parents was necessary at every moment of her growing life. We have no hesitation in believing that Divine Providence saw to it that it was so—which is another way of saying that Joachim and Anne must have been the most highly endowed of parents. This cannot perhaps be found crystallised in any writing apocryphal or divine, but it is a plain deduction from their unique office in Mary's regard.

And what of their parental influence on the mental development of their unique child? For the moment let us turn to ordinary children. There is no doubt that some children are more highly gifted than others. They display at a very early age very acute observation and also a depth of thoughtful wisdom which reveals itself in the questions they ask. But even apart from genius or exceptional talent the average child is observing almost all the time and endeavouring to increase its knowledge by a fund of questions of every variety.

It is here that too many parents fail. Their love for their

children's physical well-being is quite sufficient to prevent them from withholding material food. But they are not quite so anxious to provide fodder for the mind. Often tired, and as often quite unable to answer the torrent of questions, they exercise their parental rights by stopping the child's mouth. More psychological defects of after life may be traced to this repression than we can imagine. Moreover the delicate budding of the young mind has been rudely blighted. Happily it is not always so. And there are found many parents whose minds are not less richly endowed than their hearts, and who take a laudable pride in helping the young mind to develop. Now let us return to SS. Joachim and Anne. Once more the Immaculate Conception has its most practical sequels in the domain of Mary's mind. Here is a mind never clouded by the mists of original sin. Here is an intelligence not only made for truth but without any intrinsic obstacle towards its attainment; an imagination which will do the perfect work an imagination is destined to do without mixing up delusion with reality; here is a memory which can be a most perfect storehouse of experience. Think of the words which will come out of the abundance of that heart, what deep and searching questions, what a winnowing of thought, and collation of experience. And her parents had to be equal to all this. Because as we have said God will not multiply miracles when the nature of which He is author has the wherewithal. This ought to assure us of the mental calibre of Our Lady's parents. We will now examine their influence on her moral development.

We are accustomed to associate innocence with that period of life which precedes the age of reason. Substantially we are quite right in so doing, but we must define what we mean by innocence. If it means only a physical and moral impossibility of those darker crimes which can stain adult years, we are stating a fact which only precocious perversity could contradict. But let us take the root meaning of innocent, namely that which does not hurt. Then we must admit that few children deserve the term in its fullest meaning. For childhood can inflict pain, whether on animals or on those humans who are closely connected with its upbringing. We cannot get away from the fact of original sin and watchful parents will see constant signs of the cockle which the enemy has sown. As we have already insinuated these corrupt tendencies will show themselves in very small matters. It need only be a case of petulancy spring-

ing from self-love which will demand everything and loudly—
literally—resent any refusal. In other words it will cover all
that very varied field known simply as boldness.

Even in children original sin while asserting its existence does
not do so with a similar scope in each soul. By special preventive grace, sometimes consisting in a nature where good
tendencies far outnumber the bad some children are endowed
from their earliest years with most excellent dispositions. Yet
even with those, when they reach more adult years the cockle
even if sparingly sown has nevertheless to be dealt with.

But what shall we say of a child in whose fair soul there is
no such cockle? A child in whom by a nature altogether sub-
limated by grace there are only good tendencies without the
slightest opposing ones. There need not be postulated the
highest imaginable virtue in each thought and word and deed,
but at any rate the highest virtue called for in the circumstances
and without any vitiating alloy. Now let us remember that
almost all that can be expected of the best of parents is that
they be virtuous enough, and wise enough, and sufficiently
alert to detect both the good and less good qualities of their
children so as to develop the one and eradicate the other, what
must have been the qualities of soul and heart and mind of
those parents who were privileged to call Mary their daughter?
In her case there never could be the slightest blameworthy
tendency calling for checking, while on the other hand every
thought, word and deed was as limpidly pure and perfect as
the immaculate fount from which it had its rise. What we
ask may be postulated of such parents? Simply that they should
themselves be so virtuous that their child's virtue did not at
least occasionally shine out by too telling a contrast. And
here let us rebut an objection that may be urged against our
line of argument. Someone may be found to say that we are
creating a whole series of immaculate beings, for if Joachim
and Anne were so perfect, their respective parents, and their
parents' parents must have been equally perfect. We answer with
the Church that as Mary's privilege of Immaculate Conception
is unique, so we only claim a special Providence for those who
are brought most nearly in contact with this chosen lily of God.
At any rate we only claim congruity, but theologians have never
shrunk from using the argument. Very often when a dogma has
been defended it has been found that the arguments from
congruity when soberly marshalled paved the way for the final

definition. It has become regarded as a clear fact that we know very little about the parents of the Blessed Virgin. We contend that God expects us to use our heads, and that He could well say to us that He has said a great deal about those two privileged parents when He said " Mary " and entrusted her to them as their child.

CHAPTER XI

A CHILD IS BORN TO US (Isaias ix, 6)

WE know that the Child of whom Isaias speaks is the only-begotten Son of the Eternal Father. Yet in using this Messianic cry of joy as the heading of this chapter, thus appropriating the text to Mary, we are only following closely in the footsteps of Holy Church who constantly appropriates such oracles to the Mother of God. Mary is born. There is a little infant in the household of Joachim and Anne. In beginning this humble work we complained that most spiritual writers present Mary to us for the first time in the wonderful scene of the Annunciation. But what of the years in between? We, at any rate, intend to kneel in spirit beside this little cradle and rejoice our heart with the fragrance of this immaculate lily before it even unfolds.

This is the time, however, to stress our dependence on dogma. We would not allow mere sentiment to dictate praise even of Mary. We beg our readers to note carefully this assertion and follow us in our deductions only when they have examined our premises by the light of revelation. And so we kneel by the side of this little new-born infant. We do not know how much her parents knew of her privileges and destiny. Would one who was totally ignorant of these see anything remarkable in this tiny babe as she rests in her cradle? Let us indulge in some considerations. We would explore a rich mine, too little worked—we refer to the practical consequences of Mary's unique privilege of the Immaculate Conception.

The least result of this privilege was that her soul was adorned by grace and the object of the Divine complacency from the very first moment of her existence. And let us remember as we gaze on the little form that nine months have elapsed since that blessed moment. Already we begin to see how different this infant is from every other. Should we see an infant before the waters of Baptism have flowed over the little brow, we would see a soul from which the Divine gaze is averted, as from an object of repulsion. Never, never was that Mary's condition.

47

As we kneel in spirit by her side may we not experience the fragrance of grace which envelops her? True, she is in many respects as other infants, small, weak, helpless. But look into those baby eyes. Do we not see in their depths some reflection of the peerless soul which looks out from them? The smile of an infant always gives joy, but surely the smile of this infant must have awakened strange unplumbed joys in the souls of those who were its recipient. O blessed parents, Anne and Joachim, you could tell us so much of the graces that came to you through your little baby. One smile from Heaven's queen was sufficient to cure Thérèse Martin of the strange malady of her childhood. In the light of that first visible smile in the springtide of her life she ran like a giant to the peaks of sanctity. A similar smile from Mary encouraged Mgr. Mazenod when he was about to give the Church the new family of the Oblates of Mary Immaculate. What, then, must it have been to have this gracious child as one's very own for fourteen or fifteen years until Heaven's ambassador stood before her and traced the path which was to lead her away from Anne and Joachim to her Divine destiny as mother of the Most High?

One of the qualities attaching to genuine interior holiness is to create an atmosphere wherein wicked thoughts must wilt and die of very shame. And may we not believe that those who came to visit the home of the newly-born were conscious of a strange sweet lull of passion and a subtle appetite for holiness? Knowing who she is, we at any rate will keep near her in spirit and consciously drink in this new wine of purity which had so utterly failed us heretofore.

It is at Mary's cradle, too, that we will learn the lessons of reverence for childhood, even for infancy. This reverence for childhood is a very beautiful trait in the Christian character and we should all strive to possess it. But, like all good things, it has its counterfeits. Most normal people feel an attraction for the very young. But only too often this attraction is purely natural, and if we honestly analyse our motives we may find them of the flimsiest. The characteristics of childhood which make an appeal to us are its helplessness and what we are pleased to call its innocence. But let us bravely analyse these qualities and we will see that they can afford very unstable foundation for a lasting and reasonable reverence. Perhaps what we laud in childhood is not so much its helplessness as the pride awakened in us by anyone who is forced—even physically—to look up to us. As regards the innocence of childhood it is possibly verified only in this that owing to immaturity none of the dark passions which disturb adult years can come into play. But this is a poor sort of innocence and in the moral sphere is identified with that helplessness which marks the physical side. The child does not do great evil just because it cannot do it. On the other hand, a child may sometimes do as much evil as it can, and with petulant will, too. At any rate, these childish qualities cannot furnish us with anything more than a sentimental regard for this period of life. People who are only motivated so far do not really possess a genuine love of childhood. In fact they can do great harm to children, for they regard them almost as little playthings to be always caressed and fondled. This is a very bad training for natures vitiated by original sin.

Here by the side of God's very own infant we will try and dig better and more enduring foundations for our love of the young.

Look at her. See how tiny she is, just like all new-born infants. Already we see that size ought to have no significance either for our regard or our withholding of it. Already we are entering into the very views of God for we realise that He loves and even respects us, not so much for what we are, as for what we may yet be in His Divine Plan for us. This is only a little frail infant, yet she is chosen out of all women to be God's own mother. When that sinks into us we do not feel quite so impelled to fondle her. Here, too, we will learn well-based reverence for womanhood even in the infant state. For it is precisely because this is a girl-child that the Divine motherhood will be possible. We see, therefore, how holy a thing sex is when we see it through God's eyes as something most deliberately created by Him for purposes rich in glory for the Creator, blessed for ever more. What, in general, is the manifestation of life in any infant? There are smiles and there are tears. But we must never forget that with one unique exception these little innocents are in full possession of a tainted nature, the sad heritage of our first parents' fall. Consequently even in infancy traces may be seen of that cockle which an enemy had planted. How much self-love, even at that tender age, may contribute to the smile? How much petulancy and downright bad temper may make those infant's tears to flow? What will it be with an infant, whose nature is absolutely untouched by the hellish blight?

E

The smile of such a child will be heavenly and not the compound of a satisfied though young sensuality. The tears of such a one will be the fruit of creaturehood with its limitations, but there will be no admixture of an assertive and corrupt will. How beautiful, therefore, the infancy of Mary. How practical the endowment of her Immaculate Conception. O blessed parents whose privilege and duty it was to hold her in your arms and press her infant form to your hearts!

How blessed were ye, in ministering to all her infant needs, in drying those tears that needs must bathe her baby eyes, and in receiving so often in recompense that ineffable smile which has worked so many wonders for those who were only her servants and her clients.

CHAPTER XII

MARY'S BIRTHDAYS

WHEN we speak of Mary's birthday we are speaking with Holy Church. Sentiment as such has no place in the Church's liturgical acts. Never for an instant can the bride of Christ lose sight of what we may call hard facts. And one of the hardest of these is the fact of original sin. So far as the ordinary law went each birth of a child of Adam is a day of sorrow rather than of joy. For there is ushered into this world a soul stripped of its original supernatural endowments. Consequently the Church will never celebrate this sad anniversary as the natal day of her holy ones. Rather does she term that day their day of birth when by a holy death they are born into the possession of eternal life. However, two exceptions are made. And we find liturgical celebrations of two birthdays, celebrating the actual birth into this world. One is St. John the Baptist. He, too, fell under the law of inherited deprivation, but was cleansed therefrom in his mother's womb. The other is the ineffable birth of the immaculate virgin. However, we are not speaking of Mary's birthdays from a liturgical standpoint at all. Having pointed out the Church's example we hasten to say that we are motivated by the self-same ideal which inspired these lines from the first. We will not lose one second of those golden years which preceded the Annunciation. And so we still linger by the infant Mary. A year passed bringing with it the first anniversary of her birth. The saints as we have seen have sometimes been honoured by a smile from Heaven's queen or a vision, fleeting at best. But what must have been the ever increasing joy of Joachim and Anne to see how truly theirs was this living treasure. Not for a brief ecstacy as in the case of St. Bernadette but for minutes and hours and days and years this wonder child was theirs.

Mary will have yielded to the law of all babyhood and she will have grown with the years. Although she will be still an infant must we not believe that the development of that perfect

51

body must already be a source of indefinable and purest charm? Although we have not claimed for her a continued miracle of awakened reason, yet the reason is awakening. Let us never forget the sequel of the Immaculate Conception. In Mary more than in any other pure creature is verified to the highest degree the slogan which is also an ideal. " A sound mind in a sound body." Here is a body which inherits none of our ills. It has one limitation only, that of creaturehood. Here are no seeds of disease which can only too often cloud the very threshold of life. In the development of its faculties the soul finds its unique perfect instrument. With other children the cockle keeps pace with the good seed. Here all is good. And even negatively there must have been a striking absence of all these sallies which mark infancy as being far more helpless than innocent. To say the least of it, we may well believe that the neighbours soon discovered that it did them good to even gaze on the little infant daughter of Joachim and Anne. And in the fulness of our revealed knowledge we know how well based was their conviction, and passing over the centuries between we, too, in spirit may taste their joy.

CHAPTER XIII

DIVINE HERITAGE

DEVOUT clients of Our Lady raise the question, what was the initial grace of the Blessed Virgin? As Mary's predestination is of an order superior to that of every other creature, it follows that her initial grace is likewise superior to theirs. Among Marian theologians it is agreed that this initial grace was not less, was even superior to the consummate grace of the angel or saint highest in glory. This is a very practical point for our special purpose. It is claimed that a biography of Our Lady is impossible because of the dearth of historical factual information. We would retort that in the lives of all the saints, where those lives are most transfigured by grace, we have a faint, indeed yet a true index to what we may and must predicate of her.

Grace is a quality inhering in our soul. And as a quality can grow with regard to the subject in which it inheres and also in itself, it follows that grace in Mary increased after both these manners. Grace is also a vital quality. It is the very life of the soul. Now the growth of life, life itself is a great mystery. What a mystery must be the divine life in Mary and its growth. This divine life began in her with her Immaculate Conception, and from that very moment it grew without obstacle, nay, with every possible help. We must not lose sight of this when with love and reverence we study this ineffable child. It is because of this theological basis for Mary's growth in grace that we have always considered it a loss to meditate on Mary, beginning only with the Incarnation.

Let us now consider the virtue and gifts of the Holy Spirit as they abound in Mary. Virtues are habitual good dispositions which render the powers of our soul capable of executing promptly and easily what right reason demands in the natural order or what God invites us to in the supernatural order. There are natural or acquired virtues, and also those which are supernatural or infused. These gifts have reference explicitly

53

to the supernatural order. These are dispositions produced in the soul by the Holy Ghost and added to the virtues in order to render our faculties more supple and more docile in grace. As effects flowing from their cause, the beatitudes and fruits of the Holy Spirit flow from the virtues and gifts.

The Blessed Virgin possessed all the natural virtues, for in her no perverse inclination ever raised its head against right reason. Moreover, as sanctifying grace was in her an element, inseparable as it were from her very being, it follows that she was endowed with all the infused virtues which flow from sanctifying grace. These infused virtues attained in Mary to a sovereign perfection, because her grace rose far and above that of any other creature. As regards the gifts of the Holy Ghost we may say that their measure in Mary was their possession without measure. How clear this appears in her fiat, in her visitation and very particularly in her compassion. We come now to the theological virtues. They must have been in Our Lady to a unique degree. In regard to charity she was the living image of her Son, uncreated charity. This mode of comparison may not be extended to the virtues of faith and hope because neither of these is in accord with the dignity of the God-Man. Mary had both. As we have seen she did not enjoy here below at least habitually the beatific vision. What may be claimed for Mary's faith during that most painful interval between the death of Jesus and His resurrection is that it remained perfect with integral perfection. While the faith of others at that time suffered some eclipse yet it is going too far to say that during these three days the faith of the Church resided only and wholly in Mary.

The powers of Our Lady's soul, by virtue of the abundant grace which penetrated her entirely, were endowed with all the theological and moral virtues compatible with her condition of original purity. Where circumstances prevented her from exercising certain virtues, such as liberality in bestowing alms, nevertheless she possessed these virtues inrooted in the noble sentiments of her soul. We may not attribute continence to Mary, in the sense of a resistance to the urge of concupiscence. Neither had she the virtue of penitence if we mean thereby sorrow for personal sin. But in so far as it means hatred of sin, regret and displeasure to see God offended, coupled with an ardent desire to repair by sacrifices the affronts to the Divine Majesty, then Mary was the most penitent of creatures.

Let us now consider the beauty of Our Lady. We have taken just a peep at the exquisite qualities with which the Immaculate soul of Mary is endowed. Now we shall feast our gaze, more the eyes of our soul than our carnal ones, on the endowments of her virginal body. For though the soul is the spring and principle of all life and of all perfection in man, it is not of itself the whole man. The body too is constitutive of human nature. So a study of Our Lady would be incomplete did it not include the contribution of nature and grace to her body, making it as also her soul a tabernacle worthy of the Incarnate Word. The very perfection of soul which belongs to the Immaculate argues to a remarkable perfection of body. To this we must add Mary's predestination to the divine motherhood. Of what grandeur in every sphere is not this unique destiny the root and source! With regard to Our Lady's endowments this predestination has a negative and a positive significance. It excludes from her everything which could derogate from this maternity, and it makes hers by very right everything which could help towards the perfect fulfilment of this highest of human offices. Now we must remember that by her fiat Mary delivered over her corporal being to the action of the Holy Spirit, and in so doing she became the mother of God. Her body therefore, no less than her soul must have been gifted with qualities worthy of that Spirit who fashioned a body for the Word, worthy, too, of that Word who appropriated this body to Himself.

Mary sprang from the most illustrious race in the family of mankind, namely the royal line of David. In these days of ours perhaps royalty is at a discount. And one is often tempted to ask just what constitutes the so-called blue blood. If a dynasty bases its pride of place on length of tenure it may have to admit an illegitimate usurpation at some point of history and then royalty is based only on a successful rapine. Be that as it may, the kingly line which can claim God as its inaugurator is truly regal. And such was the royal line of David to which Mary belonged. The Holy Word of God abundantly attests this fact, which provokes the question, as to how our separated brethren who claim to be conversant with Holy Writ can yet maintain that Mary was just an ordinary woman. They make a regular fetish of royalty and yet they will not honour this most royal of women. We need not waste arguments on the objection that the Saviour's genealogy is traced through

Joseph without any mention of Mary's name. The Law of
Moses demanded that the woman who was the only heiress
should marry a man belonging to the same family stock. For
the same reason both Mary and Joseph obeyed the edict of
Augustus and proceeded to enroll themselves on the census list
of Bethlehem, the City of David. We in Ireland can see no
objection to their royal lineage that Mary and Joseph were
reduced to such humble estate. Moreover, since Mary was
related to Elizabeth she would by that fact have contact by
one side or the other with the noble family of Aaron. So in
Mary we find united the glorious blood streams of a sacerdotal
no less than a royal race. The virginal body of this truly
noble maid was of an incomparable perfection taken as a whole
and with regard to its several elements. According to Tertullian, when God modelled the body of the first man, He had
in view the body which His Son Jesus Christ was one day to
possess. By analogy it is easy to conclude that in the form-
ation of the body of the Blessed Virgin, of this body in which
Jesus would personally dwell after the Incarnation, God the
Father, laid under contribution all the resources of His Divine
art so that it would be in keeping with its high destiny. The
corporal perfection of Mary was therefore incomparably superior
to that of the first woman, and this perfection went on daily
increasing until the great day of the Incarnation dawned. The
human soul does not essentially depend on the body for its
spiritual acts. Nevertheless it needs the presentation to it by
these organs of the first objects of its cognitions. In fact, these
corporal organs lend it a certain co-operation. It follows, therefore, that the better one is endowed with regard to sensitive
faculties the less obstacles will one encounter to the full flowering of the intellectual faculties. Now after the mind and human
will of Our Lord Jesus Christ, no mind, no will was as perfect
in its acts as that of the mother of God. So that after Jesus,
no rational creature had a corporal organism comparable in
perfection to that of the Blessed Virgin. The perfect balance
which existed between all the elements of the corporal being
of Mary resulted in an immunity from every malady, an
immunity analogous to that enjoyed by Our Divine Lord. Here
was an absolute submission of the reason to God coupled with
a complete submission of the sensitive faculties to reason. There
reigned a perfect harmony of all the energies of the organic
life with the government of the soul.

What then shall we say of our mother's beauty? Obviously the interior beauty of the soul holds pride of place. Yet this beauty could not but manifest itself exteriorly, for naturally the face is the mirror of the soul. And it was the spiritual perfection far more than the integrity, proportion and harmony of her corporal being, which shone on her serene brow, in her clear eyes and in all the exterior of the august virgin. As Denis the Carthusian and Tertullian suggested, owing to the fact of the Divine maternity it is legitimate to deduce the beauty of the mother from that of the Son. Let us remember here that Jesus received His sacred humanity from Mary and only from Mary. His Divine body was formed from her by a power which owed nothing to any other agent, namely, the power of the Holy Ghost. Jesus will, therefore, resemble His mother and His mother alone, and in the most finished manner. Must we not, therefore, proclaim beautiful in the highest degree —tota pulchra—the happy mother to whom it was given to bring forth into this world Him whom the Prophet calls " the fairest of the children of men "? Since Mary's beauty was primarily the reflection of the beauty of the soul it stands to reason that her appearance was provocative of only the noblest and purest sentiments.

CHAPTER XIV

WE know that in all hearts which have retained any of the human sanctities there is an instinctive love for the young. Even the corrupt find in the sight of innocent childhood a reminder of the happier years before the poison of sin embittered their lives. But both nature and grace combine to make the child the very apple of the parents' eyes. If this be true of all normal parents it must have been incomparably true of the parents of the immaculate child. As a little one grows up there is for those who have intimate dealings with it an ever growing wealth of incident awakening the warmest love. The child's life, like the adult's, is the combined play of thoughts and words and deeds. For the majority of parents it would be criminal folly to look for perfection in any of these three spheres. In fact, original sin warns us rather to be ever on the look out for the cockle. Are we not beginning to realise better what practical results accrue from Mary's Immaculate Conception? So quite soberly we will try and ascertain just what we are to expect from this unique child, what in fact Joachim and Anne must have found in her above measure.

We have already disclaimed any miracle raising Mary's faculties to a permanent and adult activity. But as the merest results of her privilege we are faced with the most extraordinary situation. Let us take first the domain of thought. The thought world of any person has as ingredients the products of reason, memory and imagination. Because of original sin these powers are radically clouded in all ordinary mortals. There is, moreover, the added impediment of immaturity. On the asset side even of fallen human nature there may be a budding of genius easily discernible in the young child. Later on we will ask ourselves the question: where does Mary stand in relation to knowledge? But we will ask it concerning her when she will have attained maturity, not when she is still a child. For the moment it will suffice to examine her unique advantages in the acquisition of

58

knowledge with its inevitable repercussion on her words and deeds. In addition to endowments specifically supernatural there are also purely intellectual qualities which, if they are not necessary for salvation, are very helpful thereto. In fact they are often an indication and an effect of supernatural excellence. These qualities are grouped under the heading, science or knowledge. Theologians distinguish three kinds of knowledge: acquired, infused, and beatific. The first is natural to man and serves to enrich his mind. It is the fruit of application, study and all personal effort which has increased knowledge as its end. Infused knowledge is connatural to the angels and is communicated to them directly by God. They bask, as it were, in a ray of the Divine Light and no effort of their own is necessary thereto. Finally, the beatific knowledge is proper to God alone. In fact it is one with Himself, being the act whereby God knows Himself, and as His Nature is infinitely simple this act is identified with that Divine nature. As we stressed in our very first pages, we are only honouring Our Lady when we emphasise her limitations as a creature. So unique a character is she that the most and least we can say is that she is not divine. Mary did not enjoy the beatific vision. While revelation has most decidedly not stated that she did, in many ways it clearly insinuates that she did not. Mary's interrogation of the Archangel Gabriel and her words to Jesus when she found Him in the Temple are cases in point.

But we would be slow to deny her what was accorded to Moses —God's servant—and to St. Paul, that is, a momentary elevation of the soul to the contemplation of the Divinity. Perhaps the ineffable moments of the Incarnation, the Nativity and a post-Resurrection manifestation might be regarded as congruous occasions of such celestial favours. Her sufferings, too, would seem to demand just that which God so often grants to the humblest of His servants, namely, some compensatory consolations. And the sea of sorrow in which the compassionate mother was immersed would find its counter only in the highest favours such as we suggest.

Infused knowledge is not natural to man. Certainly it was not natural to the Blessed Virgin, perfect in all her natural faculties. However, there could have been moments, such as we suggested above, when Mary's soul was illumined in a superhuman fashion, as are the celestial spirits.

May we not accord to Mary other direct divine illuminations, truly infused yet proportioned to human nature? God would give her such to prepare her for her destiny. The knowledge of God and of herself was infused, which enabled her meritoriously to accept grace, infused also her Messianic lights and yearnings. After the Incarnation that clear view of the Divine Plan of Redemption was infused, her own place in it and the qualities and duties incumbent on her as mother and associate of the Redeemer. Even our first parents did receive from God a wonderful knowledge touching all which regarded their dignity and office. What treasures of knowledge may we then regard Mary as receiving, Mary destined to be our mother by a title a hundred times more true than that enjoyed by the first woman?

From all we have already said concerning that which Mary most definitely had not, or had only by privilege and momentarily, it follows that like all other children of men, she could and must needs acquire knowledge. We must remember, however, that all her organs and faculties were incomparably perfect. Her intelligence was tranquil and calm and had no intrinsic weakness capable of turning it from the contemplation of the true, error could never be accepted by such an intellect. Her love for God and for her neighbour led her to employ every possible means for loving both and serving both.

So we will not hesitate to claim for Mary a knowledge second only to that of her Divine Son.

The first source of Mary's acquired knowledge was the assiduous study of the Word of God. Undoubtedly celestial communications furnished her with another. Revelation has told us of Gabriel's embassy. But the Gospel is fragmentary and we may be sure that angelic visitants were not rare in this most privileged life. Her third and principal source of knowledge was no other than her Divine Son. What must have been, therefore, the extent and degree of Mary's knowledge! We may say that she surpassed in Divine wisdom King Solomon, and our first parents. But we need not maintain that she surpassed any of the masters in the arts and science of the purely material order.

CHAPTER XV

IN the two preceding chapters we have endeavoured to set down what theology teaches of Mary's endowments of mind, soul and even of body. But we are far from satisfied with theory, true though it be and beautiful though it be even in theory's domain. We are going to ask the parents of Our Lady to let us dwell with them and see for ourselves their immaculate child as she grows up before our eyes. We will watch God's lily unfolding and will drink in the fragrance of that divine bloom. Did we stand by the cradle of even an ordinary child of earth upon whose brow the regenerating waters had flown we should kneel down in reverence before this divinised soul. But now is the time for us to recall what we have already said about the initial grace of the Blessed Virgin. In the lives of God's favoured ones it occasionally happens that the force of the predestinating grace is almost palpable, at least to such holy souls as are completely in harmony with the divine. As in the case of the infant precursor such souls find themselves forced to ask "What a one, think ye, shall this child be?" (St. Luke i, 66). May we not well believe that Joachim and Anne experienced such things in the presence of Heaven's unique gift? And remember we have already stated that in Mary grace increased in the two manners in which a quality can increase. Taking the time factor, therefore, it comes to this, that every second, every hour, every day made this child lovelier in God's blessed sight, and lovelier in the sight of His creatures too. Grace also grew in her in that mysterious way in which all life grows. Mary possessed all the natural virtues. Let us watch these blossom and bloom. Already, by her Immaculate Conception we are introduced into a wonderland of utter loveliness. In the ordinary children of Adam there is always the cockle. And if a mother is not wholly blinded by a mother's love she will see that cockle raise its ugly head even at life's dawn. Mary will be a true child. She will not be a precocious monster.

Yet owing to her unique privilege she will be completely free from the slightest perverse inclination, even such as can mar infancy. Do we not feel the charm of contemplating such a child? Over and above this Mary was endowed with all the infused virtues which flow from sanctifying grace. She possessed the gifts of the Holy Ghost without measure. In order to witness the full play of all these virtues, and especially of the theological ones we will let Mary grow up before our eyes. We will watch her with reverent and loving eyes, we will listen to her words and try and get some idea of the grace springs which are their source; we will also observe her acts.

Before we try to penetrate into the interior of this Heavenly child we will begin, as we must begin, by admiring what first greets our eyes, her beautiful person. It is a common-place to exclaim when beside any cradle " what a lovely child." Generally this eulogy is an effort to please fond parents rather than any specific testimony to truth. But we can say it concerning the child of Joachim and Anne. As we have already said, nature and grace had a very special duty in the forming of a body no less than the soul which informs it to be a tabernacle worthy of the Incarnate Word. Oh, let us look on her! Already her Immaculate Conception ensures in the practical sphere a body vitiated by none of those ills which may mar human beauty and perfection. Moreover, this little child is to be the worthy Mother of God. Even corporally this destiny argues an exquisite perfection of body and of every member. How perfect must have been this virginal body, when later on, in answer to her consent, the Holy Spirit will find in it the adequate instrument of His great masterpiece, the fashioning of a body for the Divine word. The fairy tales of the world love to place us in the company of charming and exalted princesses whose dignity is only equalled by their goodness and beauty. But this is no fairy tale but the very truth of God. We are looking upon a girl-child who is more truly royal than any heir or heiress of the blood. She is sprung from David's royal line which holds its patents from the Most High God. If earthly royalty has any distinction at all perhaps it may consist in this, that centuries of privileged position and gentle breeding do issue in a nobility such as any nation might wish, for at least one family of all its children. Here we have not only a royal child but one endowed with all the qualities of soul, mind and body for the production of which the very dynasty was divinely inaugurated. We see, therefore, that on every title this little infant before us possesses an incomparable perfection even of body. And this perfection went on daily increasing until the great day of the Incarnation dawned. With ordinary children it is often quite otherwise. Are they favoured as infants, then they often disimprove as time goes on. How many are the maladies of childhood which may retard health and even blight the promise of the early days. None of those things could touch this privileged daughter of David.

So we see that the perfect soul of the infant virgin possessed a perfect body to minister to it. We will need to remember this when we try to assess the marvellous progress this child will make in her intellectual development. There are many elements which go to make up the beauty of a little infant. Sometimes it is a sweet smile playing on the baby countenance. Then, again, even physically Mary being totally immune from the pains incident to ordinary childhood—we mean those resulting from a fallen nature subject to corruption—her visage must have reflected a tranquillity mirroring the peace of God. This corporal beauty will also go on increasing until it will make Mary the living image even physically of the " fairest of the children of men " (Psalm 44, 3). As we have said, the divine life of grace beginning in Mary with her Immaculate Conception grew not only without obstacle but favoured with every possible help.

Owing to original sin, the rôle of parents is normally to nurture virtue in their children by carefully weeding out the evil inclinations which show themselves. Joachim and Anne were dealing with a child endowed with all those good dispositions which even in the sphere of right reason make virtuous acts easy. Take out of a child's life the whole sphere of the merely bold or naughty and you are eliminating a very big and recurrent sector. It is totally eliminated in Mary. This is likewise true of her life in the supernatural order. Let us try and figure out the actual situation. Since we are destined for the supernatural order, we can give the unqualified name of good only to that system which takes into consideration the two elements as they are meant by God to interact, that is, the supernatural with the natural as its basis. It is in this matter that parents must find their grading. We will leave out of consideration evil and depraved parents. But even amongst the children of God how many there are who live in a practical disregard for the supernatural? This attitude will have the most baneful effect on the training of the young. Let it suffice to say that Joachim and Anne were not of this category. In every possible way suggested by nature and grace they energised the full supernature of their treasure child. The holy name of the God of Israel would not have been given poor precedence in the names uttered in their infant's ear. And with the mention of God what a wonder-world would spring into life in this paradise of the infused virtues!

What happens when a mother breathes the sweet name of God into her baby's ear for the first time? We must remember that baptism has been a new birth for the child. There is now a new and celestial organism which is as real and more real in itself and in its acts than the merely human organism. This new being is the fruit of the infused virtues. The theological virtue of faith has been infused. This is as it were the very light of God. To the mind is given this Heavenly light so far and away above the mere flicker of human reason, and to the will is given the sweet strength to embrace this light and live by it. The theological virtue of hope enables the soul to hope directly in God, to aspire to His perfect possession. Charity is the nuptial garment enabling the soul to take its place at the Divine banquet. It not only makes the soul beautiful in the Divine eyes, but it divinises it, giving it a share in the Divine nature and making it a true son of God by adoption. When therefore this Divine organism is stirred into activity by its proper object, namely God, there is always at least a Divine response. God always echoes God. But in the majority of infants the immaturity of the internal faculties and of the external sense interposes a temporary obstacle to any conscious reaction of the child itself. But this was not the case with Mary. And when Anne spoke the incommunicable name of the Holy One of Israel into her baby's ear all that wonderland of grace vibrated with celestial harmony.

What did Mary look like? She would have been dark with the colouring of her race. Her features would have been perfectly formed with that perfection which we have said was the mere right of her immaculate being.

When Anne in the way of all mothers, pressed her darling to her heart, she must have been conscious of the stream of grace which flowed from her babe to herself. How radiant must have been the smile of the little one, and how often must she have

smiled. We all love the smiles of babyhood. Would there
never have been tears in those dear eyes? She is a real infant
and will feel everything incidental to her frail state. Yet she
will be spared all those sufferings which are the result of sickness. Never in her will petulance and peevish temper make
her a difficulty to those caring for her. And so we may say
that this chosen child is most often smiling.

The days merged into weeks and weeks into years. The
child of Joachim and Anne is a year old, is two, is three. We
can promise ourselves a feast of delight in contemplating her
development, physical, mental and moral. That is what must
now occupy our attention.

F

CHAPTER XVI

IN all infants the speedy physical development is most palpable.
There is a little new-born babe. In a week, in a month, in a
year it has grown almost out of recognition. This is a period
containing many joys for the fond parents and sometimes alas
keen, keen sorrows. For even at the very threshold of life those
maladies may be met with which the sin of our first parents has
sown in our corruptible nature.

Often it is the hard duty of doctor or nurse to acquaint the
young mother of the sad fact that already death has claimed the
little being to whom she had just given life amidst such pains.
Or is it even harder to place in her trembling arms an infant
already handicapped by this or that deformity? How different
it was with the child of Joachim and Anne. Already she
possesses a body perfect in every way. And every day added to
its perfection. Here we are tempted to inquire if these privileged
parents were aware of their child's destiny. We cannot know.
Revelations have occasionally been made at the cradles of God's
holy ones and it would not surprise us if He had enlightened
these parents on their ineffable privilege. Be that as it may, we
have already regarded it as a legitimate deduction, that Joachim
and Anne were perfectly endowed by nature and grace for their
high and holy parenthood. And so we may be sure that the
perfection of their child in every way was not lost on them. At
the very least they would become increasingly more conscious
of the fact that such unwonted gifts pointed to a rare destiny.
They would, above all, see in these gifts as they unfolded an ever
new claim to all the care and love placed in their hearts by God
for the living lily of which so far they had the fashioning. Step
by step with a child's physical growth proceeds the development
of the mental powers. Here again a very different scene presents
itself where ordinary children are in question. To take things at
their very worst, how many parents must watch in vain for the
slightest glimmer of intellect in their little one? That must

surely be a cruel agony to loving parents. Apart from special precocity of genius, parents can expect very little from their infants and must wait a long time for that little. Now let us resume our place beside God's privileged little one. Like all mothers Anne will be anxious to help the mental powers of her child to unfold. For a time the labour of love will be altogether hers. Then Mary utters her first baby words. Were they those which are traditional with all babies, the holy words which identified both loving parents? Or would there have been an exception in this case and would God's Holy Name be the first to hallow those divinely hallowed lips.

We cannot know. But this much is certain. If all souls, created by the Most High belong first to Him, this immaculate soul belongs to Him in an altogether ineffable way. And as we have already suggested, it is likely that Joachim and Anne were supernaturally enlightened on their child's destiny. Both of them, therefore, and very particularly the mother would be jealous of God's rights and would leave nothing undone to procure these for Him. So Anne would have spoken of God into that baby ear, and may we not believe that the fruit of all this repetition was the first fruit of all Mary's human words for the God who had favoured her.

From this moment Mary's mental life developed at a prodigious rate. Anne would point out people and places and objects to the growing child and she would never have to give the same information twice over. It is now that we can see the fruits of her Immaculate Conception in the domain of the mind. Hers was an intellect undimmed by sin's foul heritage. And its light was focussed clearly on its proper object with all the more power according as the material instrument increased in perfection. How retentive would that memory be, what a beautiful storehouse that fair and powerful imagination. Above all, what strength was in that will as it unerringly seized on the good, as unerringly pointed out by the intellect as the true. Add to all this the continued and perfectly enlightened help of the most highly endowed parents and we can look for a ravishing joy in the contemplation of this little girl's growing-up in body and mind and soul.

But if her mental development is speedy and admirable, what are we to think of her supernatural development?

What happens in the rearing of any child? There is first of all the almost purely physical sphere. We have treated of that in Mary's case. Then with development of body would come development of mind. There would be the first stumbling steps, the first articulate sounds. At this point, even in ordinary children, at least if they be not defective, progress is rapid. The helping factors would be the mental and physical perfection of the child, coupled with the perfection of the parents in parent-craft, which normally reduces itself for a long time to mother-craft. It is at this stage that when treating of Mary we must take leave of ordinary children, be they ever so well endowed. All we may do is to use them as analogies. So we will proceed. There would be Mary's first words. We have already suggested what they would be, Anne would be filled with such a love for God that there would be no danger of her trying to monopolise her child's attention. On the contrary, we believe that she would breathe the name of God over her child so often that His Holy Name would have been the very first to strike the outer ear of His chosen one. What would that name be? It would be the Holy Tetragrammaton, namely, the sacred consonants which enshrined the incommunicable Name of God in the Hebrew tongue. Never were they pronounced but in their stead the word Adonai, meaning Lord or the Hebrew word for the Divinity, Elohim. What never could be uttered by frail and sinful human lips was the personal name of the God of Israel, probably Yahweh. Was there an exception made for this child? We do not know. Two things we do know, first, that Anne would not have uttered the personal name, and second that this infant was destined to call her God by the sweet personal Name of Jesus, her God and her Child. But that is not yet.

CHAPTER XVII

NOTHING better shows how far we have put Our Blessed Lady into the clouds than our repugnance to associate with her such very human actions as eating and drinking. Such a topic is either left completely out of discussion in her connection, or there is an effort to portray her as sublimely different to us in this matter. Sublimely different she was, but seldom have spiritual writers probed the real source of the difference, or analysed it in action. And yet it is an incontestable fact that whatever about the human mother, the Divine Son did eat and drink. So little secret did He make of it that the Pharisees accused Him of being a wine-bibber and a glutton. They add that He dined with sinners. Not that we are allowing ourselves to attach any significance at all to the hypocritical calumny as such, but it could not even have been made if Our Lord either did not exercise those human functions at all, or did so only in most sacred seclusion. Was not a meal with His Apostles the setting of the institution of the great central sacrifice and Sacrament of the Christian Faith? And when He rose from the dead, Our Lord used His human powers to prove the utter reality of His corporal resurrection.

Are we not then to as much as think of food and drink in Mary's connection? Was she fed by celestial spirits on some ethereal angel-stuff? If so, angel-stuff was her body and angel-stuff the flesh she gave Him. See now where our nonsense would lead us, even to rank heresy. For one of the first heresies was actually that of the Docetæ who maintained that Christ had only a seeming body. Thus they would get rid of the scandal of the Passion, but thus also they would also get rid of the truth of our Redemption.

Indeed, Mary did eat and drink. And never were the lowly elements of sustenance more ennobled, more worthy of their creation than when they were assimilated into that immaculate body from which later on the vesture of the sacred humanity was to be woven.

Let not the reader imagine that this is too trivial a fact to merit discussion. When starting this book we made an open avowal of our purpose. Knowing that Our Lady was a flesh and blood reality we decided to regale ourselves by the detailed though reverent attention to all the sweet reality of her as it unfolds before us in her life from her Immaculate Conception to her Dormition and glorious Assumption. We maintain that this is nothing less than what God Himself wills who has created her thus. Moreover, it is only by such a true study of our mother that her glories can have practical repercussion on our own lives. This is most true in connection with this matter of food and drink, for it gives us an opportunity of revising our views on the vital questions of the appetites, indeed the question of good and evil. It is a matter upon which men readily erred from the beginning. The sect of the Manicheans proves that. Even to-day when human science considers it has plumbed all the depths there is crass ignorance displayed on this matter by so-called savants. Moreover, even among the faithful there is a lot of misconception with very practical and harmful reactions on their spiritual lives.

The worst of it is that there is a very full Catholic philosophy on the matter. We are the heirs to real intellectual giants who have shed all the light on the subject which the human intellect at its best possesses, and these truly great philosophers conducted all their researches under the white ray of Divine revelation.

The first cardinal point to make is that actuality in every shape or form is good. Evil is not an actuality, it is a defect. We are taught this primal truth by God Himself. For in the first inspired record of creation God emphasises by repetition the essential goodness of creation. Six times in the first Chapter of Genesis occur the words " and God saw that it was good " and His final approbation of His own handiwork is in the form of a crescendo. " And God saw all the things that He had made, and they were very good" (Gen. Chapter I, verses 10, 12, 18, 21, 25, 31). This divinely attested truth of the inherent goodness of all creation ought to motivate our attitude to this latter. And we must not forget that creation includes ourselves and every part of ourselves. The tragic fact of sin does not and cannot undo this truth. It is true that owing to the change wreaked by sin in rational nature created things though good in themselves may now be very easily perverted in their use or rather abuse and thus be made points of departure from God rather than direct avenues to Him, which of themselves they are. But there is no positive evil ingredient in creation leading us from our final end. Now let us take a brief look at the sphere of appetite.

Man finds in himself a twin urge, one towards the preservation of the individual and the other towards the preservation of the race. Here again we must clarify our attitude. These urges are implanted by God Himself. Therefore, they must be radically good, good in themselves, and good in all the media, physical, mental or emotional through which they operate. But it is in the field of human appetite that sin has made itself felt most intensely.

Before the fall there existed a beautiful order. God was at the top, supreme. Then human reason came, absolutely subject to God and, therefore, absolute master of the powers inferior to it. This held true for the great appetite of reproduction, but this appetite was not called into play before the fall. But the appetite of self-conservation was in use and we can measure the enormity of our first parents' crime when we realise that in their faculties and senses there was absolutely no deordination, making temptation alluring and sin palatable. Then came sin. Man's revolt against God by a peculiarly just retribution produced a revolution in the kingdom of his own being. Reason lost none of its validity but its light was dimmed. The will not only became weak but was infected with a positive inclination towards evil. The faculties and senses tended to attempt autonomy each in its own sphere. This anarchy is nowhere so apparent as in the region of sexual appetite. Here is where we must go slowly. It is a delicate subject, yet there are truths about it which may not be shirked and indeed which need not.

The first thing to re-emphasise is that sin has not made the sexual impulse evil in itself. It has come from the holy hands of God. It is harnessed to the designs of His omnipotence and His love. But here, perhaps, more than in the whole being of man has anarchy and revolution raised its ugly head. This imperious appetite is in itself blind. But it now offers itself as good to the will—and good it is in itself—and as true to the intellect—and in itself it is true. But the weakened intellect no longer reflects on all the elements which must be considered if God's Holy Will is to be done, and the corrupt will regards as good its own present pleasure without regarding the good-pleasure of the Great Creator. And so this divinely implanted urge has become the source of countless sins against God and neighbour. This whole sad state of affairs induced by original sin has different reactions from different classes of people. In those outside the Church it takes the form of a practical denial of original sin in itself and in its effects. And, perhaps, obviously the denial is loudest where the lie is most patent—precisely in the sex domain. Hence the cult of the nude—either more or less—and in the matter of dress and fashion it is always less than more. These people would maintain that if we could only get used to it the body would cease to excite inordinate passions. The most we will say about this doctrine is that its votaries can be sincere only for a very short time. For hard facts are against them. And original sin is one of the hardest facts of human experience.

Amongst those who comprise the household of the Faith there is too often found quite another swing of the pendulum. They are perhaps too little acquainted with the dogmatic background of the whole matter. Consequently they lack clear-cut principles of thought and action. If they are thus bankrupt of principles they experience like all men the interior revolt and they commence to harbour a constant distrust of the flesh and all it stands for. This false attitude results in a lot of foolish prudery. Such people consider even the natural necessities of life as something almost shameful. If they write spiritual books their treatment of sex is coloured with mere resignation if not reprobation. And it is people like this who shudder at any reference to flesh and blood facts in the lives of the saints—above all in the life of the Queen of Saints.

What on the contrary is the fact? Just as we have endeavoured to state, namely a radical goodness inherent in creation, and an ever possible vitiation stemming from original sin. We own that sin has made of human nature a dark turbulent ocean. But thanks to the Great Creator that stormy sea is neighboured by an ocean of light and peace—even the immaculate virgin. As we suggested in the beginning many spiritual writers are content with praising Mary with a wealth of metaphor. But Mary is no metaphor. She is a woman, a mother. She is the grandest reality under God the Divine source of all reality. And now we are going to translate the dogma of the fall and the Redemption into terms of Mary's flesh and blood reality. In the full light of creation's primal goodness, in the glorious light of her immunity from all infection of sin we will boldly face our task, shirking nothing, but looking with reverence and love upon this masterpiece of God, who has our human nature in all its integrity, who has that nature as it was first designed by the all Holy God.

We will first take the reproductive appetite and see what we may say of it in Mary's regard.

Let us boldly assert that Mary did indeed possess this appetite. But let us hasten to add that it was such an appetite as existed before the fall. It was an inferior power which was absolutely subject to the command of reason, and of reason itself under the perfect sway of fullest grace. In saying so much we have said what the Divines say when they exclude from Mary the "Fomes peccati," or concupiscence. It is in understanding this matter that our previous considerations will be found helpful. Let us hold grimly to the truth that the urges implanted in human nature by God are holy in themselves, in their workings, in their objectives. Only we must remember that sin has introduced a disturbing element. What now happens is that these appetites move and move strongly without consulting the reason, not to speak of God. In the domain of sex this inordinate stirring of an impulse which is good in itself provides as it were the ready material to sin. We call this deordination concupiscence and when spiritual writers sometimes seem to be reprobating the divinely implanted instinct, it is rather concupiscence which is the object of their rebukes. Owing to her unique privilege of Immaculate Conception there was nothing of this in Mary. But here is where we would recur to our dominant theme. Mary was no spectral creature, still less was she a monster as any human technically is who lacks something integral to human nature. Mary was not only a perfect woman, she was the woman of God's primal design. What does this mean in terms of flesh and blood? Mary was endowed with every spiritual, mental and physical characteristic which go to make up our concept of womanhood. That is to say she was perfectly endowed for wifehood and motherhood. Not that she was made for those things precisely because she was a woman. There are people who reprobate the Catholic attitude to celibacy and who strive to support their view by pointing to human nature itself. They say: "Look at human nature. Has not the Creator stamped His designs upon it? Has He not even added His command to increase and multiply which cannot be achieved unless one utilises the powers bestowed?" These people are lacking in true faith, but no less in common philosophy. And Mary is an admirable example of the truth of the whole matter. For before she is a woman she is a creature. That is to say she is made for

God's good pleasure, not for her own.   Then as a rational
creature she is bound to ascertain by the light of reason what
God's good pleasure actually is in her regard.   As a supernatural
creature raised to a share in the Divine nature by adoption, she
is all the more bound to consult the Divine will.   How little
merely physiological structure or created appetite has a right to
assume the rôle of dictator!

We are assured by pious tradition which has the factual backing of Holy Writ that as soon as Mary was capable of a human
act she fully embraced all God's designs upon her.   These were
not revealed all at once.   The peak point was reached with the
archangel's embassy.   But we are certain that from the very
beginning Mary knew well what God wanted of her perfect
womanhood.   He wanted, that is, the supreme dedication of all
these most real and magnificent and holiest powers to Himself.
And Mary made that total dedication.   It was because of it that
her question to the archangel was so legitimate.   The queries
of Zachary were not so, and received an altogether different treatment.   What a stupendous reward was conferred on Mary, for
her wholehearted immolation!   In her more than in any other
of her sex before or since, womanhood blossomed and bloomed
and brought forth its fruitage.   Her holy womb closed forever
by her vow was not by that fact barren but bore God's Only
Begotten Son.   Her virginal breasts dried for ever by her self-
immolation were filled from Heaven with milk to suckle the
Divine Infant.   Every womanly instinct received its perfect
fruition.   Mary was wife in the truest sense.   She was supremely
mother.   She retained withal the priceless pearl of virginal
integrity.

Let us get back again to the little daughter of Joachim and
Anne.   For Gabriel is still gazing into the eyes of God and not
yet does he read in them his mission to Nazareth.

We spoke of the appetite of self-conservation.   And this was
most surely in Mary.   Indeed in her it was more than self-
conservation.   It was the remote building up of that dear flesh
and blood material from which one day would be miraculously
framed a Man-God.

Like all other appetites in Mary that for food and drink was
under the perfect sway of reason, illumined by faith.   But this
is not to say that Mary never ate at all, or that she did so in a
Divine way which forbids us to make it a subject of our meditation.   A Divine way it was if by that we mean that it was the

exercise of an appetite by a creature untouched by the fall. In Mary there was no precipitation in eating. Never for a moment was she motivated by anything save the Divine will speaking through her needs and indicating the means of bodily reparation. But for all that, the meals in the household of Joachim and Anne were as normally conducted as those in any house on earth. Nay, it is only Mary who could be absolutely normal in this matter as in every other. For original sin has made all the rest of us fevered, sickly—in a word, abnormal. Mary also felt the need of sleep, and what we have said about eating and drinking in her case holds good for this matter also. For this whole matter of Mary's reaction to creatures—taking creatures in the fullest sense—we must never lose sight of a cardinal fact resulting from her Immaculate Conception. And it is this. Never for a moment did she forget or could she forget God. We do not refer to a more or less pious recollection of His presence but to the all-pervading fact of God as the first cause and the conserving cause. We have sadly strayed from this our true centre, owing to original sin. With Mary it was absolutely different. She never could rest in the creature as such. Her soul was too saturated with the realisation that God alone is, and that the creature—including the creature who is Mary—is of itself just nothing at all. This basic truth, could we make it the compass of our evaluations, would in itself save us from that stupid and even impious worship of the creature so characteristic of our age. What is all this advance in science but a deeper and deeper drawing upon God's subsistence and in particular upon His attribute of wisdom? In the light of this truth science would be a noble avenue to adoration, to gratitude, to love. This was precisely how it always was with Mary. When she experienced through sense and faculty anything delectable, anything admirable, she referred it all to its author. And so we can see with what tranquillity and with what thanksgiving Mary could use, as she did use, any and every creature which came within her experience. To our mind, the mistake made by too many preachers and writers on Our Lady is that while they are talking of the immaculate virgin they are keeping their eyes too much on corrupt human nature as we all experience it. Hence their reluctance to analyse Mary's human reactions. But, as we have already said, that is to regard the Immaculate Conception as a true but ethereal endowment without practical repercussions on every human thought, word and deed of the mother of men.

CHAPTER XVIII

SPIRITUAL writers, especially in the meditation genre, have quite obviously an axe to grind. It is always a most edifying axe, but there it is. The inevitable result is that no matter what setting or what personages they choose for the occasion, the setting embellishes, the personages say, precisely what the writer has in his little mind. It is a very pious marionette show, but it can be boring and it may be to some extent harmful. As an example very pertinent to our general theme let us take an average meditation on silence. Of course, the very best exponents of this very negative virtue are the members of the Holy Family. Now watch the axe. The holy writer does not even want to discuss speech. Silence is his theme. And it is silence the Holy Family must exemplify.

So we are first told, as an axiom to be sure, that very few words were used by the Holy Family. Indeed! If the author of the meditation dared, he would say that they never spoke at all. That would give a splendid edge to the axe. We are introduced to the three holiest figures in the world's history and they are little better than the statues in any church requisites shop. And these dumb holy ones are to be an inspiration to us who can so easily say too much but who must say something. What is the root error behind such presentations? We would say that it stems from faulty philosophy and faulty theology. We should have added faulty history, for we think it will be easy to show that the facts are against the scribes. First of all, to take the philosophy of the matter. These writers forget that in itself silence is a negative thing. The mere absence of sound is not thereby a virtue.

They are afraid to allow these holy people to speak, because they consider every topic too trivial for them. Bad philosophy again. God cannot be trivial. Yet He thought of a whale and He thought of a shrimp and He quite definitely created both. So that a discussion on shrimps would not be a discussion on trivial topics. God thought a shrimp worth making. And the nearer a soul is to God the more surely will it recognise the intrinsic dignity of created things, the more easily will it be able to talk of them with gravity. So we see that the faulty philosophy led to jim-crack theology. And now to history. The Gospels do not even pretend to be complete. They are fragmentary. Yet they make Our Lord speak quite at length on occasions. Also, if you watch out for it you will see that He does not confine Himself to what we would style the loftiest themes. He speaks of foxes, and sparrows and seedlings. He gives directions for the successful throw of a fishing-net, asks about the prospects of a meal for the disciples and prepares one for them Himself. So the Gospels, as far as they go—and they do not pretend to go the whole factual way—take us very far away from the silent statue theory, even when the Incarnate Son of God is in question.

We think that we have sufficiently cleared the ground for a reverent, yet realistic enquiry into what conversations may have taken place between Mary and her parents. Further, we will discuss the possibility of contacts between Mary and other children of her age and place.

Before we discuss this matter we had better dispose of another argument which would put Our Lady quite out of the ordinary in daily life. It is said that her consciousness of her own privileged nature, coupled with her realisation of how different everybody else was, created in her a great isolation, a great solitude, and great loneliness as it were. We are not concerned so much with asserting or denying subjective dispositions to Our Lady. We are dealing with practical reactions. And we would say that she could not have been other in this than her Divine Son. Despite her unique privilege, Mary was still a creature. Her Son was God. What an isolation, what a loneliness was not the result of hypostatic union! Yet as we already stressed, if the Divine nature caused all the reactions which it could have caused, the very end of the Incarnation would have been frustrated. God was to become accessible to His creatures. And so we find Him restraining as it were the legitimate over-flow of His Divinity, so that in His human life Thabor was an episode and not the normal situation. Surely we may claim as much for His Mother? We can maintain that in all the reactions of daily life she acted in the sweetest human way which was none the less immaculate.

Generally speaking, the biographies of the saints help us little as even analogies for the life lived in Nazareth by the Holy Family. For, as the authors of these biographies were obviously not the saints themselves, emphasis was laid on the exalted to the almost total exclusion of the human and ordinary. However, our own days are indeed blessed in a singularly sweet and human document of consummate sanctity, namely, the auto-biography of the Little Flower. And among the many books written around and about that unique self-revelation we would say the crown is the recent *Story of a Family,* by Father Stephane Joseph Piat, O.F.M. In its delightful and edifying pages we hear saints in real live converse. And they can talk about almost everything.

So we have our desired analogy, and in its light we will ask ourselves what conversations may be believed to have had place in the holy home of Joachim and Anne.

As we saw already, despite her immaculate endowments, Our Lady learned from experience. Of course, there never was a quicker learner. Nevertheless she would ask her parents all the really necessary questions of childhood. Greater than she will employ a similar method with the doctors of the law, when the Incarnate Lawgiver was but twelve years in reckoning of human time. And so, according as Mary grew up, her parents and particularly her mother, would tell her the names of objects, especially those in domestic use. They would likewise tell her the names of animals and birds and plants. Very rapidly the conversation would cease to be one-sided and the little girl would take her part. When such topics became possible we can well imagine conversations dealing with the good God and His dealings with His chosen people. Surely the Messias would be a constant topic and His prospective coming. If matters dealing with the Jewish nation as such, or with their Roman masters came up, it would not be in any narrow political sense but with regard to the flowering of the Messianic hope. And Mary would have these easy lessons in geography and topography, which consist in hearing place names from warm living lips that pronounce them with love. And surely at some time or other the little maid would be told of where the City of David lay, sweet little Bethlehem. Had Mary any social contacts out-side her own home? We may be sure she had. How can we believe that she was totally segregated from all other company? Of course, the best possible parents, guided surely by the Spirit of God, chose Mary's friends very carefully. But we may be sure that she had dear friends, not only of her own kin, but among the other maidens of Nazareth. Is it not a stupendous thought to realise that human eyes once saw a little girl who was destined to be the very Mother of God? It opens our eyes to the value that God attaches to human creatures. It is a source from which we may draw true and intense respect for childhood and for girlhood. And although earth will never again see Mary's peer, yet each child of earth whom we see to-day has a stupendous destiny. For he or she is certainly called to the adoptive sonship of the great God and to a high place in the Father's Kingdom hereafter. It is only in the light of this truth that we can really fathom the horrors of sin which lays its unholy hands on those Divine destinies and turns them from their course. This is the horror of heresy which takes the young mind and gives it false information about itself and its destiny. This is the blasphemy of uncleanness which blasts the temples built for the Divinity. And do we not appreciate it all when among a group of little children of Nazareth we see a little girl—even the daughter of Joachim and Anne? But it has not yet appeared what she will yet be.

Had Mary a recreational life? The bad philosophers will raise their eyebrows. But they forget that animals have no ordered recreation devices which are characteristic of rational beings as such. And as reason has God for its author, so also is He the author of all that is reasonable. If Mary did not live in complete isolation from the young Nazareth girls it is certain that she shared in their play. Of course, in this matter, too, Mary was perfect. And so we must exclude from her recreations anything which would arise from mere exuberance of animal spirits. But she could be no kill-joy as a child who would become the mother of joy. There would be nothing stilted or affected about this child. Always she would exemplify God's perfect creature, God's perfect daughter, God's destined mother.

In this, as in so many other matters, St. Thérèse has brought us to our own senses. And we know that a saint in the making may enjoy her swing and play with her bantams or little lamb. If a princess of God's court could do this, we cannot refuse to believe that the incomparable queen also honoured those dear characteristics of childhood in her young though august person.

CHAPTER XIX

THE BEAUTY OF MARY

IT is in perfect keeping with the object of these pages to ask ourselves just what Mary looked like and of what nature and how great must her beauty have been. For it is our avowed object to make her real for ourselves, though no more real than she actually is. In order to see how vague we have allowed our ideas to become on this point of Mary's personal appearance we have only honestly to ask and as honestly answer this question. What image comes to our minds when we think of Mary? Only too often it will be just a pious blur with baby angels perhaps and a crescent moon and, of course, some sort of woman who will be the central figure. To take only this one picture it may shock us to realise that the only thing in it with shape and substance tallying with reality is the crescent moon. We have seen that too often in real skies to be satisfied with any counterfeit. The angels are quite like chubby children of earth but have not got the slightest resemblance to real angels. As Saint Thérèse said with her truly Divine commonsense, angels are pure spirits and, therefore, cannot be seen as they really are by the corporeal eye. So we are left with the central figure and we ask you is it worthy of one who had a very definite appearance, as appearance is reckoned by humans, and who, moreover, retains that appearance, almost infinitely glorified in heaven? So we will clear up our ideas and ask ourselves with reverence and love—and commonsense—what Mary must have looked like.

One fact which will tell us a lot is that she belonged most authentically to the Chosen People, that is to the Jewish Race. Mary was a Jewess. If that were kept in mind we do not think that her sisters of to-day, or her blood-brothers would suffer affronts at the hands of professed Christians.

She would then be dark in colouring. We are in no lack of modern models for our instruction. Jewish maidens are almost without exception beautiful. Since God's primal plan must be discerned in the mean rather than in the exception we can believe that Mary would not have been under-stature or over. She would have attained a height and general development which would give the impression of perfect balance and harmony. Already we have stressed her royal lineage. In any royal line which has been safeguarded there would be expected a poise and a physiological perfection answering to perfect breeding in the physical, mental and moral sphere. Humans who have expected all this from their royal dynasties sometimes get some of it, and often less of it than they imagine. But David's royal line was safeguarded more by Heaven than earth. And Mary represented it at its zenith. So this child would be every inch a queen.

The blush of health contributes very largely to personal appearance. In Mary perfect physical health was a sequel to her Immaculate Conception. Let us try and see all that this means in practice. Since God is infinite wisdom, power and love, it is obvious that every creature as designed in the Divine mind reflected these attributes. However, two factors enter in capable of minimising and even of destroying the perfection of the Divine ideal when actualised by creation. The first factor is creaturehood as such with its essential limitations. To this we may ascribe all that there is of imperfection in the sub-rational universe. We see all this animal creation subject to pain, deformity and death. In their case this does not, as it cannot imply sin. It only underlines creaturehood. God alone is. God alone is immutable, eternal, the source of His own unalloyed bliss. Perhaps also we may regard it as showing the mysterious solidarity of all creation, thus interpreting the holy writer who says that all creation groans—lamenting in its own way the sin of its rational interpreters and feeling also in its own way the effects of that crime of crimes. Even in irrational nature much must be attributed to the secondary causes to which God has permitted free play, notably to human free wills in their action and interaction.

In the domain of angel and of man we have the creature's contribution of sin. Here we are no longer puzzled. No longer need we ask why innocence must suffer, for guilt is over all. And so it is that it is here the Divine Plan is most distorted. God did not design death or its baneful messengers, disease and pain. These have come in the wake of sin and continue to take their toll of fallen nature. In fact humanity is so much altered by sin that we might despair of even conjecturing what a sinless creature might have been. But praise be to the God of all mercy, we are not left to conjecture. We have before our eyes a creature absolutely untouched by sin and its consequences. It is Mary. It is the young girl we are now contemplating. Here we see God's original plan in perfect fruition and that in every detail. Mary is not like one of those works of art, beautiful, yes, but not permitting a too close or too near a scrutiny. And that is why we are exultingly contemplating her in these pages.

Her Immaculate Conception preserved her from all those seeds of deformity and ill-health which more or less blemish everyone else. And so, in general, Mary is perfectly proportioned. Although we may not analyse it, such perfect symmetry goes far to produce the subtle fact of beauty. How perfectly formed each member, each feature. You hear people say she has beautiful hands, or what lovely eyes. Those who saw Mary, and let us remember that countless human eyes beheld her—would not even be able to seize on one feature for special praise. There would be the radiant perfection of an integral whole. Surely those whose privilege it was to see this little girl as she blossomed and bloomed into perfect womanhood must have always felt struck by her appearance. They would look at her. They would look after her when she passed. And voiced or unvoiced their sentiments must have been " what a beautiful child." Here it is opportune to stress that privilege claimed for Mary by her Divines, namely that owing to her own unique perfection, she never aroused in anyone sentiments or emotions other than those of the purest admiration. Would that her daughters of to-day cherished such a noble ambition! In this matter, too, of inherent feminine attraction they would be true to their vocation to be helpmates of men. And they would only embellish their natural attractions like other Judiths to honour God and save His people. How much then of beauty adorns Mary from a merely physical corollary of her privilege! But her loveliness has deeper roots, far, far deeper.

Mary's immaculate soul was the soul of a perfect believer. Her faith was perfect. Now you will wonder how this could affect her appearance. Recall the incident of Peter's walking on the waters. There we have a wonderful epitome of all life. With our human and natural sight we see only the waters and their raging billows. Waters were never designed for walking on, never. And left to themselves our human faculties and

senses assure us only of that fact. And we feel ourselves sink-
ing. Terror is written on our countenances. Well, terror is
no ingredient of beauty. We may be sure that poor Peter
looked his worst at that moment when he felt the waves engulf-
ing him. How different when he heard the gently chiding
voice and felt the strong warm hand uplifting him. Then
serenity returned. Then was that rugged brow smooth again.
Now let us return to Mary. She always heard that voice within
her, calling her to Himself in a way that God has called no
other to Himself. Never a doubt disturbed her faith. And all
this issued in the serenest brow that was ever seen on earth.
In those dear eyes the light of perfect faith and confidence was
ever at its zenith. Our Lord Himself seems to attribute all
fear to doubt, to a faith which wavers. It was so with Peter,
and the disciples in general. It is so with us all. Why do we
so easily yield to depression when we know that we are in the
hands of a God all wise, all powerful, and above all, all loving.
And so it is that our fluctuating faith is written large in the
shadows which so often darken our countenance, in the worries
which line our brows, in all the storms within our poor hearts
which chase serenity from our visages. But think of her. How
radiantly beautiful must have been the eternal peace which
ever shone in her eyes and lit up her countenance! Mary's
beauty has another deep source. Her faith spontaneously
enkindled adoration. She was such a perfect adorer in spirit
and in truth as the Father ever seeks.

Now we often use such expressions as adoration without
analysing their meaning. Perhaps we do associate with it a
posture more or less abject. This half-way analysis has also
done harm to a full understanding of the saints, and to even
an attempted understanding of their queen. For neither she
nor they were always prostrate on the ground, nor even always
bowed in a perpetual externated doxology. They could never
have done the duties of their state under such conditions, and
they became saints precisely because they did these duties. We
forget that such necessary creature attitudes to the great Creator
are first of all interior and only exterior by accident and on
occasion. Now what is the internal act of adoration? It con-
sists in the more or less vivid realisation by the creature of its
creaturehood. Whatever about the degree of realisation the fact
is constant and it is just this, that of ourselves we are nothing.
We were not, and then by God's creative act we are. But so

radical is our nothingness that God must create us at every instant, otherwise we would slip back into our native nothingness. Perhaps there is no fundamental truth so forgotten by us, so ignored in practice. And yet from it alone we could deduce many of our obvious religious obligations.

Men there are who are quite unaware of this truth. Others refuse to acknowledge it. Even amongst the faithful, few keep it before them as the lodestar of their lives.

But Mary had it in all its perfection and always. Never for a moment did she forget her native nothingness. And for this very reason she could never be the victim of that morbid self-consciousness which is the basis of so much modern neurosis. Obviously she could not suffer from megalomania. Nor could she be a victim of inferior complex. For by a beautiful paradox when we do not purloin false titles to self-respect, we find good titles thereto in the Creator's respect for the creature He has made and keeps making. Now let us see how all this would affect Mary's appearance. In her there would be no posing, none of that clutching to prerogative which often mars human dignity. On the other hand there would be no cringing, no affected servility of look, or gesture, of word or act. Of all God's creatures Mary could best look her fellow-creatures in the face without arrogance and without impudence. How easy it must have been to deal with her. She knew what she was not. She knew what she was by God's command. She knew what other creatures were. And so there was perfect ease, perfect tranquillity. And all that was written on her brow and radiated from her person.

Let us try and plumb yet another Divine source of the loveliness which is Mary. This time it will be her perfect immunity not alone from sin but from all the corrupt motions which are the very fuel of the latter.

In every child of Adam, with the exception of Mary, there is a corrupt nature to be dealt with. This is always radically true even when by special preventive grace the domain of concupiscence and inherited corruption is at least circumscribed to some extent. Let us first take things at their worst. Imagine a person who from the dawn of conscious and deliberate responsibility yields fully to all the perverse instincts of vitiated nature. Would we not see viciousness written in every feature of such a one? Happily it is seldom as bad as that. Let us rather take the more common case, which will indeed be very

likely our own. From the time that we have become aware
of the two laws within us of which even the great doctor of
the nations was sadly aware, do we not find our soul and our
body an arena where good and evil are ever locked together
in a truceless combat? Up from the depths of our being surge
impulses which must be controlled if the life of grace is not to
be strangled within us. It need not always be a matter of
serious sin. We all feel the worry of these urges to pride and
vanity, to anger and petulance and seeking of self. This is
the warp and woof from which every life is woven. In fact
it is almost the very basis of sanctity. Take for instance the
angel of our own age, St. Teresa of the Child Jesus. How
strong was her faith. And yet, and yet, what was its background, the darkness of doubt seething up from the bowels
of hell. And it will be only on the last great Reckoning Day
that we will see how often it was thus. That dazzling purity
will perhaps be seen to be the fruit of a life-time of carnal
temptation, that charity bloomed from the very temptation to
hate, that meekness was a holy soul's response to the urge of
anger!

But what has this all to do with our purpose? Well, far
be it from us to say that such a noble struggle against corrupt
nature militates against the beauty of the human person. On
the contrary it issues in a very marked loveliness which can
transfigure countenances unfavoured by nature. But all the
stress and storm must have some effect even if it be only
momentary. If God's holy ones keep smiling eyes for all the
world, the shadows are at least no secret to themselves. Now
let us get back to God's chosen lily. From her very conception
she is endowed with a nature which knows no taint. From
whatever moment her conscious deliberate life may be said to
begin all is perfection. The only change is in the line of
increase. Like the orb of day her virtue rises at every moment
until all is radiance. Every thought from this limpid source is
perfect. Perfect is every gesture and movement. Each word,
each deed is a thing of beauty ravishing the very heart of God.
Surely we can readily realise that the sweet face from which
such a soul shone forth must have been exceeding fair. And
let us remind our readers it is not the face of the paintings,
even the greatest of them. For the artists were limning Our
Lady with their eyes on human corruption. They knew that
daughters of Eve who look one straight in the eyes are often

more impudent than modest. And so if you notice they seldom
let us look into Mary's eyes. Either she has them cast down,
or her face is in profile. But as we said, Mary above all would
look you in the face. And we, dear immaculate child, we will
not be deprived of that gaze into your dear eyes. We are not
worthy. We are unclean. But we would drink in purity from
those wells of innocency. We would learn adoration and love
and gratitude from the light shining in your eyes and revealing your immaculate soul.

What after all is beauty? It does not belong either to the
scope of these pages or indeed to our philosophical stock in
trade to analyse the notion of beauty from the point of view
of strict philosophy. But even if we do not or cannot
analyse our concept we all know intuitively what beauty is.
That is to say when we are brought into its presence we
recognise it immediately. It may be scenic beauty or beauty
of person. Of one thing we feel sure and it is this, that beauty
is the resultant rather of an ensemble than of a detail. In a
landscape we are caught by the varied play of light and shade
flitting over the whole scene, rather than by this point or that
which for the nonce is flooded in light or left in the sombre.
And this is true for personal beauty too, far more true than
we even suspect. For if it be a detail which charms us, and
every surface is a detail in relation to the whole, we show
by our speedy disillusionment that we were wrong in ascribing
beauty to a part when it could not be fairly ascribed to the
whole. This disillusionment generally follows speedily in the
wake of our admiration for mere prettiness. Our senses, our
eyes may appraise. But the soul of us probes deeper. And if
a want is detected our soul gives our eyes the lie. And the
strange thing is that when this happens our eyes capitulate on
the moment and admit the error of their former judgment. If
folk were only more aware of this truth they would never
court inevitable disaster by decking themselves out in order to
create the illusion of beauty.

In Mary's case we have no fear in viewing the ensemble.
We have already suggested that moral loveliness leaves a more
definite trace on the features than we can even imagine. And
if a beauty be born of the constant struggle against moral ugliness what are we to think of a beauty which is the exterior
shining of an immaculate soul? Can we be surprised at the
effect of Mary's beauty on those who have seen something of

it? When we read the account of the apparitions to St.
Bernadette do we not see striking testimony to the loveliness
of the immaculate one?

The bystanders were not privileged with the vision. But
they could see the visionary. In the beginning it would be
just the homely features of the little Pyrenean maid. They
were good, honest features. Certainly they possessed the beautiful reflection of the untarnished soul within. But what a
change when they also reflected the beauty of her to whom she
spoke. She would become transfigured. And her sense would
be wrapt from her. Bernadette was in ecstasy. How unanalys-
able was the virgin's loveliness! Afterwards, during her interrogations, Bernadette was asked if her Lady was as beautiful
as Mlle. So-and-so—noted belles of the district—and with a smile
she would answer that these ladies were not in it in comparison
with the Lady of her vision.

And Mary's beauty extended to details. The famous sculptor
who took on himself to reproduce Our Lady of Lourdes
endeavoured to catch in his hard medium that wonderful raising of eyes and of whole visage to Heaven which accompanied
Mary's revelation of her name. And what was Bernadette's
reaction? "But Our Lady has not goitre!" she cried.

It is the same in the case of the smile bestowed by Mary on
the sick Thérèse of Lisieux. The lines describing this miracle
belong to the loveliest of the whole lovely autobiography. Read
them for yourself. For our part we will simply draw attention to Thérèse's avowal that no words of hers could describe
the loveliness of Mary and the radiance of her smile.
Ah, her smile! It was an expression like that which made
us resolve to write this book. For generally speaking we are
presented with a virgin who does not smile. She will look so
virginal, yes, so gentle, so majestic, but smile—oh, no. But,
we say, oh, yes. We can be sure that Mary often smiled during
her years on earth. Would that St. Joseph, St. Elizabeth, St.
John the Evangelist and a host of others would tell us of how
often Mary smiled on them! What heavenly music would we
not hear!

It may be objected that in all such apparitions there is question of the glorified Mary. But as grace does not destroy nature
but perfects it, so we may make a deduction even from glory
to the nature which possessed it in the germ of grace. At any
rate it is delightful to see the little human things emphasised

even in visions, as for example when Père Lamy notices even the rise and fall of Mary's fair breast in rhythmic breathing.

We may finally ask ourselves if Mary's deep-sourced beauty expressed itself necessarily in what we style prettiness. Well, we would say that in so far as this latter is a necessary corollary of the most perfect interior loveliness, then Mary must have been pretty in the extreme. This is all the more certain when we take into account her perfect physical endowments which resulted in perfect development and harmony of every member and feature. But we must add this. The beatitude which reserves the vision of God to the clean of heart was applicable in measure to Our Lady. If people could be so blind to beauty through their preference for ugliness that they could not only pass by the virgin's Son, but even lay hands upon Him and kill Him, we may be sure that not all were able to appraise the loveliness that was Mary. And as merely external prettiness is quite capable of attracting even evil men we may exclude it from Mary in this superficial sense. Let this be our final word, Beauty is that which God styles beauty. And when His eyes rested on Mary and searched her very being, they found in her no stain. How fair therefore must she be in whom the very eyes of God find no defect. "Thou art all lovely, oh, Mary. And no stain of original sin is in thee. Thou art all fair."

CHAPTER XX

At a most ineffably solemn moment in His life Jesus gave us to Mary as children and Mary to us as mother.

This altogether Divine donation was enveloped with all that sacrosanct solemnity with which the universal sense of mankind has always invested a last testament. Jesus Christ, the Son of the Living God, gave Mary to us to be in very truth our mother. Since He is God His words are ever creative and, moreover, owing to Mary's Immaculate Conception there is no fear that the Creator's words will ever return to Him void and fruitless. But what does it mean to be a mother? Despite the accumulative corruption of our race we have managed to keep intact certain concepts in all the innate sanctity inherent in them. Motherhood is one of those. It is not that motherhood has escaped the universal assault of immorality. It is refused. Its holy duties are either refused or shamefully reduced. But at any rate the concept has remained intact to show men how far they were failing in its due fulfilment. Now there is something universal in the idea of motherhood. We are accustomed to limit most duties, to certain times and places. We consider our teachers to be in place so long as we need them. But if they do their duty and we do ours we won't need them always. Even fatherhood seems to have its term. We know that it will always involve filial conduct on our part. But we do not always expect the duties of fatherhood to be exercised on us. How different is our view of motherhood.

We never grow out of that. We expect mothering at every hand's turn and at every crisis in our life. And the glory of it is that we always get it. It is the unceasing devotion of the mother that gives much poignance to those closed tired eyes, to those weary folded hands on a frozen breast. Most of us have gone through that. And we know that we have met an irreparable loss. We have lost a mother. Now it seems to us that precisely in this matter of Mary's motherhood of us we have sustained one of the major injuries from a piety which, if it may not be called downright false, is at best incomplete. For if we ask ourselves the question we will be forced to admit that current Marian literature makes us regard Mary as a mother rather for certain classes of people and for certain very respectable periods in their lives rather than for all and in all. It is true that she is styled the Refuge of Sinners and that would seem to gather us all into its sweep. But does the current jargon encourage the young affianced person to feel for the warm clasp of the hand of her who was also affianced; does the wife realise that if Mary was a virgin she was also a married woman in all the senses that are necessary to the fullest connotation of the term? Even her motherhood which, of course, can never be called in question, is too often reduced to a cold plaster statue holding out cold hands to an infant which those cold hands never really reach, never really fondle. Yet what are the facts? Mary was engaged. Should we really call her engagement espousal and keep the plaster statue intact? But Mary is no plaster statue. She was, she is a perfect flesh and blood woman and she was engaged. Moreover, her engagement issued in marriage, and in the most perfect marriage ever made in Heaven. In all these statements we have theology on our side, for scientific theology can never be blamed for the cold lifeless statuary sculptured by a piety, well-meaning but unenlightened. And as we want our flesh and blood mother, we will dare to look into her heart and mind as these big and biggest things in her life approach her, take shape and ultimately happen for our salvation.

As we emphasised in the beginning of these pages, the idea of womanhood is God's creation. No one was more thoroughly aware of this than Mary. And although her eyes were ever directed to the Creator she saw herself for what she was—a woman. The Creator's idea of Mary existed in the Divine mind prior to her creation. But not thus did Mary now see herself but as a living, breathing person—and a woman. This wisest of women was there and then also aware of the correlative notion of womanhood. She knew that woman in the Divine Plan stood in a certain immutable relation to another creature—called man. We say immutable relation. For there could be a deepening of this relationship, in terms of spirit, and in terms of flesh and blood. But such potential development left the primal relation unchanged. God made woman to be man's helpmate and nothing could change that Divine ordinance.

Mary knew all that as no woman before or since ever knew it. She could not live in an unreal world where only maidens existed. She knew that God had created a world in which men and women existed and that the women were for the men—only in God's sense. Already we hope that we are getting away from the plaster statue.

However, Mary was immaculate. Practically speaking that means that she put first things first, quite naturally and normally. And we may well believe that there never was a moment in her blessed existence when she was not under the fullest dominion of that choice written down by the inspired pen of St. Paul: "And the unmarried woman and the virgin thinketh on the things of the Lord, that she may be holy both in body and in spirit . . ." and "He that is without a wife, is solicitous for the things that belong to the Lord, how he may please God" (Cor. vii, 32). There is the authentic trumpet-call to all Christian virginity! How clear it rings out from the highlands of the Spirit and how it gives the lie to all the mistaken interpretations. In this matter above all do our separated brethren protest against a figment of their poor imaginations, against the foul legacy of the lying heresiarchs whose sad heirs they are. The Christian knows God's plan for man and woman but he knows first and foremost God's plan for his creature as such. The heart, with all its capacity for love, belongs to God. Marriage in the ordinary sense tends to divide the heart. And when God wills marriage for an individual He accepts that tendency. But He can never surrender His right to be wholly loved and so He permits, He counsels certain chosen souls to love Him with an undivided heart. What does this mean in practice, not only for God but for all humankind? Just this. A person marries. Then love is lavished first on the partner and then on the blessed fruit of children if they are granted. But necessarily it is a love pretty well confined to the family group. A person renounces marriage for God's sake. What is the result? A heart undivided for God and big enough for the world besides. This is the glorious epic of Christian celibacy. This it is which has multiplied the beautiful feet over the mountains preaching the gospel of peace. It is to this that the poor owe their countless helpers in many a congregation, to this that youth can trace its devoted teachers. This, above all, was Mary's way. And because she was wholly His has she become wholly ours. Because for His sake she renounced the motherhood of earth has she become His mother. Because she chose virginity for His sake, has she become the mother of men.

But once more we will descend from the peaks and stay beside a gentle maid for whom a wondrous destiny is opening. We can be quite sure that the Spirit who filled Mary inspired her to a vow of perpetual virginity. We may go further and presume that the same Holy Spirit directed her to enter the most beautiful of affiances. And so we are brought into the presence of man, a flesh and blood man, as little a plaster-cast as our peerless maiden. And, of course, his name is Joseph.

The Holy Spirit has deigned to tell us of the embassy sent by the Triune God to the humble virgin to treat of the plan for man's redemption. We are not told of how or when Mary learned of Joseph's part in this Divine Plan. But once more, without yielding to any extravagant imaginations, we can form a very safe estimate of how it must have been. There is, first of all, the fact of Mary's vow of perpetual virginity. She reveals this herself in her words to the Archangel Gabriel. For only such a vow could give meaning to her query. With such a vow then how did she acquiesce in human espousals? The answer suggests itself. Very obviously the two parties, either by mutual communication or by interior inspiration, were made aware of their perfect identity of purpose. So that St. Joseph had made a similar vow. This divine and mutual pact in no way militated against the true nature of the marriage which they were about to contract.

There is very little said about St. Joseph in the sacred text. But we have only to remember that what is said has God for its Author in order to invest the paucity of information with an almost infinity of significance. But this scantiness of factual information has had its usual misuse in pious thought and literature. For the impression is that if ever there had to be a statue, it was in the case of St. Joseph. And it had to be as silent as a statue normally is and very, very antique.

Now we have tried to show that all the wonderful truths about Our Lady, in their last analysis issue in a most wonderfully real flesh and blood woman. And in like manner we assert that no matter what divines may say about St. Joseph—and it looks as if they will always have something fresh to say about him—the truths will not be draped round a statue, but will take flesh and blood and life in a most authentic man—if ever there was one worthy of the name. So we need not imagine that

Joseph came into Mary's life all of a sudden and out of nowhere. Nor are we to think that he moved around her person like a dignified ghost, doing a very few big things in complete silence and then walking off the stage almost as if he had never been in the scene at all.

If St. Joseph was real for anybody it was for Mary. And nothing could be a better remedy for all faulty and incomplete views of him than to try and see him through her dear eyes. That is exactly what, with all reverence, we shall now try to do. When we are dealing with Mary's interior we must first write down the word—God. It is because of this axiom in things Marian that the viewpoint of those who assert that Mary could come between us and God is so indefensible. If ever in practice it seems to be so, we are dealing with a Mary who is the figment of our imagination. She is not the real one at all. We see it here and now with regard to St. Joseph. We want to know how Mary regarded him. The question is answered if we find out what designs God had on Joseph in Mary's regard. For these will determine both Joseph's special qualities and Mary's regard for him.

Enlightened as no creature ever was before or since, Mary was perfectly aware that God willed this man Joseph to stand to her in the unique position of husband. As we said already, we do not know, nor does it matter much when and how Mary became aware of this.

At the very same time she was also informed, to her supreme joy, that this new alliance willed by God was perfectly consonant with her personal vow.

See what a flood of light streams in with this assurance. It means that Mary knows that Joseph has already a similar mind on this intimate matter. This fact alone creates the purest love in the virgin's heart for the man of God's choice. And it was primarily because he was the man of God's choice that Mary loved him. For wherever Mary saw God's interests involved, there all her interest concentrated. How worthy of esteem was a man in whom God has inspired such a will—before the law of grace! What designs must not the Almighty have on such a one! Now Mary can be also glad that Joseph is God's choice—for her. For it means that she, too, has some part to play in the great rôle for which Joseph has been obviously chosen. All this wonderful balance of motivation is the fruit of Mary's Immaculate Conception. In the case of all other creatures self-love would at least need a careful watching.

But this is not all. Joseph is to be Mary's real husband. Now this is God's ideal woman. She therefore, best of all, will understand God's primal plan for man and woman. If she is to have Joseph for husband he is going to find in her the helpmate par excellence.

We think that we are breaking all that elegant statuary. It is becoming obvious, we trust, that these divinely chosen pair are going to be very, very real, in relation to God, in relation to each other and, God be praised for it, in relation to us.

So Mary is coming to Joseph, first as God's woman, but then, and because of that, as Joseph's wife. She is not coming as a most sacred friend, not even as a sister but as a wife. Her love for him will therefore be the love of a perfect woman for the most perfect man of God's fashioning. And while we are on this terrain let us win back all those sacred terms which the world has filched from truth, such a term, for instance, as love. The world is always bandying about that sacred word. But it has no right to it. It does not even understand it. What it has put in its place is a foul parody and criminal caricature. And we, all too weakly, have yielded up our legitimate vocabulary and fear to use those sacred and intimate words. We shall have no such fear in these lines and our readers will not misunderstand.

One fruit of Mary's love for Joseph will be absolute abandoning trust. We must never allow ourselves to think of Mary as a timorous thing always ready to swoon away at a man's footstep and always fearful of malicious designs. Because of her Immaculate Conception Mary had perfect peace in the house of her own person, spirit and body. From her own untainted nature she had nothing to fear. God's Providence secured her from all possible hurt from her less-favoured entourage and, as regards St. Joseph, part of his providential set-up must have been integrity which came nearest to Mary's own. Mary knew that, as the Church has always equivalently proclaimed it when lauding the chastity of this greatest Joseph. We can easily see that all these considerations made for the easiest and happiest relations between these two. How privileged was this man! Mary's voice was the instrument of the Baptist's sanctification and of Elizabeth's joy and illumination. What must it have been, in terms of further sanctification, light and joy to hear the sweet voice of one who was his very wife? A smile from her cured little Thérèse of her mysterious malady. What must it have meant to have her gracious eyes so constantly upon him, so often in smile of utter gratitude and love?

Only at Judgment Day will it be plain how the mere thought of her has kept men pure when passion's flood seethed in their tainted breasts, what must it mean in terms of whitest chastity to have been her husband—the witness and the inviolable guardian of her peerless virginity!

CHAPTER XXI

JOSEPH THE HUSBAND OF MARY

It cannot be regarded as a digression if we devote a special chapter to that wonderful man who was chosen by God to be Mary's authentic partner in the great mystery of the Incarnation.

In arriving at even some estimate of his moral stature we shall have the advantage even over Mary herself. For, as we saw, she knew enough at the outset to fan her love for St. Joseph into a living flame. But in spite of all Mary's prerogatives she need not have seen all the road. We hold that her knowledge at any given time was perfect in view of what was necessary. But she was not bound to know everything all at once. We, on the other hand, puny minds though we be, live when the great events connected with the Redemption have passed into history. We know now what God's designs were, and as we contemplated Mary herself in the light of those designs and saw that the dogmatic facts square with these, so now we will use the same approach to St. Joseph. Let us hope that thus the statue will not only come to life but that the grandeur of the great just man may shine upon our eyes with all the greater brilliancy.

As in the case of Mary, so in Joseph's case too, we must choose as the starting point of our enquiry the very life of God in the Most Adorable Trinity.

There is one thing which St. Joseph possessed in no less measure than his immaculate spouse. And that is—have you guessed it?—the radical limitation of creaturehood. In other words, St. Joseph is wholly God's idea. God thought of him before we could have. And in our investigations touching him we will be simply walking very reverently after the Creator.

We can use the same approach as we did to Mary. In the inaccessible depths of the Most Adorable Trinity there is an eternal generation. The Father eternally begets His Word, the Son of all His love. The Incarnation of this Son in time is decreed in the Triune Counsel. As regards the mode, the

Incarnate Word is to have a human mother, but He is to have no natural father on earth. Nevertheless, and this is a cardinal point, He is to have all the love and solicitude and caring that the first-born of many brethren has a right to, a right no less than the least of these possesses, a need greater than any of them. And so God the Father will shape a human heart. Into it He will pour as much of His own Divine Love for His Word as a finite heart can hold. It will, before all, be the heart of a father, of a human father who will be the very shadow of the Father—God. It is the heart of St. Joseph.

Here we must consider a matter which is full of significance for our enquiry. After all, in a very real sense God the Father gave His Son into the keeping of us all. He delivered Him up for me and to me. It is likewise certain that God willed from us all the most perfect love for His Son—" they will reverence My Son." But at this point theologians introduce an idea which may seem subtle but is very practical in explaining very hard facts. They say that God's Will must be distinguished—by us at least—from His permissions. For instance, God hates sin with all His Godhead. He cannot will sin. But permit it He does. So also, when He delivered His Son to each member of the human race His permissive Will opened up the possibility of a very varied treatment of the only-begotten. He delivered Him up to Pilate. God did not will the sin whereby Pilate in his turn delivered Jesus up to His foes and the Cross. Yet, as things were, God willed the Redemption of the race precisely through that Cross and therefore indirectly through Pilate's weakness and sin. In the same way He delivered Him up to Judas. We need not repeat ourselves. But God wanted a human father for His Son who would be every inch a father to Him—and that gives a clue to the magnificent endowments which were God's bounty to St. Joseph. This heart, truly a masterpiece of God, will be first of all the heart of a man. If ever one had a man's part to play it was Joseph. His statues may not always bring out this virility, but the statues just are not Joseph. He will be a man perfectly conscious of his manhood and of God's designs upon it, potential and actual. And when Joseph made his private vow of perpetual continence he knew its significance both in the goods renounced and in the goods involved. Joseph by that act made his heart big enough to embrace the world—perhaps he could not have guessed that it was to embrace the world's Creator—and His virgin mother. He would have to be

a man in the fullest sense of a rational being. Every sense would
have to be keyed up to perfection, every interior faculty. For
this man would have the total responsibility of guarding the
treasures, greater than which were not to be found in the
treasure-trove of God. Perhaps we have never even tried to
deduce all that St. Joseph's rôle involved even in the physical
sphere. The guardian of the Holy Family could not fail them,
say, through bodily indisposition. He would be the bread-winner
for the Bread who had come down from Heaven and whom the
Father had sealed. The man who could be told at a moment's
notice to flee into Egypt; the man who would know that the
greatest powers which were at the time had set all their state
machinery against him and his, could have nerves—yes—but with
perfect reactions. Then, again, what must have been the mental
equipment of St. Joseph? We must remember that the Incarnate
Word functioned as a real Child. Before He had sat in the midst
of the doctors He had sat on Joseph's knee and at it. And can we
doubt that He was any more sparing with His questions than
He was with those who were not likely to have the answers?
Christ added to his experimental knowledge in the ordinary
way. And surely in this case the mother did not occupy the
whole scene. And what of Joseph's soul? God Himself through
His Church has told us what He has done for Mary. And we
know that her privilege is unique. But revelation also attests
to the anticipated sanctification of at least John the Baptist, with
whom divines consider we may place Jeremias. Had God not
told us of John's sanctification in his mother's womb, it would
have been a fact all the same. We may well believe that these
examples do not exhaust the Divine preventive kindness. And
if there was anyone for whom we could congruously claim a
privilege coming as near as possible to the unique one, that one
would be St. Joseph. What integrity must we not believe to
be his to whose chastity God entrusted the fairest lily of His
creation. If all of us even when striving to keep God's laws,
are only too conscious with St. Paul of that other law which is
not His, if we could blush to have our first motions detected in
all the shameful and merely mean risings of our corrupt nature,
how can we believe that Joseph could have even lived beneath
the gaze of that Child who was God, not to speak of her
immaculate eyes if he were just as we were?

   Perhaps the greatest indication of St. Joseph's spiritual stature
lies in the fact that he had the right to direct the activities of

his Divine foster-son. Here we must recall what we said about the permissive Will of God. Wherever a sinner abuses his free will, God, as it were, obeys by material co-operation with the sinful act. We could not even sin without drawing on the Divine Power. And so in this sense God willed His Son's obedience to Cæsar, to the synagogue, nay, to the very spirit of evil who brought Him to the pinnacle of the Temple. But with St. Joseph it was completely different. God wanted His Divine Son not only to obey Joseph but to like obeying him—all the time. He wanted the Incarnate Word to obey St. Joseph with the same joy as in His human nature He would obey His Eternal Father. All this has one tremendous significance which is the very root of Joseph's sanctity. For it means just this that St. Joseph's will was ever in conformity with that of the Eternal Father! This must have been so, for during the hidden life Christ not only obeyed St. Joseph in this and that, but he lived in a state of constant obedience to him. It is in the light of this truth that we come to see ever more clearly what the Holy Ghost meant by styling St. Joseph a just man. On the lips of a human, even of a saint, the appellation just might admit of some more or less, particularly less. But the Holy Spirit both knows the full meaning of His own expressions and means them fully.

What is justice in the Divine and comprehensive sense? Is it not holiness? And if we want to define holiness we must further ask what it means in God himself. For He is infinitely holy, the source of all sanctity, even holiness itself. Well, holiness in God is God's oneness with Himself. It is God's identity with His own Will, the norm of all holiness. Can anything higher or greater be said of St. Joseph than that he was at every moment one with the Will of the Eternal Father? Once more let not the stupendous truth drive us back to the beautiful though mute statuary. This holiness is created. It is in terms of a soul and body, of faculties and senses. It is a living, breathing man. And his name is Joseph, the husband of Mary.

CHAPTER XXII

SENT FROM GOD (St. Luke i, 26)

IF we were asked offhand from whom we would be likely to receive the best instruction in devotion to Our Lady our answer would be coloured by our own particular setting. Certain grand names would surely occur to our minds, such as St. Bernard for instance, St. Alphonsus Maria de Liguori, and that remarkable slave of Mary raised to the highest honours of the altar in our own very days, St. Grignon de Montfort. What is particularly certain is that we would hardly think of the Angel Gabriel in this connection. Nevertheless, it will be our easy and very pleasant duty to point out that no one is better qualified than this great angel to teach us how we should regard the Immaculate Virgin.

It is a pleasant duty because it fits in so perfectly with our general plan, namely, to show Mary, not as she has been portrayed by a pious art or literature which sprung up after Heaven had received her, but as she was when among men, as she was when Gabriel stood before her on the first Annunciation Day.

It will be an easy duty because only a little consideration will suffice to show us how utterly qualified is Gabriel to be our mentor in all that concerns Marian devotion.

" I am Gabriel, who stand before God, and am sent . . ." (St. Luke i, 9). There are Gabriel's credentials. He stands before God. He is of the number of those loyal and glorified spirits who always see the face of the Heavenly Father (St. Matthew xviii, 10). Wrapt in ecstasy and gazing on the lovely countenance of God, Gabriel found his mighty intelligence marvellously illuminated and his angelic will impelled by an ever-deeper love which if it always centred in God had also a reference to a creature outside of God. We will most reverently beseech the great angel to make us, too, sharers in his illumination and in his love. Looking into the eyes of God he read a marvellous design. It had reference to the thrones left empty by Heaven's first defection. It regarded the race of man. Above all it regarded one member of that race, a little maiden in Nazareth. And in those Divine eyes Gabriel read his own commission: "Who, stand before God and am sent." What does this Divine sending involve for Gabriel in terms of special endowments for the due fulfilment of his new office? We have suggested some of these in general—a great illumination covering the ground of the Divine Plan and a great love reaching out to all whom the plan involved—but especially to one central figure. And it is the figure of a young girl at prayer. But Gabriel was given even more precise gifts for his mission. In a flash of intuitive light he saw the unique predestination of Mary. Think of it. Gazing on the Triune God he sees the Divine Trinity. Thrilled through and through his angelic being with adoration and love ineffable he sees the Triune life, the Eternal Father ever begetting His Word, the figure of His substance, the splendour of His glory, one with Him in Divine Essence. He sees the third person, the Spirit proceeding from the Father and the Son, their mutual love, a substantial person. He sees, and as he gazes in rapture he sees the infinite designs of the Eternal. The second person will become man, will become an authentic member of that lower race. And how? It is all clear to the angel, because God has made it clear. And in that light he reads his own commission, to go to that kneeling virgin, present God's designs to her and—oh, God—to ask her free consent.

We can be even more precise. All this is God's work. Only He could conceive it. Only He could realise it. Even an angel could never draw up from his own created being words adequate to frame this stupendous plan. So God must give Gabriel the words. And let us never forget it, He did. It is from the Triune God that Gabriel will bring his message. God will do more. He will fill His celestial ambassador with that respect which is the due of this predestined being. Do not think that this is only a matter of fair speech. In nature Gabriel is immeasurably superior to this child of Adam to whom he is sent. And yet he will stand in her presence not as a pure spirit in the presence of a lower organism but as a subject before his queen. God has shown Gabriel that. So God Himself has instructed Gabriel on what he is to say to Mary and how he is to say it. He stands before her.

The Annunciation scene is a familiar theme with artists. And some of their interpretations are not without a rare beauty.

But in this case, too, we would dare to say that art's last word is not a fraction of what might be said. We will try to elicit some of the secrets of this truly epic scene. And the angel Gabriel will be our informant. What did he see when from high Heaven he entered that modest abode in Nazareth? To borrow the information of the paintings we would answer that he saw a young girl in prayer. What robs us of inestimable treasures is just that capacity we have of saying the most wonderful things in the world, and then hurrying on to trivialities. This is because we are humans and complete and clear vision is not our birthright. But it is the birthright of the angels. So we will look at this familiar scene through the eyes of Gabriel. Let us remind ourselves of who he is and whence he comes. "I am Gabriel, who stands before God . . . their angels in Heaven always see the face of my Father Who is in Heaven." . . . So Gabriel is gazing upon the unveiled splendours of the Godhead and yet when, without turning his eyes from the vision splendid, he gazes upon Mary as she is absorbed in prayer, Gabriel sees something which thrills his mighty being with a newer ecstasy. He sees this young girl, of an order lower than his own in the hierarchy of creation, wrapt in an adoration deeper and greater and grander than his, deeper and greater and grander than the highest seraph of the most exalted choirs. He sees a love breathed forth from every fibre of that fragile being which makes the united loves of Heaven pale as the stars when the orb of day is risen. And the most remarkable feature in the whole glory of it all is that Gabriel sees that Mary's adoration and Mary's love is kindled, not by vision as his own is kindled, but in the obscurity of purest faith. The prayer of Mary, how wonderful it must have been! And Gabriel found her thus, communing with God. For what is prayer? It is the ascent of the mind to God, it is a conversation with the Most High, or it is an asking of seemly things. For thus and thus have the masters defined it. What then will be the ascent of that immaculate mind to the God Who is her all in all? No obstacles to be overcome as in the case of even the greatest saints, no dark regions to traverse to reach the region of light! Just a perfect, speedy and unimpeded ascent to the Godhead. And it is fourteen or fifteen years since that ineffable ascent began when Anne felt life stirring in her bosom. What a Heavenly colloquy will this prayer be which is a conversation between Mary and her Creator.

What range of subjects, what heart to heart intimacies. And Gabriel came into the middle of that. What seemly things will Mary ask for in her prayer? Ah, can we doubt it? Does not the future supply the key to the present and can we not be certain that over and over again she says to God, " they have no wine "? " They have no wine." But it is not the wine of earth she craves. It is rather that draught of salvation for which poor humanity thirsts. It is the Saviour for whom Mary pleads. Little does her humility know the living gift which she thus asks—and impetrates for us all—but first for herself. And God can no longer resist the pleadings of His immaculate one. Oh, Gabriel, you have come into all this, and for this have you come!

When piety strives to depict prayer it generally seizes upon certain accidental features such as a wrapt expression which only too often is—at least for us—expressionless. Once more sober truth is the adequate corrective. Prayer is the attitude of a creature at the peak point of its creaturehood. To be a creature is to be a prayer by essence. To fail in this great duty of prayer is to be false to one's essential nature. Prayer is virility at the highest—taking manhood as indicative of a rational nature. To possess reason, to become even more and more conscious of our utter dependence, and not to pray is to lower ourselves to the level of criminal lunatics. And so true prayer is something noble, virile, beautiful. Artists often miss just those traits in depicting the saints at prayer. There is too often an effeminate note, a weak languorous expression, an ethereal suggestion of other-world make-believe. God does not see prayer so. Gabriel saw it not thus when he saw Mary at prayer. He saw utter loveliness, supreme strength, illumination, he saw a perfect creature, a perfect woman. He saw Mary. And what did Mary see? If we are going to look reverently through her eyes we must first get rid of our own. They will not serve us at all. It is because pious people have been looking through their own eyes at Mary that the pictures they have given us of her are so unsatisfying. Instinctively we feel that they are far from the truth, if well-meaning enough. In the matter which we are about to consider Mary's outlook is totally different from ours. We are children of Eve who have not been the object of any privilege comparable to her unique one. We have our roots in a race of conscious exiles. In our first parents we were driven from Paradise, and even now the glare of the flaming sword seems to be on our eyes. Of course we are redeemed. The Son of the virgin has deleted the handwriting which was against us. No merely earthly garden of delights is reopened to us, but Heaven itself. That is so, and we bless God for it. But our wounded nature has not been healed as our souls have been. We are wayfarers with all the barriers down and a clear road. But it is a long one. More than one lion is in the way. And the turrets of the city of peace are very distant yet. We are exiles who have a home to go to, and we know the way. Yet while we are en route our exile presses sorely upon us. Never can our newly-restored sonship make us forget that we are prodigals. And the memory of our unfilial conduct makes us even a little shy of the Father who awaits. We feel almost strangers to Him and strangers to all those who are our brethren who remain always with Him in love and loyalty. And so we are affrighted if that true home of ours reveals itself too suddenly. We are not prepared for visits from its inhabitants. We even doubt such. And perhaps we are wise.

How different it is with Mary. She is, it is true, an authentic member of our race. But she did not fall in Adam. The exile's psychology was never hers. From the first moment of her conception she was perfectly at home with God, perfectly at home with all His friends. And so her reaction to Gabriel's presence will be something quite other to what our human experience might suggest. How did he appear to her? We can only surmise. In the angelic appearances of both Testaments comely youths are the form generally taken. So we may suppose that Gabriel stood before Mary in this guise. But here we must register our wonted corrective to the moralists. We have said enough already to dispose of the idea that Mary was a timorous, shrinking maiden. No corruption was latent in that most pure heart to prove even a warning indication of danger from without. When any man stood in Mary's presence he stood in the presence of one absolutely untouched by that " other law." Neither could she have been in danger of illusion. The evil one, multiform traitor though he be, has no mask through which those pure eyes would not penetrate. Moreover, angels, true or false, act completely under the Divine command. If either must adapt a form it will be the one permitted by the Most High and most calculated to further His designs—which are never the devil's. For instance, when the enemy of our race wished to tempt our first mother he had to ask God's permission. If further he expressed a preference for the serpent's guise it was because that was the form which God was ready to permit. And we may venture the opinion that Satan did not relish the disguise at all, for in itself it was quite capable of giving the whole game away on him—with one such as Eve. The same lesson is taught by the herd of swine mentioned in the Gospel. The devils asked to be allowed to enter them, precisely because in God's Plan the swine were there for that purpose. In the rational creature their malice was not so obvious. In the irrational pigs the devils found themselves unable to withhold an object lesson to mankind for all time—the devil has only an abyss for his dupes. So God's chosen ambassador came in the form willed by God. And we may be sure that his appearance was such as to win perfect and fearless trust from this most wise virgin.

What did Mary hear? Why, you will say, that question is answered by the Gospel itself. So, dear readers, you are sure you have really grasped the significance—for Mary—of the Divine Message. We are not so sure. It is only when one thinks long and carefully on such matters that assurance weakens. Let us see.

"And in the sixth month, the angel Gabriel was sent from God into a city of Galilee, called Nazareth, to a virgin espoused to a man whose name was Joseph, of the house of David, and the virgin's name was Mary. And the angel being come in, said unto her . . ." (St. Luke i, 26, etc.). Slowly now, . . . "Hail!" There are words which epitomise huge periods of history. There are words which unleash the dogs of war or which cry halt to death and misery. This one word "Hail" in the mouth of God's ambassador and addressed to a member of the human race, is one of these words if there were ever such. For monosyllable though it be, it cries truce to the only war worthy of the hellish name, the war made by mankind against its good God. Far more than truce it cries. For it says peace, and restoration and a new beginning and a better one. We may help ourselves to realising all this if we turn to the far different plight of the angels who had sinned—and sinned but once. Even to us it is clear that no salutation of friendship can ever fall upon those reprobate ears never . . . never. And yet, so far as the radical effects of sin are concerned the human race was as finally severed from the Divine friendship as the evil one who had tempted. Nevertheless we hear this celestial greeting from high heaven addressed to a member of this fallen race. See why we have said that in itself this blessed word signified redemption? For it could not be addressed to any member of the human race unless in view of the Just One who would justify. And it was spoken to Mary because she was the chosen, undefiled way by which He would come who would say of Himself, "I am the Way." Nor was it any niggardly pardoning that would be the ransoming. For even in her whose fiat was to deluge the world with the torrents of God's mercy, it was indeed a copious redemption. "Hail, full of grace." "The Lord is with thee. . . ." The Incarnation showed up human relations to God just like a photographic snapshot fixes the scene which is before it. It did not create those relations. It found them there and translated them into terms of living flesh and blood. God was in Mary's mind and heart before He entered her chaste womb. But the only physical relation which could interpret her union with her Creator was precisely the one effected by the Incarnation. Where is there a closer union to be found in all nature than that which exists between a mother and the living fruit of her womb when that fruit is still part of herself? Because Mary was so close to God in spirit He will be her very Child in the flesh. "The Lord is with thee." "Blessed art thou among women." Is not this a résumé of all that has been said about womanhood in the Divine Mind? The Holy Ghost does not employ verbiage. And here He salutes the woman *par excellence,* the woman after God's own heart.

Now that we are approaching the study of Mary's own reactions to the wonderful salutation we must remember our duty of getting rid of misconceptions, due to our own corrupt nature or even to excess of after-knowledge: "Who having heard, was troubled at his saying, and thought within herself what manner of salutation this should be."

One of the most difficult virtues to recapture by fallen though redeemed humanity is the virtue of humility. Nevertheless it is by no means a complex virtue. It is simply truth, a true appraisal of ourselves in all our varied relations, to God and to creatures. There is so much darkness clinging to us that we find it difficult to arrive at this simple view of truth. So for us humility means a constant strain, in the sense that we must be always correcting self-love—or even correcting self-depreciation. It was quite otherwise with the immaculate virgin. From the very beginning of her conscious life she saw herself for what she was in relation to God and therefore in all other relations. She never for a moment lost sight of her radical nothingness. And precisely because of this clear light on what she was not she saw perfectly what God had raised on this humble basis of utter nothingness. It was not even possible for her to take complacence in her dignity. Consequently we cannot say that it was Gabriel's expression of this very dignity which troubled Our Lady. Being an angel of light he could say no less if he said anything. But does not the inspired text point out exactly the source of Mary's trouble? She thought within herself what manner of salutation this should be. What Gabriel had said tallied with her knowledge of herself. But why had he come from Heaven to say it? In other words, what was the precise significance of the salutation relevant to Mary here and now, and relevant to what else . . . relevant to whom? Now we must look at things not merely through Mary's eyes but through the eyes of the chosen people represented so signally in her. We remember the scene which was staged in Eden. We have already reviewed it. Following instantaneously on their weak surrender to the liar our first parents became conscious of their sin and that in every fibre of their being. There was no intrinsic reason why God should deal otherwise with them than He had dealt with the angelic offenders.

Judge, then, with what heartfelt joy they grasped at the first indication from God that their fall was not irremediable. He would find in His mercy what He could not find in any extenuating circumstances that they might plead. He spoke of a mysterious woman and of her conquering seed. From that moment mankind in our first parents, and particularly in the race that would be set apart, was moulded by that Divine Promise. The whole history of the Jewish people revolves round it and has all its meaning from it. It is a human line of eyes straining after the Promise and saluting it from afar. Since Mary represented in herself all that was highest and best in God's designs on this people may we not be certain that in her, above all, the Messianic hope attained its most vivid flame? More than any other of her race she would interpret all events in the light of God's promise of a Redeemer. She knew all the Scriptural references. She knew what Isaias had said of a virgin who would be a mother, thus even in prophecy constituting a sign worthy of the Omnipotent God. Think, then, of her unexampled clarity of mind and sureness of judgment. A deduction must have been forced upon her did not her humility cry it halt. And so from a situation always productive of anguish to the created mind trouble was born for Mary. But see how the angel answers her very ponderings. " And the angel said to her, fear not, Mary, for thou hast found grace with God. Behold thou shalt conceive in thy womb, and shalt bring forth a son, and thou shalt call His name Jesus. He shall be great, and shall be called the Son of the Most High, and the Lord God shall give unto Him the throne of David His father, and He shall reign in the house of Jacob for ever. And of His Kingdom there shall be no end " (St. Luke i, 30-33).

Fear left Mary when in God's Name Gabriel told her to fear no longer. Therefore to the remainder of the most momentous message she brings a mind the most tranquil that ever could exist in a pure creature, and a judgment the surest and most unerring. Mary was the woman *par excellence* and, as we have stressed, perfectly conscious of her womanhood with all the obligations and potentialities involved. She knew how much fruit a woman may and must bring forth by being true to her divine destiny. She knew that normally fruitage of children is a woman's most honourable treasure and pride. By the anticipated light of the Gospel counsels she had already renounced the gift of progeny. And, moreover, she had perfect assurance of the Divine good pleasure in her resolve. God had even underlined it by inspiring her husband, Joseph, with a similar vow. Yet upon her ears fell clear and crisp the words from Heaven : " Behold thou shall conceive in thy womb, and shall bring forth a son " . . . so she was the woman of prophecy, the real sign foretold by Isaias! Now let us try and follow the quick workings of this peerless mind. The angel had mentioned very significant words which lost none of their meaning for this most authentic woman. Conception was mentioned, and the womb, and a bringing forth. This Son who was to be hers would not descend from Heaven in the full stature of manhood, standing by her side and proclaiming at once His heavenly origin and vindicating her virginity. Conceive . . . womb . . . bring forth. No. It will be by the ordinary human road, so far as gestation and birth were concerned. But it would not, it could not be by the ordinary human road that He could enter her womb. See, Mary is in no doubt about the fact, but hers is a most legitimate

query as to "how." It comes. "And Mary said to the angel,
How shall this be done, because I know not man." Quicker still
comes the Divine response. "And the angel answering, said to
her, the Holy Ghost shall come upon thee, and the power of the
Most High shall overshadow thee. And therefore also the Holy
which shall be born of thee shall be called the Son of God. And
behold thy cousin Elizabeth, she also hath conceived a son in
her old age; and this is the sixth month with her that is called
barren: Because no word shall be impossible with God" (St.
Luke i, 35, 37).

Mary listens. Never had she feared for that virginity which
God had inspired her to embrace. God is consistent with Himself. But now she has the Divine assurance of the very mode
of her miraculous motherhood. If the motherhood of Elizabeth
is cited as a help to assurance, notice how God underlines the
precise nature of the prodigy in Elizabeth's case. It lay in the
conception of a child when age had precluded such a possibility. Mary knew how it would be with herself. But before
we come to her glorious "fiat," let us look deeper into her
thoughts. Already the mystic sword of Simeon's prophecy is
refracted from the very near future! We have said that Mary
is the woman *par excellence*. No other woman before or since
so realised the full implication of her vocation as woman. And
it was not merely to men in general that she was to be a helpmate, but in God's designs to one man, to Joseph. Can we
doubt that when Mary realised the import of the angel's
message her thoughts went out to Joseph? For all the world
besides, her putative marriage with him would safeguard her
honour. We say putative in contrast to the consummation that
was never to be in this Divinely arranged marriage. But what
of Joseph? Mary loved this pure-souled man whom God had
placed at her side, having first prepared him for such a privileged position. Would God reveal the heavenly secret to
Joseph, and when? It is in such a delicate situation as this
that we must put out of our minds all misconceptions of Our
Lady. She was the most human of all God's human creatures.
After God Himself no one was less likely to inflict pain on
anybody, not to speak of a loved one. And Mary could fore-
see the greatest mental anguish for Joseph unless God
enlightened him. But when she had assessed that and accepted
it, tranquillity reigned in her virgin heart. God's will must
be done, cost what it might to Joseph or to anybody else.

At this very time there is a strange controversy in progress in a doctrinal publication. A worthy member of an illustrious society sponsors the view that at this stage Mary need not have known that the miraculous fruit of her womb was to be very God.

We have not got the qualifications to enter into this duel of learned divines. We only say quite humbly and without any intention of offending that this view is most repellent to us. In fact we are tempted to believe that the worthy object of its protagonist is to force theologians to defend the traditional position with scientific precision. We think that a consideration of Gabriel's rôle will assure us on the point. He was an arch-angel. This means that not only was he entrusted with very important embassies from the Most High, but also that by his proximity to God his illumination was of the highest degree. In particular he was perfectly enlightened on the import of this extraordinary message and it is a small thing to say that he certainly gave the full Divine message in the clearest possible way. Now a good instructor may be nullified by a poor pupil. But what a listener Gabriel had in this privileged one! We have all too easily forgotten the practical results of the Immaculate Conception. But let us recall them now. Here was a young girl of the chosen people who by a unique privilege was preserved free from original sin and all its effects. Her mind was unclouded and had behind it fourteen or fifteen years of unimpeded development. She knew as no one else the implications of the Fall. She knew that the sin of our first parents had rendered the race radically bankrupt of the very possibility of repairing it. Far speedier than our best ascetics she realised the import of Heaven's salutation to herself. But —far better than even the sectaries, God help them—she knew that as a creature she could not effect the redemption. But her child would. Then he must be able to not only buy back but pay in full. Pay in full to God! Mary knew what that involved. And it was in the full light of the proffered Divine maternity that she uttered those momentous words which can be said to have saved us because Mary gave us the Saviour. And Mary said: "Behold the handmaid of the Lord, be it done to me according to Thy word" (St. Luke i, 38).

There is no creature of adult years who is without responsibility. At the very least he or she will have that of their own

immortal soul and destiny. Since this is so it is a fair division
of mankind to say that it is composed of those who accept their
responsibility and those who shirk or evade it. Of the first
class a further division may be made into those who rise to
the full exigencies of duty and those who do not take things
quite so seriously all the time. Then again it is obvious that
some people have comparatively light responsibilities while
others have onerous ones which press heavily upon them all
their lives. Now there never was and there never could be a
responsibility so onerous, so exacting and so permanent as the
one accepted freely by Mary on that first Annunciation Day
long ago. And in union with the Catholic instinct of all the
ages we emphatically assert that she knew the nature of the
responsibility imposed on her. It was nothing less than the
mothering of God in the flesh. It was, moreover, to be a
perfect unflagging mothering of Him from the first moment of
His conception until He could do without it. And although it
is looking ahead we know that He needed His mother sorely
when He came into this world, and when He went out of it.
If His mystical body has any meaning in fact He still needs her
mothering. We do not claim for Mary a knowledge of details.
In fact some of her dolours will arise from God's permission
that she should not know everything all at once. But what she
did know was more than enough to invest her *fiat* with the
greatest merit and dignity and make it claim our heartfelt
gratitude. If this has not been always so clear to us it is
because of the unfortunate statuary which we rejoice to grind to
powder. It will help us if we make a short review of the past.
Let us again take our stand in the first garden of delights.
There we see our first parents in the full flush of their creation
and clothed with innocence and sanctifying grace. Here before
our eyes is the first loving plan of a God who can only love.
There is Adam the first flesh and blood realisation of manhood
in the Divine mind. In soul and in body he is a true king.
Master of his soul and equally master of his body, his dignity
lies in his conscious subjection to his great Creator. What a truly
noble subjection, and how utterly rooted in his nature as a
creature! All the universe and all its lower inhabitants are
for his use and pay him obedience. To complete his happiness,
see by his side the fair helpmate designed for him by God.
Bone of his bone and flesh of his flesh the holiest love unites
the twain with each other and with God. Nor does God ever

do things on a small scale. These two privileged beings are to
be the forerunners of a mighty race of humankind and when
physical life is handed on by God's wonderful and holy plan, all
the magnificent endowments of soul and body are to be part of
the inheritance. Bliss here, supernatural beatitude hereafter.
What a programme of gratuitous love!

We will not dwell on the sad story. That helpmate betrayed
her husband and he betrayed us all.

Another scene opens before our tear-blinded eyes. Once again
we see a woman. God's plan has not miscarried. This woman
represents perfectly the Divine idea and she, too, takes her stand
beside a Man. She will not fail Him. Nor will He fail us. But
as we stand in loving reverence in the little room at Nazareth
we see that ideal woman. But we do not yet see the Man. No,
we must wait for a hillside cave in David's city of bread. But
for all that, He is there. Not yet beside her, but within her,
beneath her immaculate heart. For the Word has become
Flesh!

To conclude this chapter let us revert to the truth with which
we opened it, namely, the peculiar aptitude possessed by the
Archangel Gabriel to instruct us in true devotion to Our Blessed
Lady. From the uncreated source of light he was enlightened.
He was instructed as to her great destiny. He was taught how
to stand in her presence, and what to say to her. He is the
precentor of that golden rosary of Hail Marys which has scented
the world and will girdle all time. We live in an age when the
wonderful power of the radio elicits our admiration. But was
there ever a more necessary or grander message flashed from
Heaven to earth than Gabriel's one, and where was there ever a
greater relay than is ever realised by the Hail Marys which have
been on Catholic lips ever since. Truly the Church of the
Incarnation is the Church of the Angelus bell, of the never idle
beads. "Hail Mary! Full of grace, the Lord is with thee,
blessed art thou among women. . . ."

Could we not recommend serious and reflective devotion to
the Archangel Gabriel to our separated brethren who have such
a strange attitude to the Lady to whom he was sent? They claim
to love the Holy Book. Well, it is all there. For here is the
thundering truth. Who is Mary's first devotee? Was it Gabriel?
But he was instructed by someone else. Oh, God can it be!
Yes, of a truth it can be so long as God's Word stands. The

very first devotee of Mary, He who put those words of light and love upon the angelic lips is no other than her Creator, the Triune God. What will we have? If God thinks so much of her, can our poor tribute ever be excessive?

Hail Mary, full of grace!

CHAPTER XXIII

"AND THE ANGEL DEPARTED FROM HER"
(St. Luke i, 38)

WE trust that in the preceding chapter we have given sufficient proof of our reverence and love for the great archangel of the Annunciation. Otherwise our words now may be misunderstood. For we are glad that he has taken himself back to Heaven! Since he entered the room where Mary prayed we have been surrounded by light from on high. There was the great archangel bearing on his radiant brow the reflection of the uncreated Light upon which he ever gazes. There were words the most momentous ever uttered by celestial lips into human ears. And there was the holy virgin herself, with all her heavenly endowments rising up in splendour to meet this moment of grace for which they were bestowed. In the chamber inviolable of that freest of human wills counsel was taken and the *fiat* uttered. Our Redemption has begun. But all this has again placed Mary in the clouds. And we want her where we are, so very far beneath them. So Gabriel goes. And we are glad. For only Mary remains. She rises from her knees. Even if her interior communion with God is never interrupted, for her, as for us, liturgical postures must often give place to the ritual of the pots and pans. She rises from her knees. Is she changed by the stupendous thing that has happened? Not very noticeably—yet. She is still our dark Jewish maiden, beautiful beyond compare, simple as God Himself is simple. Perhaps there is even a greater, grander serenity on her unfurrowed brow, a newer light may shine from her frank eyes. But she is no other than that dear child at whose cradle we watched, by whose side we tarried as she grew from infancy to childhood and on through fresh girlhood until her present ripeness. But if we have dared to stay with her until now, surely her presence is too holy for us now! If we asked her she would reproach us for so soon forgetting the angel's message. " And thou shalt call His name Jesus." The Child within her virginal womb is the Saviour. His name, given not on earth but in the Triune Counsel, states His very office. He has first of all been a Saviour for Mary herself, only by a prevenient salvation which held off from her all taint of sin. He is hers for herself. But He is no less hers for each and every member of the fallen race, for you and for me.

Least of all will we leave her now, when she possesses Him. We need Him, we need Him. So we will not leave Mary's side.

The Annunciation took place. And it was five minutes after. It was the next day and all the to-morrows. What was Mary's life like? We still refuse to invent fairy tales or even angel stories —unless the angels are real. And Gabriel was real enough and the story about him is the good story which we call the Gospel.

But it will not be calling on our imagination if we presume a proximate meeting between Mary and her husband. What a meeting that must have been. Shall we picture it? Mary stands mutely before Joseph with hands folded on her breast and eyes cast down. Drivel and nonsense. No woman ever stood like that before her husband when he wanted a meal or at least a word. The helpmates have little time for posing. But this much we can say. Mary sought to read in Joseph's eyes if he too had a revelation from on high. And his eyes told her plainly that Joseph had not. A revelation he will have, but it will be in terms which have made a similar revelation to many a husband before Joseph and many a one since. For his part Joseph has become so accustomed to the atmosphere of utter perfection surrounding and permeating his girl-wife that he probably did not try to analyse why the light seemed even more lightsome and the fragrance even more rarefied. Oh, sword of Simeon!

The days grew into weeks, and the weeks became months. St. Joseph was coming very near his revelation. And now a change is coming over Mary. A very palpable change. As days merge into weeks and weeks into months, the gentle lines of girlhood take on a richer, fuller contour. The ever growing maturity of motherhood makes its appearance. And now we are face to face with Joseph's anguish and we will not shirk its analysis. Two schools of spiritual writers here cross our path and neither are without great names. One school accepts the situation on its surface value and says quite simply that St. Joseph was tortured by the prima facie evidence of his wife's infidelity. Of course those who take this view make the kernel of Joseph's pain his unwillingness to believe what his eyes told him. Let us state with emphasis that such a view offers no verisimilitude to us. Happily there are holy writers equally worthy and learned who propose another and a far more satisfactory solution. With these latter we maintain that, knowing Mary as he did, St. Joseph never entertained, never could entertain a doubt touching her virtue. Solid proof is adduced for this statement. The Holy Ghost solemnly proclaims Joseph to be a just man. Now God's own law gave no opportunity to take a mild view of conjugal infidelity. Where the fact was proved, the course was clear—and it was no merely private dismissal of the offending party. Very well then, what was the source of St. Joseph's most real anguish? We believe that parallels can be cited from ordinary spiritual experience. We have faith in God. Yet temptations to doubt may abound. To the true believer these constitute a real martyrdom of heart and by no means a verdict of wavering faith. That was the case of St. Teresa of the Child Jesus. Her black night agonised her soul and all the agony was the very fruit of her intense faith in God's Holy Word. Even in our common lives it happens in measure. We believe in God's assurance that He will answer prayer. We pray and the heavens are of brass. Then it is that to our love of God and our faith in Him the temptation to lose confidence is full of pain. St. Joseph had two certitudes. One was that Mary was the purest virgin who ever breathed. The other was that she was about to become a mother. So far God had not deigned to give him any special revelation on this most extraordinary situation. What was in effect St. Joseph's deduction? It was one full of honour both for God and for Mary. Joseph recognised the finger of God. But he was not as yet enlightened as to the mode or meaning. One thing was clear to him. He was standing on the holiest ground. And with the humility of this greatest of saints Joseph decided that the ground was far too holy for him. He would relieve it of his clumsy unenlightened presence. " Now the generation of Christ was in this wise. When as His mother Mary was espoused to Joseph, before they came together, she was found with Child, of the Holy Ghost. Whereupon Joseph her husband, being a just man, and not willing publicly to expose her, was minded to put her away privately " (St. Matthew i, 18, 19). This decision of St. Joseph no matter how nobly motivated only turned the knife in the bleeding wound. For let us ever remember it, Joseph loved Mary with all the warm love of a man's pure heart, a heart framed by God for this flaming love. His proximity to her since their marriage had certainly not decreased this affection. And now he saw his wonder world falling to pieces around him. Good reader, could you or I do without our "Lady?" Well, then, how could Joseph face the impending separation without the laceration of his whole being? And this sorrow of Joseph's was Mary's sorrow, too. Can we imagine that this wise virgin was unaware of the struggle going on in Joseph's soul? Yet she would not anticipate God. No word from her would ease the situation. God Himself must speak. And God will speak. "But while he thought on these things, behold the angel of the Lord appeared to him in his sleep, saying: ' Joseph, son of David, fear not to take unto thee Mary thy wife, for that which is conceived in her, is of the Holy Ghost. And she shall bring forth a son, and thou shalt call His Name Jesus. For He shall save His people from their sins ' " (St. Matthew i, 20, 21).

Not all the ministering spirits who exercise their beneficent mission in both testaments have revealed their identity as the great angel of the Annunciation. We do not know by what name the angel who thus appeared to St. Joseph is known among the choirs. But this much is certain. He has a claim on our deepest gratitude. He certainly won the gratitude of his queen and of the patient Joseph. For he was God's instrument in restoring perfect tranquillity to that great heart. If we love Mary and Joseph must we not also feel indebted to this angel? And we must remember the essential freedom of these angelic wills confirmed in glory.

They made choice of their Creator's will in the vital flash of their trial and never again can they turn aside from it. But their proper choice did not deprive them of their freedom but rather consecrated it forever. In other words, they love doing God's holy will and, therefore, deserve our gratitude for their ministrations. Moreover, an angel is always specially endowed for its mission. We have seen that in the case of Gabriel, and it is not less so in the case of St. Joseph's angel. He had the special God-given power to dispel fear and instil peace and joy. He dispelled fear in this case by removing the lack of due knowledge which was the source of Joseph's anguish. We may be sure that he has not lost this Divine aptitude. We would be well advised to invoke his special intercession when we too suffer in mind because of our lack of vision. We see so little at a time and none too clearly at that. Often we shall stand in need of that heavenly light which will solve our perplexities and establish us in peace, and even joy if God so wills. The angel of St. Joseph's holy slumbers will help us as he once helped a mother-maid and her trusting husband.

CHAPTER XXIV

INTO THE HILL COUNTRY

ALTHOUGH by His glorious assumption of her into Heaven, God raised His Blessed Mother to its highest throne, He did not put her out of our reach or even sight. It took our spiritual panegyrics and our own lack of commonsense to do that. In this book we have made it our avowed object to portray, however feebly, the sweet humanity of our mother. And as we have probably said already, one motive for our audacity was that we wanted to provide such a book—for ourselves. For although there may be such, and even many such, we have not seen them. Perhaps lovers of Mary may not be blamed if they have not wished to anticipate our handiwork. And one who has the nerve to make Our Lady a warm flesh and blood woman who ate and drank and slept and talked is certainly inviting a storm of criticism from disedified devotees. Such is the lot of all pioneers. Theirs it is to blaze a new track and although wayfarers will one day bless them, there are many who will accuse them of destroying the primeval forest and robbing it of its hallowed mystery. But perhaps mystery is not much good to weary travellers. At any rate, it takes some courage in the face of prevailing Marian literature to suggest and even assert that Mary lived the fullest possible human life. Did we say that she was not a Divine solitary who stepped down from Heaven, then might we further deduce for her a very human milieu with relatives and friends involving quite definite social duties and contacts? If we went further and denied that she spent her hours in immobile ecstasy but even visited her relatives, holy eyebrows might be raised. But the limits of our rashness might consist in the assertion that Mary might be so glad to visit a friend or relative that she went in a hurry. Now, who ever contemplated our beloved statuesque virgin in a hurry? But perhaps we have said all that when we have so unctuously repeated "the second Joyful Mystery, the Visitation." Yes, indeed, we have said it. And in saying it we are only echoing the inspired word which said it before us: " And Mary, rising up in those days, went into the hill country with haste into a city of Juda. And she entered into the house of Zachary, and saluted Elizabeth " (St. Luke i, 39, 40).

We intend to extract all the honey we can from this most human and most beautiful episode in the life of Mary and her cousin Elizabeth. To do so we must again adopt our method of getting outside our puny minds into the minds of that holy couple. First of all, let us see what motivated Mary in this visit and why she went on it " with haste." One motive which was most certainly not hers was a doubting anxiety to verify the angel's words relative to her cousin. We have seen already that the one query made by Mary to Gabriel was a perfectly legitimate one, having as object not the fact revealed but the mode. And that is why the archangel found himself instructed in the complete answer. Moreover, he added the fact of Elizabeth's motherhood, not to bolster up a weak faith but to reward a perfect credence with the astounding sign of the Divine omnipotence. It was quite different in the case of Zachary. Gabriel's message to him followed closely the lines of the annunciation of Mary. In both cases there is the human reaction of trouble and fear—though Zachary had sources of fear within his nature unknown to Mary. But it is in the question put by each to the Ambassador of God that we see the great difference. Mary accepted the fact, vouched for by God. Zachary asked for some proof of the fact likely to convince an old man that his old wife would become a mother. And this time Gabriel finds himself possessed of an answer—and a rod. The expression of his diffidence was the last vocal utterance of poor Zachary until his eyes had assured him of a fact for which God's assurance was not adequate.

In this visit to her cousin Mary was impelled by charity. The failure to use, if not the positive abuse of our Christian heritage, is nowhere better shown than in the unpleasant meaning so often ascribed to the word charity. There is even a saying coined " as cold as charity." If this be so to our shame, there could be no Gospel scene better calculated to invest the royal word with its true and Heavenly meaning than the one we are considering. Mary, we have said, was motivated by charity. And how could it be otherwise, seeing that she carries substantial love incarnate within her? God has defined Himself twice. He has told us by His Holy Spirit that He is subsistent being: " I

am who am " and that He is love—" God is love." How allied
are the concepts! Everything that is, everything positive is
good, coming from the great source of uncreated being. On
the other hand, sin is no thing. It is a defect, a lack, a negation.
God is. And eternally God is love. Creation is the over-
flowing of that love on creatures outside of God. And creation
is one long drama of never-ceasing love, bringing into being and
conserving in being. When God is in a soul, that soul must
live a positive life, must ever love. It need not always love by
external action, but if external action is demanded by love, then
that person gets busy on the moment. That is the story of
Mary and her visit to Elizabeth. Even when we retain a worthy
concept of charity we are inclined to strip it of all warm
humanity. That is obviously wrong. Even with fallen nature
our business is to strip love of what is counterfeit. We do not
attack nature but rather the corruption which seems to be our
nature but is not. Here again the dogma of the Immaculate
Conception holds a delightful sequel. For Mary alone can love
with her whole being, just as it is, without the necessity of all
the vigilance exercised by even the greatest saints. Let us enjoy
the contemplation of her love for Elizabeth. First of all, it is
rooted in God. And this motive is intensified by the fact that
Elizabeth has been the privileged object of a tremendous exercise
of Divine power. She has been even brought into the very
orbit of the Incarnation itself. This only goes to emphasise that
the miracle was not worked to strengthen Mary's faith. It had
its own *raison d'être* and it is to provide Mary's Child with a
precursor. Then Mary's love was a love of kinship. Ties of
blood are created by God and the consequent affections willed
by Him. But, above all, Mary's love is the love of the perfect
woman. And now it is fanned to flame by another woman's
need. God has made woman the child-bearer. And only
feminine resources can help a woman's spirit when that moment
comes for her. It was coming for Elizabeth and under
strange circumstances. She was to bear a child at a time in her
life when such a crisis need not be feared by ordinary women.

Her child was in her womb by a miracle. But it was a
miracle which did not affect the mode of conception, nor need
it be hoped that it would notably affect the travail of delivery.
Elizabeth will need a woman's consolation in those months of
waiting. Well, a woman is coming, across the hills—and in
haste.

The Gospel takes up the narrative. " And she entered into the house of Zachary, and saluted Elizabeth " (St. Luke i, 40). Even here let us pause. The virgin of our pictures and poems and statuary is so silent. Certainly one would never imagine her speaking first. Here again we might picture Mary arriving at Elizabeth's dwelling and standing mute before her, telling in language of downcast eye and prayerful pose how favoured she is. The truth is something quite different. Mary spoke first. And her speech was a salutation to her less privileged cousin. As we said already, her smiles from Heaven have melted hearts and healed bodies. We may take it that those who were privileged to receive them from her when she was still on earth wondered why jubilance seized upon them. Certainly her salutation of Elizabeth had a most remarkable effect " and it came to pass, that when Elizabeth heard the salutation of Mary, the infant leaped in her womb. And Elizabeth was filled with the Holy Ghost. And she cried out with a loud voice, and said : ' Blessed are thou among women, and blessed is the fruit of thy womb. And whence is this to me, that the Mother of my Lord should come to me. For behold as soon as the voice of thy salutation sounded in my ears, the infant in my womb leaped for joy. And blessed are thou that hast believed, because those things shall be accomplished that were spoken to thee by the Lord ' " (St. Luke i, 41-45).

All these wonders were effected in Elizabeth at the mere sound of Mary's voice. How beautiful must have been Mary's speech. Consider its source. Our words are the expression of our thoughts and these latter well up from our hearts, for out of the abundance of the heart the mouth speaketh. And our Divine Saviour Himself has assured us that the good in us and the evil have their source in the heart. Then think of the purity of thought and word issuing from the immaculate heart of Mary. Then, owing to her physical perfection her very utterance and articulation would be charming. As the radio proves even a voice may hold you, as a voice may repel. She would speak without precipitation, yet without that slowness which can irritate. So perfect would the harmony be between her thoughts and their verbal expression, and so perfectly would the latter be served by the physical apparatus of voice production that Mary would achieve without affectation and without straining after it the very perfection of elocution. Her voice would be a woman's voice, with its sweet delicate timbre. In her days humans were near enough to their origins to keep the vocational duties of the sexes distinct. The voices of women were not then given the hard metallic clang of a barrack square where women drilled and women gave the words of command. Post-war problems are making Ministers of State wonder if their calling up of women was justified either in results or in aftermath.

This visitation scene ought to be studied by our separated brethren who smile on the Bible but frown on Mary. God could have done all that He did for Elizabeth without any human intermediary. Moreover, the instrument remains always an instrument and secondary cause—yet be it remembered—a free cause. The fact is that God did not effect these wonders until Mary came to her cousin. And that involved a journey in haste and a journey over hills. Mary might have elected to stay at home. It was well for Elizabeth and the babe in her womb that she did not. When we realise that it is the Holy Spirit who is recording the episode through St. Luke we can see what significance it must have. The most perfervid Catholic would not attribute more to Mary's instrumentality.

Jesus is the only name in which we must be saved. This was true for John the Baptist too. Yet sanctification came to him in his mother's womb when, and precisely when, Mary by her own physical proximity and verbal greeting, brought the unborn Saviour to His Precursor. Mary was even the secondary cause why God poured forth on Elizabeth the substantial love proceeding from the Father and Son, the Holy Ghost. Whoever possesses this Spirit cannot praise Mary in a whisper, still less can such a one think or speak against her. In this Elizabeth is their forerunner of whom it is written that " she cried out with a loud voice." How futile have been the efforts of heresy to silence the prayer forged in Heaven and on earth. We may be sure that Gabriel did not mince his words when he began it, and now we hear Elizabeth continuing it, " in a loud voice." " Hail, Mary. Full of grace. The Lord is with thee. Blessed art thou, among women and blessed is the fruit of thy womb." Poor, poor Protestants. You claim to love and reverence God's holy word, and you are forbidden to lisp those blessed words after Him. Truly the Church of the Hail Mary, is the Church for little ones. And Heaven is for these same.

In reference to the controversy about Mary's degree of knowledge at this stage, we may assert that Elizabeth's words leave us in no doubt about her illumination. "And whence is this to me, that the Mother of my Lord should come to me?" Elizabeth was a better theologian than the reformers. She knew that sanctification could come from God alone. And she had been made feel—almost physically—the sanctification of her unborn child. It was not Mary's voice in itself, but the voice of Mary, Mother of the Redeemer—the Theotokos of Ephesus—Deipara! Elizabeth found that out before the council—because she was full of the spirit which directed its decision. How inspired Elizabeth was is shown by her allusion to "those things . . . that were spoken to thee by the Lord. . . ." She had no knowledge of the annunciation secrets from Mary. But quite obviously God had granted her an illumination on the matter. We then have Mary's inspired hymn of thanksgiving. Every word of it must be almost a torture to those who will not call Mary blessed. Ever since Holy Church has chanted her evensong or vespers she takes up again on countless consecrated lips the Virgin's Magnificat. Truly the Church of the Magnificat is the Church of the Incarnation.

God be praised for it, the Heavenly radiance although always enveloping Mary, is not always of such a blinding light. And we meet our little flesh and blood girl-mother again in those significant words: "And Mary abode with her about three months" (St. Luke i, 56). If ever we could maintain that any three months in Mary's life were lived humanly it must have been these. What conversations must have taken place between her and her cousin. And if the prelude was so fraught with wonder surely that wonder went on increasing with the hours and days. What did they talk about? Oh! we can well guess what Elizabeth would talk about. And she would not be slow to notice that all her years of married life had not given her the knowledge and judgment of this most wise virgin.

We can be sure that Mary prepared her aged cousin for the coming crisis with such words of consolation as would come natural to a woman, and as would come so natural to one full of God. Nor would she confine herself to words. There would be so many services Elizabeth would need and Mary anticipated her every need. If she was preparing the swaddling clothes for someone else, perhaps she helped to prepare the first garments for Elizabeth's child. At any rate, we need not draw on our imagination to fill these three months with the most loving human and delicate words and deeds. Never was Mary less a statue. It is with her as it is always with those who are moved by the Spirit of God. He inspires the initiation of their good deeds, He carries these through to their term, and He teaches them when to withdraw.

" And she returned to her own house." We will return with her and await His coming.

CHAPTER XXV

SINCE the angel had enlightened St. Joseph touching the mystery of Mary's motherhood, a heavenly tranquillity reigned in the humble dwelling at Nazareth. There were two hearts united in adoration of the holy who was incarnate beneath their roof and united also in the holiest and strongest love of each other. The days were punctuated by all the simple yet vital duties which make up home-life everywhere and although the world of that day had its special centres of excitement and stirring occurrences no one dreamed of making a little Nazarene dwelling the pivot of all global and all temporal history.

Here we are brought face to face with that truly Divine humility which is quite incapable of looking for the applause of creatures. God and His angels knew that Mary and Joseph were united by the bond of the truest, yet the most virginal marriage conceivable. Yet when in the course of time it became evident that Mary was bearing a child, everyone thought, if they gave it a thought, that it was a marriage similar to all human unions. Did anyone know? Did Joachim and Anne? We cannot say. The Holy Spirit has told us of Elizabeth's enlightenment and there may have been others. One thing is certain, as it was certain during St. Joseph's anguish. God must do all the revealing. No word of Mary's will betray the secret of the king. And in this, too, she and Joseph are well mated. This is an interesting point. Because the great glory which has transfigured Mary since her Assumption is inclined to be transferred by us to her mortal days and is thus partly responsible for our interpretation of her in art and script. We wish our virtues to be known. We stand on our rights. Alas, it is well that these virtues are not known for what they are, that these rights are not too closely scrutinised.

Another question now suggests itself. Since Mary, and in his measure, Joseph, were very conversant with the law and prophets, were they aware or alert to the fact that Bethlehem was written down as the birth place of the Promised One? We think that we could not imagine Our Lady ignorant of this fact written down by the finger of God. But this knowledge would not have disturbed them or made them anticipate the Divine guidance. We must remember Mary's unique privilege. She enjoyed that utter trust in God which was so natural to our unfallen parents. When they found themselves existing, living, breathing and thinking they never thought of looking to anyone or anything outside of their Great Creator for any needs they had. We have had a long, long trek away from the first paradise. And our exile psychology is particularly evident in our lack of childlike trust in God. The fact is that we have forgotten the native feeling of a creature, made from nothing and conserved in being at every moment and in all its being by the same Divine agent who gave it existence. Did we realise this truth in its application to ourselves and to all other creatures we would not allow secondary causes to loom so large in our thoughts and fears. While doing all that we are bound to do as rational creatures we would have learned the grand art of waiting for God with unshakable assurance. Mary had this art as part of her immaculate heritage and we may be sure that St. Joseph was also a proficient. As we have said their world was in all essentials our world of to-day. We do much the same things as the ancients only with greater speed and on a larger scale. Our own age has witnessed and bids fair to witness to a greater degree, the invasion of the citizen by the State. Actually the totalitarian States are those who make no secret of this while the democracies pay some external service to forms and orders in council. But the regimentation goes on apace and is almost all embracing.

The State rudely pushed its way into the Divine homestead at Nazareth, too. And it was an alien State. It was Rome. The Holy Land was under occupation at the time. Perhaps its plight was better than its plight to-day. For there was at least one dominant power. So one day Cæsar came knocking at the door of Mary and Joseph in the form of an imperial decree. " And it came to pass that in those days there went out a decree from Cæsar Augustus that the whole world should be enrolled. . . . And all went to be enrolled every one into his own city " (St. Luke ii, 1, 3). We wonder do angels laugh? or even smile? Or, perhaps, a yawn might answer the situation better. For what do they so often see, as looking on the Holy Countenance they see also the doings of little men. They see

the dictators framing their decrees and sending out their couriers
—or radiograms—north, south, east and west. And these poor
little tyrants have one scheme on foot. But God has another.
That's all. And it is always true for our comfort wherever the
little man may live.

One may easily imagine the different reaction to this particular
decree of Augustus. Every emotion would be stirred up from
merely fretful annoyance to a hate not less fierce because
impotent. But how was the news taken in one little home?
Mary's eyes shone. And Joseph's reflected their shining. For
God had spoken. And now they knew how the prophecy was
going to be fulfilled. They are off to Bethelehem. Good old
Cæsar. Or is it, poor little Augustus? They have not much to
pack up. Only—Mary brings the swaddling clothes.

CHAPTER XXVI

"SILENT NIGHT"

"AND Joseph also went up from Galilee, out of the city of Nazareth into Judea, to the city of David, which is called Bethlehem, because he was of the house and family of David. To be enrolled with Mary his espoused wife who was with child" (St. Luke ii, 4, 5).

Although Mary and Joseph recognised God's designs in this journey imposed on them apparently by an emperor's ambition they were not spared for all that the grave inconveniences involved.

It only takes a couple of verses for the evangelist to mention the journey and the major inconvenience " with Mary . . . who was with child," but much, very much lies in the trite words which will yield itself up to a little reflection. How necessary Joseph becomes in this and similar crises which Mary could not have faced alone. We will remember that in Joseph's breast beat the heart of a divinely appointed husband. He will not shirk any of the responsibility. And how great it was! It was his duty to bring Mary to Bethlehem at a time when her condition made such a journey very inconvenient to say the least of it. Not that she was facing the ordeal which was the lot of all other daughters of Eve who would bear children. But the fact remained that the great event was very near and caravan-blocked roads or wayside inns do not offer the ideal situation for even a miraculous birth. So Joseph would have to exercise all possible foresight and while rendering the journey as commodious as possible for his holy wife he would have to accomplish it as speedily as possible also. Then when he did arrive at David's city there was the question of accommodation. Have we ever realised how those problems of everyday life weighed on these privileged ones? But then we know that a niche is always found for a statue of Our Lady. Poor St. Joseph found it much more difficult to place the living, breathing Mary who was in his care by Divine command. We will have occasion to refer to it again, but even now we can see how the Incarnation is showing up all human relations to God. To say that God was forgotten in the world of that day is to say something which is really beyond us. But to see door after door closed in Mary's face, to see that God Incarnate cannot find a place to be born into His own creation, that is very plain, painfully so. And it is exactly what happened. How that great heart must have been wrung in anguish when refusal followed refusal. Too full already—try elsewhere. Is it the first century or the twentieth? And we must never forget how knowledge of the facts accentuated the pain for both Mary and Joseph. No one on earth loved God as these two loved Him. And they saw Him refused a place for His entry into His own universe as a man among men.

They both felt it terribly for His sake, Mary felt it also for Joseph's sake. But what shall we say of his wounded love for her, in such proximate need and refused, ever refused.

But deeper far is the agony in Joseph's heart for that he is the divinely appointed foster-father of the Divine Babe and he is unable to make due arrangements for His coming. Only love can know suffering. And we can read of that hopeless search without a tear. But it could have killed Joseph. And what of Mary? Eternity will not be long enough to fathom her love for her Son. And He was coming. What mother of earth is resourceless at that peak-point in her woman's life. The closed doors, the accents of refusal were Simeon's sword at work in that most loving of hearts. However, through it all they were conscious that the Eternal Father was watching. They must continue to do their utmost, but in the end it would be God who would provide. And provide He did. For in lack of anything better they turned aside into one of those caves destined for sheltering the passing shepherds. It was bare and bleak. Animals there were and all that goes with them. There was a manger with straw. Oh, God, can it be now! " And it came to pass, that when they were there her days were accomplished, that she should be delivered. And she brought forth her firstborn son . . ." (St. Luke ii, 6, 7). Ever since her Immaculate Conception He had been in her heart. " Hail Mary full of grace, the Lord is with thee. . . ." From the moment of her fiat He was in her blessed womb. And now, oh blissful moment, He is in her arms.

As usual the Holy Spirit says much in a few words. The

miracle of the virgin birth, due sequel to the miraculous conception of Christ is plainly stated in the very phrases used describing
the heavenly event. " And she brought forth her first-born Son,
and wrapped Him up in swaddling clothes, and laid Him in a
manger. . . ." She did all these things herself without the need
of other's aid. This is not the case of the other daughters of
Eve in similar plight.

Many sincere enough souls outside the Church who nevertheless do accept and cling to the central dogma of the Incarnation
both as regards the fact and the mode, own nevertheless to a
sense of irritation at what they deem Catholic over-lauding of
Mary's virginity. They see in this a veiled depreciation of all
other motherhood. It cannot be denied that some Catholic writers
and perhaps preachers have been found whose language in this
regard lies open to misinterpretation. In fact almost all the
hitherto current jargon about sex, and purity and vice might be
better expressed. We will try to put the matter plainly here
apropos of the magnificent mystery which we have just contemplated. As we remarked much earlier in this book the root
error lies in the fact that when dealing with this delicate topic
most people begin by saying " man " when they should say
" God." Christ Himself showed us the correct approach in His
own answer to a typical sex question—that of divorce. Let us
emphasise it even at the risk of repeating ourselves. The whole
idea of man and woman and all that concerns them is God's
idea. To grasp even this much gives us the correct approach—
one of adoring reverence and humble enquiry. It prepares us
spontaneously to ask God all the questions and receive all the
answers from Him—not from physiology, or psychology and,
least of all, from the State.

Now the first relation of man and woman to God is that of
creature to Creator. And into this the notion of sex does not
intrude. Then by God's infinite goodness that basic relation is
elevated into that of sonship. Even here there is neither male
nor female, for we all are one in Christ. But sooner or later
we do arrive at the sex conception. But it presents itself not in
horrid isolation but once more in magnificent relation to the
Divine will.

God created Adam. And then He made Eve from the
former's rib, designing her to be his helpmate. This vocation
of helpmate to man is never in abeyance. But it is not always
expressed in the same way. One very vital mode of its expres

sion is through holy marriage. In this matter, too, the Creator has left us in no doubt about either His rights or His will. In the very first pages of the Divine record we find God Himself solemnly instituting the marriage contract and underlining its indissolubility even then. So true is this that when the Son of God wished to restate the Divine law in this vital matter He had only to quote the primal charter. He Himself raised this natural contract to the dignity of a Sacrament of the New Law. Neither the Divine origin of marriage nor its objects in the Divine mind are in the slightest way obscure. God, who alone is, created beings outside of Himself. To animate life He gives the power to co-operate in His creative work. This power is peculiarly noble in the human species. Mankind has the power to effect such conditions under which God may create an immortal soul. We say may, because these conditions in themselves are not creative. But normally God does not create souls apart from them. God wills the propagation of the human race. And He is so anxious that many and even the majority of men will under-take the obligations and responsibilities of parenthood that He has made the instinct of reproduction the object of the greatest urge and the most intense pleasure. This latter must not be regarded as confined to a physical aspect only but to the whole beautiful intimacy involved in married life. This very beautiful will of the Creator is the source of sexual differentiation. Even at this stage let us ask ourselves if a single reprehensible element has entered into the whole scheme of things and the answer must be, not a single one. All is beautiful, all is honourable, in a word all is Divine. However, though the light be so bright, a shadow there is and it is all the darker because of the surrounding radiance. When the fall debilitated all man's power it wreaked its greatest ruin upon human nature at this point of sexual urge. Where God was supreme and where sense obeyed a reason perfectly subject to Him all was serene. But it is quite otherwise with us now. Precisely because the instinct of self-reproduction is so strong—at God's behest—there is hardly a point of our moral and physical being where revolt is so keenly felt. Spiritual writers often fail just at this point. They do not sufficiently distinguish between the Divine legacy and the disease induced by original sin. Hence they often appear to be reprobating what is merely natural, therefore God given, when the con-cupiscence or fevered passion is the real object of their vitupera-tion. Also they often appear to be unduly praising negative abstinence when they are actually extolling the regain of self-control under the law of grace. Now, although God manifestly wills fruitful marriage for very many people, He has not laid a specific command on any individual to marry. On the contrary, speaking through His Divine Son, He has issued a general invitation to absolute virginity. Here, too, motives count for everything. And the best interpreter of the Divine motivation of celibacy is St. Paul. He states quite simply that a virgin can concentrate on pleasing God, while the married person's heart may be divided. It follows that if God has counselled virginity no human power may filch away this free choice from man or woman. Least of all will God Himself be inconsistent. Now in Mary's case He had both inspired the vow and assured her through Gabriel that the conception of His Only Begotten Son would be without the slightest detriment to that vow.

When Mary uttered her momentous consent she became immediately conscious of the Divine accomplishment of this promise within her. Now at the Blessed Nativity she sees herself the object of the complementary miracle. He had entered her womb without detriment to her virginal integrity. When she found Him in her arms she was perfectly conscious that her virginity was intact. In the language of Holy Church, she was a virgin before the birth, a virgin during the birth, and a virgin following the birth. Notice that corporal integrity is not praised for its own sake but as the necessary sequel of God's inspiration, the virgin's vow and the Divine assurance. On the other hand, in Mary motherhood receives its crowning eulogy. We must remember that God could have come among men even as a man after other fashions. He chose virginity in a woman and made the virginity fruitful in His own motherhood. When God has spoken, have we anything to add? Above all, have we reproaches to urge against the Great Master of His own gifts?

While on this subject we would touch lightly on one other kindred one, namely, the adequate education of the young in life's mysteries. It is plain that the immature mind cannot grasp facts clothed in a language still strange to it—not merely in the mental but even in the physical domain. But we would make this suggestion. From their very earliest years children should be inspired with a very practical love of God, with love that is fed on the appreciation of the Divine in all creation. They should be impressed with the utter goodness of all God's handiwork—including themselves. Incalculable harm is done by a false jargon which divides the human body into good—and not so good—parts. They should be trained into looking for God's point of view, of appreciating it, and embracing it with their whole moral, mental and physical being. Anyone can see that thus they are being prepared for the proper attitude to the big matter of sex. If this attitude be already nurtured, factual information will come along in its own time and only serve to intensify the love and respect already planted in the fresh pure heart.

Spiritual writers like to think that Mary brought forth her Son in a rapture of raptures. This may well be. But it is quite certain that once He lay in her lap practical sequels to even Divine motherhood had prior claim to any ecstasy. And we are glad of it. For in these humble pages we are looking for our human mother rather than our celestial queen. She is both. But during her lifetime her humanity is predominant. Mary knew that her Divine motherhood was no beautiful theory but a very practical fact. And the faint cry of the new-born Infant emphasised the truth. So she " wrapped Him up in swaddling clothes." He had flung the star dust athwart the heavens. He clothed the lilies of the field with their white vesture. But now He has assumed a human nature. He needs mothering. Mary clothes her Babe. This is the first service of countless others that He will need for many a day. Oh, mothers, who have borne us all and tended our infant years, how were you willing to have this mother-maid thrust into the clouds out of your sight! The holy script tells us that Mary laid Him in a manger. It does not tell us what we will tell ourselves. She placed Him at her breast.

CHAPTER XXVII

ANGELS AND SHEPHERDS AND KINGS

OUR present purpose is not concerned, at least primarily, with either the origin or hierarchical rank of the first recorded worshippers of the Divine Babe. What does interest us is that they did come. The visitants were angelic, pastoral and regal. That has its own significance. But for us the big thing is that visitants they were. Because, as we have said perhaps too often there has been for so long a tacit conspiracy among spiritual writers to make the Incarnation so utterly divine that the human side of it suffers. And we suffer with it, because we are so human. After all, the Divinity was eternally safe in the inaccessible heights of the Trinity. If the Second Divine Person became Man, He can be trusted to look after the interests of His Godhead. We can surely enter into His will that we should reach that Godhead through the sacred humanity. And linked forever with that humanity is every human thing and most especially the humans who had first and direct contact with it.

" And there were in the same country shepherds watching and keeping the night-watches over their flock " (St. Luke ii, 8). Our modern world has almost completely lost a sense of real values. Because we have lost the key-valuation. God gave us this latter in the very first words of His Divine Letter to the human race which we call the Bible.

" In the beginning God created Heaven, and earth " (Gen. i, 1). Yes, the correlative notions of Creator and creature are sufficient to safeguard human sanctity and sanity so long as they are preserved. Proper values are immediately ascertained when these radical notions are used as norms. They have been largely lost. And our world is evil and our world is mad. Did we preserve these norms we would find ever at our disposal bubbling wells of happiness and even health—not to mention holiness. There was a man of our day who had been defrauded of the very road maps to these eternal wells. But he kept his heart pure, and that in its turn kept his mind bright. He found

the wells and the whole world rocked with his merry laughter.
Yes, Chesterton discovered his birthright and at least in his
truly big person merry England was reborn.

About these shepherds . . . watch the process of false
valuation. Take the world of fauna. Men say that lions are
noble and that rats are ugly. They do not add that the values
are only relative. No, they are fixed values. But God made
both beasties. And man could not even think of a whisker-
end of either much less produce them from nothing. It is the
same with the world of floral creation. This we say is a flower,
that a weed. Make us a few weeds, oh, man of science!
Would we not be satisfied with an atomic bomb? It is the
same with hierarchical grading. That is a position of eminence,
that a menial job. And so shepherds and sheep are so
uninteresting. Just yawns and bleats and nothing. But a sheep
is a Divine idea. And it might have remained in the Divine
mind. It need not necessarily realise itself in fleecy creatures
roaming hillsides and eventually warming the inside and outside of men. It looks as if there is a mighty big sermon in a
sheep, telling of being subsistent, of love, of omnipotence.
Shepherds are also Divine ideas. And duty faithfully performed
is a very divine idea. In fact, anything might happen in such
an interesting setting as shepherds and sheep.   And it just
did. " And behold an angel of the Lord stood by them, and
the brightness of God shone by them and the brightness of God
shone round about them. . . ." (St. Luke ii, 9).

When one studies carefully and closely the Divine record of
both Testaments one is made conscious of the remarkable rôle
exercised by angels in God's dealings with men. Already in
our study of Our Lady we have met the great Archangel Gabriel
and also the dear angel who gave peace and joy to St. Joseph in
giving him knowledge of God's dealings with Mary. Now we
are introduced to this other Heavenly dweller who is the
evangelist of the shepherds as we may term him. What we have
tried to emphasise about these various angels is, first of all, that
their rôles were very distinctive calling for distinct endowments
in the angel; and, secondly, that they still possess a special aptitude for the same rôle as exercised on our behalf here and now.
It must attract our attention that a wholesome fear is the first
reaction in humans to such visitations. We call this fear wholesome radically because it is rooted in our nature to fear beings
not only greater than us in the hierarchy of creatures but beings

from the other world. Where one is avid of visions and sees such without fear, then indeed may one be really afraid. But if fear be the first and natural reaction, good angels always allay it immediately. Other angels there are. . . . These shepherds would not be such strangers to the supernatural as their brothers on other hillsides throughout the gentile world. For they belong to the chosen people. They were of those whose fathers the patriarchs spoke with God. They were used to Divine interventions which had always punctuated their history, reminiscent of the morning of the world when the first man and woman walked with God in a garden into which as yet sin had not entered. Nevertheless, as humans they were afraid. " And they feared with a great fear " (St. Luke ii, 9). But the inevitable happens. And the angels said to them: " Fear not, for behold, I bring you good tidings of great joy, that shall be to all the people. For this day is born to you a Saviour, who is Christ the Lord, in the City of David. And this shall be a sign, unto you, you shall find the infant wrapped in swaddling clothes, and laid in a manger. And suddenly there was with the angel a multitude of the Heavenly army, praising God, and saying glory to God in the highest, and on earth peace to men of goodwill " (St. Luke ii, 10-14).

There will come a day in the earthly life of Christ when He will disclaim the ministry of Heavenly legions if these were to hinder His Passion and therefore our salvation. But whenever their ministry served the Father's will then the angels were there. We may learn a lot from these first angels of Christmas. Undoubtedly they retain their mission to point out the Divine Child. They are the special angels of the infancy. We ought to invoke them at all times, but very particularly at Christmas. For they belong to this liturgical season. As we have said, angels do not improvise their messages. If they scatter light, if they give a message, the light is reflected from the very face of God, the words are God's before they are the angels. When we remember this we will not be surprised if we find that a short phrase on angelic lips says very, very much. Have we realised that these first Christmas angels gave us once and for all the formula which our statesmen admit they cannot find— namely, a formula for global peace? Because they are angels they start with God " Glory to God in the highest "—which is a plain manner of saying that God's glory must be our first objective. Yet the agenda of the great world conferences never

starts thus: "And on earth peace to men of goodwill "—
actually, according to the original text, "men of goodwill" rather
means men who are the subjects of God's complacency. But
this is not really different from the customary interpretation, for
goodwill in men is the fruit of God's goodwill to men. Now,
is not it quite apparent in our troubled era that our greatest
need, and, alas! our greatest lack is precisely men of goodwill?
Place a man of such goodwill in the councils of each nation,
place several such if you will and the nightmare in which we
are living will be dissipated. So the angels' formula is valid.

We said that our interest in these angels and their shepherd
audience, as well as the kings from afar, lay in the fact that they
published Christ and visited Him. For if the rude cave at
Bethlehem was crowded with visitors, we are less likely to
believe in the splendid isolation of later days when the Holy
Family had a home in which visitors might be received. If
high Heaven made the young virgin mother hold levee in
Bethlehem we may form our own conclusion about the social
contacts of Nazareth later on. The fact is that God became
Man to draw men to Himself. And no sooner does He enter
Mary's womb than He starts to draw them. He will draw all.
But some will not come. But many, many will and the queue
is forming this first Christmas night.

"And it came to pass, after the angels departed from them
into Heaven, the shepherds said one to another. Let us go over
to Bethlehem, and let us see this word that is come to pass,
which the Lord hath shewed us." And they came with haste,
and they found Mary and Joseph, and the infant lying in the
manger (St. Luke ii, 15, 16).

The so-called reformers endeavoured to lend some show of
respectability to their theories by claiming Scriptural authority
for all their assertions. And, like all falsehoods, dint of repetition will give a semblance of truth to that which is utterly
devoid of it. See how the Catholic lay-world does retain the
idea that Protestantism has at least some verbal backing from
Holy Writ. That is to say, it is widely believed that the
reformers can make some class of verbal case for themselves out
of the words of Scripture. The truth is quite otherwise. How
could it be anything else? God wrote the Bible and, therefore,
the Bible cannot be a support to heresy. Of course, we do
recall the incident where the spirit of lies quoted Scripture for
the Author of Scripture. But he was soon racing for the abyss.

A sound acquaintance with the Sacred Text makes one wonder
how our separated brethren can read it with equanimity. Here
is a case in point. Suppose a Pope had written verse sixteen of
St. Luke's second chapter. He would be accused not merely of
putting Mary in, but of putting both Mary and Joseph prior to
the Divine Infant. Yet the Holy Ghost adopts just this order.
Because the Holy Ghost is aware that in the time order both
Mary and Joseph necessarily preceded the Incarnate God. Here
then is the one authentic setting. It is the Church of
Bethlehem. It is the Church of to-day—and to-morrow and of
all time. "And they found Mary and Joseph and the Infant
lying in the manger."

"And seeing, they understood of the word that had been
spoken to them concerning this child" (St. Luke ii, 17). The
question suggests itself what was said at this wonderful interview? Once again, our cribs are mute. Mary is silent. Her
Infant utters no cry. And the shepherds are beautifully carved—
but of stone. But it was not so. No, most decidedly it was not so.

Like all simple folk those shepherds would possess a natural
courtesy and politeness. Although it is recorded of them that
"they came with haste" we may be quite sure that they did not
rush in on the sacred scene but humbly begged admittance. And
so there would have been conversation. St. Joseph would bid
them welcome and lead them to Mary and her Infant. She in
her turn would repeat Joseph's words of welcome. They would
then tell of the heavenly vision which had been vouchsafed to
them and which had led them thither. And then the obvious
question would surely tremble on their lips: what is the meaning
of it all and who is the Infant? Already the angel had told them
very much. He had banished fear from their hearts and had
spoken of his own message as "good tidings" calculated to
inspire great joy. We must remember that if humans sometimes forget true values angels can never do so. Then, as now,
secular events whether touching the Roman Empire or the
Jewish people would be classed as interesting and joyful, too,
according as they suited at least some of those concerned. But
then as now heaven would have quite other interests. But the
angel asserted that his news was absolutely good and absolutely
joyful. Moreover, it all centred round a birth. The new-born
Child was precisely what Israel was longing for since Israel
became a people, nay what all humanity was longing for—a
saviour. And although it took the Great Doctor of the Nations

some time and trouble to drive home the universal significance of the Messianic promise yet the angel of the First Christmas Night said as much: "I bring you good tidings of great joy, that shall be to all the people." So we see that it was very instructed shepherds who came to the first Crib and what they already knew only whetted their appetite for further knowledge. Since the Infant and his very apparel was the central theme of the angel message we may well believe that all the interest of the shepherds was concentrated on the mother and Child. Of these two, the Child was as incapable of furnishing information as any other newborn babe. So there remained Mary. But before they questioned her we may believe that their own hearts were saying strange things to them. The angel had said "this day is born . . ." and the shepherds had come with haste. Surely they marvelled at the freshness of a mother immediately after her ordeal—but this mother did not look like as if she had experienced any ordeal. We wonder how much did God tell these simple hearts?

So they will recount their vision to Mary and she will confirm it by telling them—what? It matters little, save to emphasise the conversations that must have ensued. And now, when a proud mother shows you her first-born do you stand in impassive silence. You do not. You caress the child. If you are intimate enough you take it up in your own arms. We may be certain that this is exactly what happened on the first Holy Night. The shepherds would even mutely ask Mary for the Infant. And Mary knew well that her Infant was hers precisely to give Him to others. So those shepherds would cradle the Divine Child in their rustic arms. Truly the scene has never changed. The Church of the first Bethlehem is the Church of the Crib to-day and of the Bambino. How alien to it all is the spirit which has swept all those lovely things out of religion? And, as we said, they have done this in the name of Gospel texts. Certainly they dare not quote St. Luke, Chapter II, verses 8 to 16, in their own favour.

We can see that these shepherds received all the information which was necessary to a complete understanding of the angel's message. For St. Luke tells us: "And seeing they understood of the word that had been spoken to them concerning this child " (St. Luke ii, 17). Moreover, they were not strangers to the human instinct to broadcast all news. So, in their turn, they became evangelists. "And all that heard wondered, and at those things that were told them by the shepherds."

Even Mary's wonderful knowledge received accretion from those Heavenly occurrences. " But Mary kept all these words pondering them in her heart " (St. Luke ii, 19). The Church of Christ has never ceased to learn from this most wise virgin, whereas one of the first punishments experienced by those who reject Mary is that the wine of knowledge and love dries up and utterly fails. That is why the sects have no real theology. To see even the titles of their so-called pious books is to see either borrowed Catholicity or a barren negation owing its existence to the truth against which it protests. So our shepherd visitors take their leave " And the shepherds returned glorifying and praising God for all the things they had heard and seen, as it was told unto them " (St. Luke ii, 20). We can picture them on many a subsequent occasion chatting about the wonderful Child and the extraordinary lady who had been so gracious to them. We think that those shepherds could never, never have made good Protestants.

But the visitors have not ceased to come. It is St. Matthew who tells us of these others from a far land. " When Jesus therefore was born in Bethlehem of Juda, in the days of King Herod, behold there came wise men from the East to Jerusalem." Were the shepherds not also wise men? (St. Matthew ii, 1). They were indeed in so far as they were not incredulous to the Heavenly vision. But these now mentioned were apparently professional savants. They were learned in special lore. Tradition has invested them with regal rank. How suitable that royalty should so visit royalty. For, as we have seen, if regal blood ever had authenticity and worth it was the blood which flowed in the veins of Mary and Joseph. St. Matthew continues, saying: " Where is He that is born King of the Jews?" Moderns agitate themselves about many questions which can profit them little. These truly wise men were concerned with the one which solved life and death, time and eternity. " For we have seen his star in the East, and are come to adore Him."

The Incarnation is always sifting hearts. Even then there were those for whom the Heavenly tidings spelt grief and chagrin, not great joy. " And King Herod hearing this was troubled, and all Jerusalem with him. And assembling together all the chief priests and the scribes of the people, he enquired of them where Christ should be born. But they said to him: ' In Bethlehem of Juda, for so it is written by the prophet.

And thou Bethlehem, the land of Juda, art not the least among the princes of Juda, for out of thee shall come forth the captain that shall rule my people Israel '." Then Herod, privately calling the wise men, learned diligently of them the time of the star which appeared to them and sending them into Bethlehem, said: " Go and diligently enquire after the Child and when you have found Him bring me word again that I also may come and adore Him. Who having heard the kings went their way, and behold the star which they had seen in the East, went before them until it came and stood over where the Child was. And seeing the star they rejoiced with exceeding great joy " (St. Matthew ii, 3-10).

The shepherds have gone.   Now the new visitors have arrived. " And entering into the house, they found the Child with Mary His mother, and falling down they adored Him, and opening their treasures, they offered Him gifts, gold, frankincense, and myrrh " (St. Matthew ii, 11). We may be quite sure that in the case of the Magi, as in that of the shepherds, it was not altogether a matter of dumb show. By way of introduction they would tell Mary and Joseph of the wonderful star which had conducted them thither. They would add what their belief was touching its significance and then Mary would do what she has always done in the Church, she would corroborate their dearest convictions and point to the Child as fulfilling these latter. We cannot doubt that they told of their interview with Herod and the very remarkable interest evinced by that monarch in the Child towards whom the star was directing them. We have no reason to think that these wise men, despite their wisdom, penetrated the treacherous designs of the infamous monarch. And judging by the Divine intervention necessary to divert their journey they were not put on their guard by Mary or Joseph. Did Mary realise the danger which lay behind Herod's apparent concern? As we have already stated, despite Mary's wonderful endowments, flowing so naturally from her unique privilege, there is no need to posit in her perfect knowledge of everything all the time. Like the humblest dweller in the land she could have no doubts about the unsavoury character of Herod. But it is not likely that she feared a concentration of his wrath upon the tiny Infant in her lap. The same must be held with regard to St. Joseph. Of all present there was only one who knew perfectly what was in Herod. But by His own will he was not merely silent, but quite unable to give the slightest expression to His knowledge. Yes, the Infant knew. But he can neither speak nor act. So the Eternal Father must do both. And as a clear indication of his special rôle, it is Joseph who gets the revelation. A revelation was given simultaneously to the Magi and as both are recorded together by St. Matthew we just quote: " And having received an answer in sleep that they should not return to Herod they went back another way into their country. And after they were departed, behold an angel of the Lord appeared in sleep to Joseph, saying, Arise, and take the Child and His mother, and fly into Egypt and be there until I shall tell thee. For it will come to pass that Herod will seek the Child to destroy Him " (St. Matthew ii, 12, 13).

Perhaps after all the Magi had entertained some fears concerning Herod's motives and had made their doubts the object of their prayers. For it is said that the warning they received from Heaven was in the nature of an answer. Once more we have the blessed angels at work. Was this the same one who had removed Joseph's worries about the mystery! We do not know. But to this angel, whoever he was in the hierarchy of good spirits, we owe heartful gratitude for saving the Holy Family from the fury of Herod. It is interesting to notice how Divine Providence acted when the very Son of God was the object of its care. Had the Gospels been merely fairy tales their human authors would never have confined themselves to such sober facts, nor would their listeners have been satisfied with such. But since eternal truth is recording what did happen we notice two things. First of all, events run their natural course up to a point. Then, if it be necessary, Heaven speaks. But the implementing of the Divine directions is left to free human agents. Happily, in the matter of the Incarnate Word's safety, these free human wills are by a special grace guaranteed against failure. But they remain free. As we said, it is a splendid testimony to the calibre of Joseph, spiritual, mental and physical, that such a journey should be imposed on him and that he accomplished it to the safety of Mary and the Divine Child.

The recent war made us familiar with child evacuees. Nevertheless no belligerent nation had actual designs against the children of the enemy. Only bombs are rather indiscriminating things. But the life of this Child was sought. See the drama of sin placed within reach of God. It hunts Him down. Yes, and it kills Him in the end. But that end is not yet. The Eternal Father sees to that—through Joseph.

CHAPTER XXVIII

THE SWORD OF SIMEON

WE may find in current Marian literature an excuse for framing in our minds a virgin who never speaks and who never smiles. But not all the false reverence of pious writers could make Mary into a being who never suffered, because a text of Holy Scripture blocked the way. Yet even in this domain we seem to have surrendered our right to feel the soft warm hand of our suffering mother in ours. And God knows we need her closeness in this if in any matter touching our human lives. What, then, has happened? The sufferings are there, obvious and wide as the sea. How have we converted this, too, into statuary, impressive, reverent if you will, but cold, cold? We think that our great mistake lies in our concentration rather on the divine source of these sufferings than on the very, very human subject of them. As a Doctor of the Church has already said about Our Lord, His Divinity must not be permitted to obscure His Humanity and His Humanity must not be stressed to the detriment of His Divinity. This has an application to Mary too. She is not divine, yet she has been so caught up into the Godhead that no human side of her is interpreted aright if it is not seen in the light of the Divinity which shines all round and through her. On the other hand, if we forget Mary's essential creaturehood and flesh and blood humanity we lose the key to all her emotions, psychic, moral, mental and physical. In fact we are dealing with a figment. And Mary is the most glorious fact in Creation.

Could we have conceived a Christ to whom suffering would be unknown? Well, absolutely speaking and regarding His rights as God, even a human existence should have been for Him replete with all possible happiness. But taking into consideration the fact of sin and realising that sin ranges through this world, we can realise that if truth is going to be portrayed we will see sin attacking a God who put Himself into its reach. We have seen it. We have seen it kill Him. And what of Mary? Something analogous may be said of her. Her unique privilege of exemption from all sin, original and actual, furnished her with title-deeds to immunity from sin's effects—suffering, and even death. But she is to be the mother of the Suffering One. So for her, too, suffering will be inevitable. In fact, just as in the case of her Divine Son all the reasons which militated against suffering will become sources of its very intensification. We must keep before us all the time those sources. The first is precisely her divine motherhood—or, we should say, that she suffers because she is mother, and because her Son is very God. She will also suffer in proportion to the very perfection of her nature in every sphere. How strange, and what a commentary on the Divine indictment of sin: "Sin is iniquity." Mary is mother of God, therefore she must suffer. Mary is the best of mothers. Therefore she must suffer. Mary is immaculate. Therefore she must suffer. Truly upon her has passed the similitude of One in whom Pilate could find no cause but of whom he said: "Therefore I will chastise Him . . ."

In earlier chapters we saw that Mary's privilege of Immaculate Conception had very practical consequences in every sphere of her being, even the purely physical one. Did our deductions surprise our readers? If they did it could only be due to our confining the dogma to the purely speculative field. Of course we believed in it. But we had not faced up to its consequences. And although it gave to our mental image of Mary an aurora of celestial light it had not dawned on us that during her mortal days it gave an exquisite blush to her maiden cheek. Now we have made another statement which we think is going to lead us on a most interesting journey of discovery. And discovery it will probably be for many of us. But although a wonderland it will be, it will not be a figment of our imaginations. There is nothing so hurtful to the saints and nothing so utterly unnecessary than to make up legends about them. And this holds with still greater weight for the queen of all saints. Well, our statement was that Mary must suffer, and suffer intensely, because she is immaculate. That demands looking into. We hope to do so right now, and we will certainly see that the Heart encircled by cruel thorns is not merely a touching symbol but an idea terribly realised in suffering flesh and blood—Mary's.

As in the case of all Mary's qualities we refused to begin so late as the Annunciation, so in the case of her sufferings we refuse to begin only with Simeon's prophetic words. At this latter time her title-deed to pain was particularly the divine

L

motherhood. But her Immaculate Conception antedated that by perhaps fourteen or fifteen years. So once again we shall begin with the tiny Infant of Joachim and Anne.

When discussing Mary's privileged immunity from all interior results of sin, such as debility and disease with their attendant woes, we emphatically stated that she was as subject to all exterior assaults as any other creature. Positing a very special Providence which would reduce these latter and exclude some we must now add that in such matters she was more subject than any other pure creature. If it was merely physical cold that was in question, she would feel it more than any other, because of her most perfect and most sensitive physical get-up. The same must be said of the whole gamut of external inconveniences. Now the question is, was Mary's infancy perfectly shielded from all such? We know that the Eternal Father willed her to bring to her divine motherhood the healthiest of minds in the healthiest of bodies. But while safeguarding this objective in all essentials, may we not believe that, like the Child who would be hers, Mary, too, was subjected to quite a lot of the external afflictions which beset all infancy. If we know that regal blood flowed in that family we are also pretty certain that it was the Herods and their ilk who had the money-bags. Yes, we think that we can assume poverty as a setting of Mary's infancy and, if so, there could be real tears in those baby eyes, through which the smile was no less a smile.

And she grows up. She develops in soul, in body, in faculty and sense. Now if we have eyes to see, the page of suffering must unroll before us. Already we tried to glimpse the wonders of that immaculate soul. They may be all summed up in a love for God such as never before appeared on this earth and never shall appear again. This beautiful soul is served by perfect faculties and senses. . . . These latter develop. Now it has been almost an axiom with us that Mary was no hermit. If she later on went to a marriage feast she did not meet all her friends and relations there for the first time. It is interesting how she was singled out for the confidence touching the wine debacle. They seemed to know that she would have the good will to help, aye, and more. Very well, then. We need not labour the point. As she grew up Mary met other folk, old and young, men and women, boys and girls. In many respects the world has not changed much, if at all. The population of Nazareth would very probably represent just as mixed a grill of manners and morals as our own home towns of to-day. To say the least of it, Mary would have no escape from finding out that everybody was not the same as herself. For most of us this discovery generally meant that folk were heaps better than us. That was not the experience of God's little girl. Let us remember that the children who would be contemporary with Mary would be contemporaries later on with her Son. They would be old enough to be, well, His apostles, or publicans like (and unlike) Matthew, and perhaps priests. At any rate they would be a section of those who surrounded Him later on and loved Him or hounded Him to death. Christ would prove Israel to be rotten in the main. But that kind of universal religious and national decadence is not a sudden process. The child Mary would be growing up in full view of the ugly thing. And taking it by long and by large as a lack of love of God it hurt this child as it could hurt just One other—later on. But the pain could have been more specific. Were all the children of Nazareth cherubs—or did Mary meet only the cherubs? Suppose she found herself up against childish selfishness? She had not the root of that in her. But that only meant that she saw it for the ugly thing it was. There's pain for her that I suppose we never dreamed of. But you see, in the paintings she's always so safe with only her parents. Yes, but the paintings are not roll films. Now take her mind. Like all children, she regarded her parents as know-alls. And we have seen that God must have highly endowed these two. But when Mary came in contact with other minds, a great shock must have confronted her for she would meet obtuseness, downright stupidity or at the very best a terrible slowness. Put a genius out of his milieu. Put him among people who have no idea in common with him. You or I cannot know what a genius would feel like. But we can guess. And irritation might be succeeded by anger and anger by worse. So you would have to bundle off your guest to a big house. Now consider Mary's mental stature, between clarity and factual richness. She would not feel irritated. But she would feel terribly lonely even in a crowd. And we see that agony in the other, too—later on. Is there not a pent-up anguish in the pathetic cry of a Man-God, "Are you also yet without understanding?" So we see how much Mary's perfect virtue could suffer from her environment and how much her genius could suffer from the darkened minds which surrounded her. We have alluded to the religious decay which must have surrounded Mary's childhood. Think of her speaking with one such as Caiphas. Her son spoke with the doctors when He was twelve. Some of their questions and some of their answers may well have saddened His Divine Heart. The theology, or rather the casuistry, was crystallising which would later on break upon Him and His beloved disciples in torrents of small vituperation and heartless interpretations. Mary could have met a lot of this, too, although as a woman she would not be so exposed to discussion with the Rabbis. But wherever a false note was struck, no one would detect it with the same celerity as this immaculate one. And she would suffer.

Then, again, Mary was a royal member of the great theocratic nation—great because theocratic. Yet she would see the legions marching by. And she would see the beginnings of that national landslide which ended in the great national religious apostacy. "We have no king but Cæsar." So we think that the early years of this chosen lily were hemmed in by many a thorn.

We need not repeat the suffering potentially involved in her fiat. And her fears came true—until God sent that dear angel to Joseph. At last we have arrived at the great source of anguish for Mary: her mothering of God. "And thy own soul a sword shall pierce" (St. Luke ii, 35). So spoke Simeon to her. Now He is in her arms. Ah, Simeon, Mary's experience has anticipated your inspired utterance. For suffering came to her in billowing waves from the moment He entered her blessed womb.

We wonder how we arrived at our uncanny facility in dehumanising, so to speak, the sufferings of Christ and those of His blessed mother. We call it uncanny because it strikes at the very object of these sufferings, namely, that being like to our own they should help us therein. A general reason may be said to consist in that tendency implanted by original sin to make false judgments even when premisses are clear enough. But there is the deeper reason to which we have often alluded already, a false reverence which simply will not have the Incarnation in all its implications. This spirit, masquerading in the alleged light of shocked piety, led to one of the very first heresies in the infant Church, that of the Docetæ. They were so appalled by the Passion of Christ that they sought to dispose of it by disposing of the reality of His body. He only seemed to have a body—hence their name, Docetæ. The root error of Manicheanism is much the same. They were so averse to the corruption in us and outside of us that they posited two principles, a good and an evil. The former created all that is good and the latter all that is evil—

including the very flesh. So in this scheme of things everything human went by the board, including marriage, which has the effrontery to procreate more flesh. Now none of us would like to be convicted of either of the above-mentioned heresies. We think that our attitude to the sufferings of Christ and His mother is coloured by a conviction which may be apparently humble but is no less false for all that. We are only too conscious that for the most part our sufferings take their rise in our sin and corruption. Very seldom do we feel completely innocent martyrs. Whereas we are very aware of the essential holiness of Christ and the derived though perfect holiness of Mary. That alone seems to place a chasm between us. How can we dare equate these sufferings with our own? What we forget is that a similar suffering may be induced by a totally different cause. But similarity of suffering there can be and there is. And in our study of Mary's sufferings, as in all else concerning her, that is our avowed object—not to show how unlike she is to us—too easy a task—but how very like.

A little reflection shows that it must be so. In the bosom of the Eternal Father, in the infinite depths and heights of the most adorable Trinity, the Word was inaccessible to suffering. It was precisely the humanity which He assumed which brought Him within reach of it and, as things are, made Him vulnerable. Quite obviously, therefore, He will always suffer in a most human way. The contribution of the Divinity will be to almost infinitely enlarge the horizon of pain and add an incredible intensity thereto. But never for a moment must we allow ourselves under the pretext of reverence to lift His sufferings altogether out of the human sphere which is not only their own but outside of which they could not have happened. Do we not sometimes hear very worthy people say, in reference to some acute crisis in the Passion, "But he was God"? Here the nuance is all wrong. For they say by implication that the Divinity lessened the pain in some way. The correct note is struck by the one who asserted that there is no suffering in our lives, no matter what the source, which is not to be found in His.

We have stressed the case of the God-Man in order to accentuate the similar truth about His mother. It is a similar truth in her case—we mean under the aspect of human sufferings as such. For she was a pure creature. When, therefore, we put her pain up into the clouds and etherealised it with fine phrase and noble sentiment we have done an injury no less to truth than to ourselves.

Mary's dolours had many specific sources, and we hope to examine at least some of them. But one general source there was and it was opened by her fiat. It was, in fact, her divine motherhood. We have said it already and we repeat it here with emphasis. We take our stand with those who believe that from Gabriel's message Mary was made perfectly conscious of the identity of the Child within her womb. We do not even essay to marshall proof. Any other view is repellent to us. We remember Christ's momentous query to His disciples: "Whom do men say I am?" And the answer: "Some Elias, some the Prophet . . ." Now here is a cardinal point. Those who thought that Christ was Elias or the Prophet gave Him the treatment due to these human worthies—if their belief was not merely in the speculative order. In other words, their dealings with Christ would be coloured by their conviction that He was a human person. If they did not like Him as such, their dealings might be coloured with His Blood. They were. No. God the Father wanted His Son to be mothered, and mothered perfectly. We maintain that Mary could not have given Him this adequate mothering if she had regarded Him as less than He really was. Now we shall see how true that is according as the drama of the Incarnation unfolds before us. Mary, then, was perfectly conscious of her Child's divinity. His humanity spoke for itself. She was also conscious of her tremendous obligations as mother of God. Had she not been aware of these obligations she could not have fulfilled them. For in thought, in deed she would have been wanting in all that must be demanded by a Divine Person. Mary, then, was perfectly conscious of three great facts and they were almost simultaneous in her experience. One was her Child's Godhead. The second was her perfectly adequate endowments for the perfect motherhood to which she was called. Not that Mary analysed her gifts in a complacent way, of course not. But she was perfectly aware that she had it in herself— though not of herself—to rise to the full stature of her predestination. In other words, if her Immaculate Conception was God's gift to her Son—and to us—it was also His gift to Mary. She certainly needed it in all its implications. The third fact, and it may be regarded as the proximate cause of her dolours, was this: that from the very beginning Mary was made aware, painfully aware, that the Eternal Father's Providence for His Son was far more a matter of her alert and efficient motherhood than any miraculous interventions. In effect, what Mary realised was that God had placed very literally in her hands His greatest treasure, that precisely as her Son He was exposed to suffering, and that it would be through her mothering that He was to be preserved from any suffering not designed for Him by His Father. We will see some of this working out in detail. But for the moment we would draw the following pertinent conclusion. In safeguarding her Son from all hurt Mary experienced the anguish which confronts any and every soul that becomes conscious of its responsibilities as a Christ-bearer. The only difference is that with Mary the enemies of Jesus were all without. With us they are without and within. We ourselves are Herod, are Pilate, are Judas—at least potentially.

As we have already remarked, to realise responsibility and to rise fully to all its demands on us is to have an arduous life, to say the least of it. Mary did both in the highest degree in relation to her divine motherhood. She was fully aware of it, realised all its implications and responded fully to these every moment of her maternal life. We would make a great mistake if we were to satisfy ourselves with this general statement, however honourable it be to Mary. We will pursue our wonted course of examining with reverence the detailed working out of this maternal solicitude, and that from the very first moment of its inception.

As soon as Mary had uttered her fiat she became conscious of the Word made Flesh within her. From that same moment she brought to the divine mothering every fibre of her being, moral, mental and physical. It is here if anywhere that we take leave of the statue and meet a flesh and blood woman. We meet a woman who is a mother.

True, the Conception of Christ had been miraculous, the operation of the overshadowing Spirit. And Mary knew well that when it came, His birth would be in keeping with His entry into her sealed womb. So she was not preparing for the ordeal which is the honourable though pain-fraught lot of all other mothers of men. But there was a lot to be done in between. Here is one of the times that Mary realised how humanly would the Incarnate Word exercise His new life. So Mary experienced the responsibility of all pregnant women, namely, to contribute in every way to the development of the new life within. But she was also aware of something else, which was unique to her case. In ordinary gestation the life within is not an independent rational life for many months. It was not so with the Christ-Infant in the virgin's womb. He will develop as other infants develop. And he will tarry in his chosen prison for nine whole months. But from Mary's fiat the adorable Soul of Christ vivified His assumed humanity and this humanity was perfect in every detail from its miraculous conception. There arose for Mary, therefore, the sweet duty of constant and unremitting communication with the Incarnate Word within her breast. How near Mary comes to each one of us, not indeed in due reaction but in the fact of our Communions! Now perhaps we can make some effort at measuring her response to her responsibility as contrasted with ours. When we receive Holy Communion our faith assures us that Jesus Christ, true God and true Man, is within us with all His divinity and all His humanity. At such privileged moments our alleged best is often poor enough. Sporadic acts punctuated by distractions—or coma. Mary did not fail the Man-God within her, not in anything, not for a moment. And although her Immaculate Conception made all her maternal duties so sweet and easy, yet they were always the fruit of the most exquisite free will—and despite miraculous settings—in faith.

Our statuary experts moulded an exquisite virgin—only in marble. She was silent as marble must needs be silent. And quite obviously she neither ate nor drank. Well, dear, well-meaning sculptors, it is an excellent statue. But would you mind if we turned our attention to the living mother-maid? For her now, eating and drinking is invested with a new and divine significance. For through those so human processes she is weaving the seamless robe of His Flesh and Blood. And see in this the confirmation and illustration of a statement made earlier in these pages. We said that the Incarnation did not create relations with God so much as it revealed already existing ones. Much later on Christ will say that His food is the Father's Will. He will further assert that those who give Him that food by faithful accomplishment of that Will are His very parents and true kin. See how these divine words receive their truest verification in Mary. From the very moment of her conception she did the Father's Will as no one before her, as no one ever again. "The Lord is with thee." From the moment of the Incarnation she feeds the Incarnate Word literally with her own very substance. Had Mary not given Him the first mystic food of the Father's good pleasure, never would she have been chosen to give Him the second. But it is so. Did the precious product of fruitful earth ever receive a greater sanctification and sanction than when it became first bone of her bone and flesh of her flesh that it might build up the Sacred humanity!

Does not this provide a beautiful commentary on the Pauline injunction: "Whether you eat or whether you drink, do all for the glory of God'? Does it not give us the correct angle on concern for our bodily health? How did Mary view this human concern? Owing to her Immaculate Conception she brought to the Divine motherhood every perfect contribution of a perfect mind in a perfect body. Yet, as we saw, she was not invulnerable to external inconveniences. And all through her life she was bound to supplement a very special providence by a personal output of vigilance and care. But this became especially imperative when His heart beat close to hers. And so, without any selfishness being ever possible, not to mention neurosis, she took particular care of her health during that Divine novena of expectant months.

And thus it was that God continued to read Mary the two practical lessons. First, her Divine predestination which made her quite certain of miracles when these were needed; and, secondly, her unique endowments which made her expect no superfluous interventions.

These two ways of God with Mary combined to light her days with joy and shadow them with sorrow. See them at work. The Annunciation was the hour of miracles if ever these had their hour. But the day after came, and the weeks and months. And it was with Mary as with all expectant mothers. Would God enlighten Joseph? Not until Joseph's eyes had enlightened him with a ray of utter darkness. For he knew it was all light, but for him there was darkness. That is how the mothering of God crushed her heart by crushing that other heart. Then God did speak.

The journey from Nazareth to Bethlehem was another station in Mary's Dolours. Because, as we have said, she knew it was her duty to preserve the Infant in her womb from all those external things which are recognised as detrimental. And a journey at that time could be listed among these latter. It was not the age of speed and luxury travel either. Just a literal jog trot up hill and down dale, with Mary watchful—oh, as watchful as no one in her position ever was or could be. And it is very plain to us now that the good man of the house had his worries too. For he, too, knew that he had been gifted for just this tremendous responsibility. So he knew that any accompanying angels would be very invisible. The little donkey was visible enough and the woman on its back.

Then there was the hopeless search for an accommodation which was becoming hourly more necessary. And they knew who was coming if the world did not. We can only measure Mary's pain by Mary's love. And even God could not make us big enough to understand that. For He will never make another heart like hers. Always, too, her pain finds its biggest and most faithful echo in the heart of the man whom God had placed at her side.

We have so idealised the flight into Egypt that we have shorn it of its freezing terror. It is above all in reference to this episode that we must recall what has been said of an economy of miracles.

The miracle was necessary to get them going. So God's angel spoke. But from that moment until safe frontiers were passed it was just the perfect motherhood of an immaculate virgin and the manly resources and toil and love of a chosen man pitted against a powerful monarch controlling every resource of the State.

There are people to-day in war-scarred Europe who know what it is to be fugitives from hate harnessed to power. Ask them what such a trek may mean. Ask them to tell you how the shadows of night can take on a thousand sinister shapes, how trees and bushes and hillocks may tear the heart out of one by their cruel similarity to pursuing men. They will tell you how the very beating of their hearts took on the sound of pursuing foes. Night terrified them with its delusions, borrowing their forms from their fears. Dawn seemed to betray them utterly as its convicting light made them so visible to peering orbs of hate. And yet such victims had one treasure, their own lives. But Mary and Joseph were fleeing with the treasure of the Eternal God. Because of their endowments we may, we must spare them ungrounded fears. But all fears were not so lightly based. Herod wanted the life of that Infant in Mary's lap. And they were not yet in Egypt. Quite a different scene, dear reader, from the one painted by piety and embraced by our imaginations. The virgin in blissful slumber, the glowing embers of the little fire, St. Joseph doing sentinel, so unimpassioned, scanning—the ground, not the horizon! Away with such phantasies. It was quick march into Egypt, we tell you, with Herod's horsemen abroad. Sleep could come later—if it was not to come too soon.   Oh, it was a terrible joy to mother a God in the flesh, when that flesh made Him vulnerable to all the human instruments of that which is God's own evil—sin.   Yes, Egypt must ever stand for another milestone on the Virgin's Via Crucis. Mary knew a lot before Simeon cried aloud: " And thy own soul a sword shall pierce " (St. Luke ii, 35).

" And his parents went every year to Jerusalem, at the solemn day of the Pasch, and when He was twelve years old, they were going up into Jerusalem, according to the custom of the feast, and having fulfilled the days, when they returned, the Child Jesus remained in Jerusalem and His parents knew it not. And, thinking that He was in the company, they came a day's journey, and sought him among their kinsfolks and acquaintance. And, not finding Him, they returned into Jerusalem, seeking Him " (St. Luke ii, 41-45).   To deny the Godhead in Christ is to put oneself outside the very reach of salvation.   To forget its implications while adhering to the great central dogma is at least to lose much, very much of the doctrinal content and practical consolation of any given mystery of Christ's life on earth. We venture to think that few incidents recorded in the Holy Gospel have received such superficial treatment as this one of the three days' loss of the Child Jesus. If it is even listed among Mary's Dolours it does not seem to bear comparison with later ones as, for instance, when she stood beneath her Son's cross. Yet there is just that one vital element in all her sorrows which made each as infinite in its degree as human suffering could be. That element is, of course, her Son's Divinity.

If we give this element as full play as our minds permit in the consideration of the loss, we shall be surprised that thoughtlessness ever betrayed us into passing it by so casually.

There are those who could tell us a lot about the height and depth of this mystery. The souls who have bartered away their God forever could tell us much. For what is their most grievous torment?   Is it not the pain of loss?   " And not finding Him. . . ." But if they could chill us to the bone by telling us what His loss means, they are utterly unable to grasp or explain what His loss meant to her.   They have lost the God who made them and for whom they were made. But the eternal sentence of Divine justice which decrees that loss for them is but the ratification of their own rejection of God when free will was theirs. Death found them hating Him. And even if they have come to realise that in hating Him they have spurned their own happiness they hate Him forever, and forever are tortured by His loss.

The souls in purgatory could tell us. For it is the delayed possession of Him, that is to say His loss for a time which constitutes their greatest pain. Neither could they claim to know what she felt. Because these souls are conscious of their wilfully incurred stains. Why, it is supreme love which has created this middle state. For no soul conscious of its defilement would dare enter into His all-holy presence until love, accentuated by expiatory pain had restored full beauty to the nuptial garment.

There is yet another category of souls which comes near to understanding the anguish in Mary's heart. These are the saints while they were still wayfarers, and they are also those other souls who would be loath to be styled saints, but who nevertheless are sincere seekers after God. Many of these may be in the world, but they will be best represented in dedicated lives, especially in the religious state. Such souls know what it is to glimpse God; to see even for a moment and in faith's obscurity the loveliness that is Jesus. But what they are forced to know better still is the agony of losing sight of Him and facing instead, and facing full their own corrupt selves. That is a purgatory which the religious state provides and it is a path over which immaculate feet have gone before—but immaculate they were.

But none of those experiences can measure up to Mary's, not the worthiest of them. For alone of all creatures she was as worthy of Him as creature could be. And yet He was lost. There was no stain in her to explain His absence and make it bitter sweet. From the first moment of her being she was all fair in His eyes. Second by second, day by day, week by week and year by year she loved Him perfectly and increased in her love. At the Annunciation she possessed Him in her heart. We have the angels' word for that. After her consent He was incarnate in her womb. From that moment all the hitherto transcendental relations between her immaculate soul and Him were translated into the nearest and dearest intimacies of flesh and blood. How may we conceive did her love for Him increase during those wonderful nine months? For His humanity is not superfluous. His physical presence within her made for ever greater light, for ever stronger love. See it portrayed as the Incarnation portrays all else, in His nourishment and development from her very substance. The mind shrinks from even trying to assess what heights were reached by Mary's love when at last she held Him in her arms. That invisible God whom she loved so was rendered visible in the fair garments of her own flesh and blood. Now she finds it, not merely permitted, but obligatory to love Him in a new way, always as her God but now as her infant. Ask any mother what that means in tender service and unselfish solicitude. But this mother is immaculate and this Child is her God. Think of how the flame of her love was fed by her nearness to Him. As she had wrapped Him up in swaddling clothes as her first maternal act, so must she ever clothe that Divine form until he can serve Himself. She must feed Him at her breast who feeds all His creatures. She will lull to sleep Him whose watchful eye is never closed even when He is giving His beloved sleep.

In those years of His infancy and babyhood He was always with her, for He needed her at every moment. And it was not otherwise with His growing years, always was He by her side or within call. And she knew who He was. Knew that He was the joy of the Eternal Father, the delight of the angels. Knew that all creatures yearned for Him and that, above all, the eternal felicity of all immortal souls depended upon possessing Him—securely and for ever. Above all, she knew that she had been uniquely made for Him and for more than any other creature was He necessary for her, her all in all.

The years followed each other. He was one year old, was two, was eight, was twelve. The summer sky of Mary's happiness showed no cloud. But it is not unseldom that from out just such a cloudless blue the sudden thunder peals and the deadly lightning flashes. It was so even now. "And not finding Him. . . ."

Now is the time to delve deep into the virgin's heart if we are to make any attempt to gauge her woe. We saw that she had been trained by experience to put forward all the natural and supernatural endowments of her motherhood in defence of her treasure. Twelve years were not long enough to blot out that harrowing journey into Egypt, with the cries of Bethlehem's infants in their wake. Moreover, we have never claimed for

Mary clear and precise knowledge of the Father's plan for His beloved. That was as a scroll slowly unfolding before her eyes. Many chapters were already perused and they gave a fair indication of what was to come. The page dealing with Joseph's perplexity had been turned over. Came the refusal of accommodation, the wonderful visitants, the sinister designs of Herod. And then the scroll had been written fair—over a decade of blissful peaceful years. What might come next? His loss had come. Now let us remember that we are dealing with the wise virgin *par excellence*. No one was conversant as she with the holy writings, and no one had so penetrated their meaning. Later on He would try to force understanding on His enemies as on His friends by collating texts for them. " Ye are gods " insinuating the Divine adoption, " The Lord said to My Lord," driving home His Divine nature, and so on. May we not be certain that His holy spirit had rendered a similar service to His mother, only with fullest fruitage? And could she have passed over and missed the significance of the plain texts which showed the Messiah as the suffering one? Despite her happiness in His nearness and possession, Mary knew that He was God's own lamb, waiting for the great immolation. Here we need have no hesitation in calling a halt to her knowledge. When would it be, how would it be? God need not have told her all that. But now He was lost? Could this be the hour? This is the anguish great as the sea which is covered by just five verses of St. Luke. But might we not have understood? " And it came to pass, that, after three days, they found Him. . ." (St. Luke ii, 46).

God loves Mary too much to allow her Dolours to be unrelieved by joys. These latter can only be measured by the Divinity. For this short half verse reopens Heaven for the immaculate one. The sun shines as brightly as ever and the thunder is heard no more. . . . " They found Him in the temple, sitting in the midst of the doctors, hearing them and asking them questions. And all that heard Him were astonished at His wisdom and His answers. And seeing Him, they wondered. And His mother said to Him: ' Son, why hast Thou done so to us, behold Thy father and I have sought Thee sorrowing?' " (St. Luke ii, 46-48). Mary had supplied an omission of our own, though a deliberate omission. She includes St. Joseph in her own sorrow. And, of course, it goes without saying that it must be always so. Whenever we have limned a joy or sorrow of Mary we have done as much for that great heart which was one with hers.

"And He said to them. How is it that you sought Me? Did you not know that I must be about My Father's business?" "And they understood not the word that He spoke unto them. And He went down with them, and came to Nazareth, and was subject to them. And His mother kept all these words in her heart" (St. Luke, 49-51).

Ah, Mary, it is a grand thing to be mother of God's Only-begotten, a grand thing and a terrible!

CHAPTER XXIX

THE SUBMISSION OF CHRIST IN HIS INCARNATION

WE HAVE referred already in passing to the strange contention that Mary need not have been aware from the start of her Son's Divinity. The gifted protagonist of Mary's full knowledge in one of his contributions quoted from a Protestant exegete, Van Oosterzee, who maintained that the Divinity of Christ was not definitely revealed to Our Blessed Lady at the Annunciation. He maintains that such full knowledge would have rendered it impossible for Mary and Joseph to bring up the Child. His humanity postulated submission, yet had His parents been aware of His Divinity, such submission could have been only in appearance. This, it seems to us, is completely to lose sight of the utter reality of the Incarnation, in all its implications. Before we part company with Van Oosterzee we will utilise for our present purposes his reference to the submission which was indeed a necessary condition of Christ's sacred humanity, and we will try and show that so far was this submission from being in appearance only that it was but the very submission of God to His creatures rendered visible by the Incarnation.

And, first of all, let us face up boldly to all the Incarnation did involve of submission, remembering, too, that in this, as in all that flows from the Incarnation, there is no " make believe," no " in appearance only," but utter stark reality. In her very infancy the Church repudiated the contrary when she gave the lie to the Docetæ.

St. John in luminous words paints for us the pre-human history and status of the Word. " In the beginning was the Word, and the Word was with God, and the Word was God " (St. John i, 1).

Eternally begotten by the Father, the Word inhabits light inaccessible. One of the very objects of the Incarnation was to make God accessible. Two facts must be kept together in our minds. One is that it is utterly unthinkable that the Word should ever leave the bosom of His Eternal Father, and the second, which is the very fact of the Incarnation, is that by assuming human nature in the chaste womb of the Virgin Mary to which human nature the Second Divine Person is hypostatically united, God has willed to enter into all the relations involved by temporal and spatial limitations. At the same time, and this is a cardinal point, the Incarnation will reveal in terms of most real flesh and blood relations which already existed in a transcendental manner between God and His creatures.

Obviously non-Catholic exegetes have missed this point, but it is not certain that Catholic believers sufficiently assess it. For running through the whole mystery of the Incarnation is this golden thread of beautiful reality which can only be expected from a God who is truth itself. We find our thesis established, first of all, in Our Blessed Lady. When, at her blessed fiat, the Second Person of the Most Adorable Trinity became incarnate in her bosom, He only externated in a most stupendous way the relation which already existed between this most privileged of creatures and Himself.

Short of the hypostatic union, she was already one with Him in will and heart. Prepared by His prevenient grace, she was completely without sin, original or actual. She was adorned in her blessed soul with every conceivable grace. When all these ineffable relations with the Godhead were translated into terms of flesh and blood by the Incarnation, what do we find? We find what we expected to find, the most intimate physical union in nature's order, the union of a Child with Its mother in the latter's womb. When later on a human voice will raise itself in benediction of that womb and those virginal breasts, incarnate truth will not gainsay the tribute but will merely place it in its proper hierarchy of values. He will, in other words, divinely say what we so humanly stammer, that Mary's glory has its origin in her relations to the Godhead, before even those relations had been incarnated by the mystery.

We are stressing the note of reality, of truth, because this note will be the very origin of those most real submissions which we shall reverently examine. We will boldly say that the very first moment of the Incarnation gave reality to that first of the Divine submissions, that " Kenosis," that emptying of Himself which the voluntary acception of creaturehood involved. Yet this, too, translated a Divine submission accepted by the Deity when He condescended to create at all, especially to create free wills, angelic or human.

M

And now that Mary carries the Incarnate Word in her chaste womb, let us reverently face up to the submission after submission which it involved for the Word made Flesh.

He is now dependent upon her very substance for His nutrition and growth. He will one day state that His Father's will is His meat and drink. Who gave the Divine Word this mystical nourishment more truly than Mary, who now gives it to Him in terms of her own substance? Oh, delightful and most real submission!

The Word who dwells in light inaccessible now comes within reach of all human laws. He becomes subject to the laws of time and space. Before the Incarnation He was everywhere. Now, in His human nature He submits to a local habitation. He is an authentic member of the human race, a citizen of Palestine with all the submission that is going to involve to obligations of chosen people and self-chosen conquerors. He becomes subject to locomotion. He chose to sanctify His unborn cousin John, by Mary bringing Him over the hill country of Judea to Elizabeth's dwelling.

The Great God has now become a subject of Imperial Rome. And even while still in His mother's womb this submission claims Him. So He is conveyed from Galilee to Bethlehem, David's City.

Big business cannot avoid having relations with God. But they are not creditable to big business. The Incarnation shows up these relations as it shows up every other—exactly as they are. "There was no room for them in the inn" (St. Luke ii, 7) More human expression of that other statement of the Divine John. "He came unto His own and His own received Him not" (St. John ii, 2). The ineffable has happened and the eternal has been clothed in flesh and blood. He has been born into His own world. Now that we realise the source of His submission to Mary, we need not shrink from them. From this moment He stands in need of all the mothering which is the necessity of the humblest of His creatures. Here a capital point must be made. Once God became Man He submitted Himself most really to many creatures in varying degrees. As we stressed, these submissions suggested other submissions which were His even before the Incarnation, though then as a transcendental relation which could not really reach His inaccessible Deity.

But God willed certain relations for His Divine Son in time.

Some of these represented merely the Divine permission, as when the evil one tempted and even laid hands on Christ, such also was the imperial decree which brought Christ to the place of prophecy, the maltreatment later on in His Blessed Passion. But other relations were positively willed by God for Christ's actual good in His incarnate and passible state. Such were the Divine motherhood, and the rôle of St. Joseph. But here let it be remembered where the Van Oosterzees forget, that God prepared an immaculate mother for His Only-begotten, and that in St. Joseph He created one who was His very shadow in His ineffable love for His Word. To our mind, no words of sacred writ more fully attest the virtue of Mary and Joseph than those which say: "He was subject to them" (St. Luke ii, 51). Because these words say so much. They say that He, the all-holy, could be subject to them not in appearance only but most really, since these two hearts pulsed as one with His Father's. No thought or word or deed of theirs which was not dictated by that Holy Spirit who proceedeth even from the Father and from Himself. We need not labour further this fact that the Incarnation showed up only relations already existing between God and His creatures.

Just in passing, let us note how in this matter Christ's Eucharistic life is but a continuation of His incarnate one.

Scripture itself attests that it was on the vital question of the Eucharist that the first Protestants entered—or left—history. One thing can be said in favour of those first defaulters that, at any rate, they were no Docetæ. They believed in the very real flesh and blood of the Person before them, and when He said that eternal life was bound up with the eating of His flesh and drinking of His blood, they found it a hard saying and walked no more with Him. Of course, they had not risen to the faith in His Divinity which would win a docile hearing for any and every word of His. But they were blameworthy, for they could at least have taken refuge in the self-proposed enigma of the equally puzzled Peter. "Lord, to whom shall we go, Thou hast the words of eternal life." Far more difficult to understand is the attitude of their post-reformation successors. Many non-Catholics do claim to maintain the historic belief in Christ's Divinity. Personally, we think it is very illogical for such as they to find any rock of stumbling in the full Eucharistic doctrine. They claim to reverence the Holy Book which tells of the ancient covenant. In that imperfect law there was an extraordinary intimacy between Yahweh and His people. He could be consulted on such matters as the proposed attack on an enemy stronghold. David consulted Him so, and was answered. There was the Temple holy, there was the sacred Show Bread. There was a sacrosanct priesthood, with detailed and variegated vesture, and a liturgy with forms. For modern Protestants this noble shadow, this typical blossom has become what kind of reality, what species of flower? Yahweh is now silent. No voice on earth claims to speak in His name, the Show Bread is gone and there is nothing in its place. Gone is all sacrifice, all priesthood worthy of the name, all liturgical splendour and mystic rite. Comment is unnecessary.

The Blessed Eucharist does continue and perpetuate the Incarnation in our midst, and most palpably does it again portray the Divine submissions characteristic of the former. The average Catholic priest has served and assisted at Mass for many a year before it becomes his privilege to celebrate It himself. And all young priests admit to one experience at their first Mass and it is the stupefaction they feel at the fact that they have effected the Sacrifice and Sacrament. In other words, God had obeyed their behest and honoured their consecrating utterance. And it is a stupendous fact to which no priest need ever, or ought ever grow quite accustomed. And this submission of the Eucharistic Christ meets us at every turn. He obeys our priestly words if we say them, and whenever we say them. It matters not whether we are His friends or His betrayers, He submits to our words. If He is to be raised in blessing over His faithful it is our hands must raise Him, if He is to hold solemn court on His Altar Throne it is we who must place His Royal Seat. We and we alone can see to it, that He visits those who are afar, and if we bring Him not, He cannot go. But is not this what happened already in His human life? He the Word Divine was everywhere, but the Word made Flesh must needs be brought over the hill-country of Judea to gladden an old woman, and sanctify her unborn son.

At the outset we claimed that meditation on the implication of the Incarnation would be fraught with much practical advantage to the faithful.

We believe we can substantiate this suggestion by the final thoughts which will follow the submissions of God right into every corner of created being. For this purpose we will divide creation into the following categories: — First, the material universe as such, then created intelligences, and, thirdly, the grand world of super-nature. In each we will examine the great liberties which God Himself permits us to take with Himself, liberties without which we could not even be.

Before proceeding further we will try to clarify the object which these lines have in view. We saw that a non-Catholic exegete maintained that the Divinity of Christ was not immediately and definitely revealed to Our Blessed Lady and St. Joseph. His contention was that had they been aware of the Child's Divinity, His upbringing would have been impossible, as neither they could have exacted submission nor could He have yielded it—except in appearance only. We maintain, on the contrary, that once God created at all He has willed that creation should make unceasing demands on His attributes and, moreover, that we ourselves are constantly taking liberties with God while being perfectly aware of who He is and what we are. This Divine submission is met with in each order of the hierarchy of creation, it is most stupendous in the realm of- free wills, and the Incarnation translated all this into terms of flesh and blood. While utterly denying all " make-believe " in all this, we do feel it necessary to state that the word submission when applied to God does not, of course, involve any unworthy notion of abjection. It is the free submission of the supremely free Creator to His own laws in every sphere. But it is real when the Incarnate God was subject to two of His creatures— who, however, were so prepared by grace that His subjection was for Him a joy.

Now, let us review the physical universe. It is only necessary to remember at every step that existence in its full subsistent sense may be predicated only of God. He predicated it of Himself. " I am who am." Outside of the living God all being is created, is contingent. In other words, creatures of their essence have no hold on being. Did we see a huge boulder, nay, even a little pebble suspended in mid-air, without any visible support we should gape. Actually, each created existence is as much of a wonder, and more of a wonder each successive moment. Because creation must continue every moment, conserving the being which it has brought forth from nothing. In the light of this truth the whole universe becomes transfigured with wonder. Each shoot of wheat is the fruit of the primal fiat, each ray of light, too, which nurtures it and makes it grow. Where does God's action cease? Can we be surprised that when the Creator Himself in human language expressed the truth of God's universal and indiscriminate Providence He quoted only the beneficent sun and the nurturing rains. Or that His supreme threat to carnal peoples of old was that He would shatter on them the staff of bread. All that is must at every moment draw its being from God. And God ever submits to this ceaseless drawing on His attributes, on His omnipotence, wisdom and tender love.

It is just because God's submission can be counted on that physical laws are noted. It is in eternal if too often inadvertent trust in God's submission to His own created order that the sower flings his grains into earth's bosom and awaits the harvest. It was a great blow to pious recognition of the Divine action in the universe when we humans too readily accepted the almost personified and deified nature of which we so often speak. Nature is but the workings of God's power and love, the sweet testimony to His stupendous submissions to Himself first—but then to us.

And this is true not merely of phenomena, the legitimate field of scientific research, but also of the essences of things. All is created, the fact and the mode. When after æons of centuries men pry out some of the secrets of the universe they are discovering slight radiations of the Divine wisdom. Why is it that scientific progress is not accompanied by religious? Why does not adoration keep step with the discovery of God's infinite Being in all the potentialities of created things? We would not fall down and worship speed on land or through the stratosphere did we remember that God has created all. Man has unleashed in a flood of fire the atomic energy stored up by the great Creator for His creatures' good. Have the scientists anything more to be proud of than the mischievous boy who places a watch on the carpet—in countless shattered springs and bearings? And what of the world of rational beings? Is the Divine action any the less necessary, or the Divine submissions less marked?

Wonderful indeed is this world of human minds. Its marvels can be best appreciated when we review that other world which lies on its borders, the world that is of irrational things. The former world is not less of a creation than the latter, but how many more are its demands on the Divine fiat. That inanimate universe, the animal world, all were in being almost if not quite contemporaneous with man. Yet what a chasm separates them. On the one side stupendous operations without the slightest glimmer of self-consciousness, on the other mind, conscious both of itself and all within its range of thought. Mind, with all its potentialities, is responsible for all the progress in the world and for all the progress that yet may be. It is to mind is due all the masterpieces of human achievement in every sphere. It has produced the world literature with its gems ancient and modern, to it may be ascribed all the triumphs of the artist's brush and all the symphonies of musical genius. Mind has constructed all the engineering triumphs of our day and the victories of science are its fruits. But to what is mind itself due? To the Divine goodness which willed for man this participation in the Divine wisdom, to the Divine omnipotence which realised this participation in created intelligences. And ever since our first parents used and exulted in this wonderful power which gave them dominion over all nature, the exercise of intelligence and the play of free will has ever drawn upon the creative fiat. And God has always been submissive. He has created and conserved both man and his works, and it is only because God is, that the singer sings, and his song dies not even when the voice itself is muted in the grave.

We will now review the world of supernature. The Divine concurrence is not less necessary in the sphere of pure nature than in the supernatural sphere. But in the former this concurrence is altogether independent of our will. Whether we advert to it or not, even if we deny the fact, we live, move and continue to be through the Divine fiat. But the supernatural world presents still greater marvels. Here it is a dogma of faith that the Divine action is necessary not only to continue a salutary act but even to initiate it. It is, therefore, in this realm of grace that the Divine submissions are most wonderful, as they are most necessary. In fact it is a totally new world where God's action is first and last—from the first divinising of the soul through Baptism, through the grace development wrought by the other sacraments, with all the static and dynamic areas of sanctifying and actual grace, it is because of the sublime nature of the Divine action and its absolute necessity that sanctity is such a tribute to all the Divine attributes.

Had heretics not forgotten this they would not have so railed against the saints, so bitterly outraged the queen of saints. For in them, and above all in her, there is nothing but God's work, God's work brought to perfection. When we realise that authentic holiness is a share in the very life of God and that every further degree of sanctity is a further share in this divine life we are forced to realise at the same time how utterly God surrenders Himself to the seekers after sanctity. It is a domain made beautiful by the submissions of God, but submissions which are highly pleasing, as they are honourable to Him. But there is another side to the picture and we must face it. Here we have the submissions of God to free wills which use God against Himself. It is the black fact of sin. Man cannot even sin without drawing upon God. It is true that the essence of sin is a negation, a refusal of the will to follow God's Will. And in this essentially sinful kernel God does not co-operate. For it is nothing. But co-operate He must in all the positive acts which are the necessary setting of sin. The sin of the thief is the refusal to obey the Commandment, "Thou shalt not steal;" nevertheless God is forced to co-operate with all the positive planning and action involved in the theft. The sin of murder lies in the refusal to obey the Commandment, "Thou shalt not kill." Yet without God's co-operation the knife could not be wielded and plunged in the victim's heart, or the trigger pulled which speeds the bullet on its murderous way. What submission is this!

And it is a submission which is most clearly and terribly portrayed in the Incarnation, especially in the Sacred Passion. To take just one example, the nailing to the Cross. We see the brutal executioners fling Him down on the Cross as it lies on the ground. They seize His right hand, place it so roughly in position. Then the cruel hammer is raised on high and the first stroke falls, driving the nail through the poor palm; stroke after stroke follows until through blood and pulpy flesh and bone and sinew the nail reaches the wood. Go over all that in your mind from limb to limb, but above all remember that this Man is God. Try and realise that it is His eternal fiat of love which has brought those creatures from the abyss of nothingness and which holds them still in being, giving them the very power which they are wielding again Him. Then you will no longer be surprised when you see the sinner of to-day draw all his power of ill-doing from the very God whom He outrages.

We will now hark back to the thought which prompted this chapter. It was that the Divine Child was not only really subject to Mary and Joseph, but that they on their part were perfectly well aware of who He was and yet exercised their parental rights over Him and, moreover, that He gladly subjected Himself to them, because He had prepared their hearts for their tremendous responsibilities. In other words, Jesus Christ, who was God, subjects Himself to all His creatures in the measure in which their very existence demands, subjected Himself to His own perfect Will when He was subject to Mary and Joseph.

We have seen that the Incarnation only rendered visible relations which already existed between God and His creatures. It may be finally asked if His sweet subjection to Mary and Joseph has also its parallel in the world to-day. It has. It is perfectly reproduced in what is known as the religious state. When people are anxious to know God's Holy Will in every detail of their lives it means that they are anxious to use God's continuous creative concurrence for God's own interests. In other words, they want God to be subject to them gladly. For the religious state has just this prerogative as its essential treasure. It matters not what form of activity is exercised by a religious order or congregation. The essential thing is that by the immolation involved by religious vows, particularly that of obedience, God is enabled to seize on all man's activity of soul, mind and body, for all man's life. Then indeed is God subject with joy! And He has promised a hundredfold reward to the one who gives God this dominion over him. Can we be surprised if we see God's joy in subjection palpable in the health and happiness of those privileged creatures who draw in God's riches only to enrich God? Before our eyes once more is enacted the Divine and whole-hearted subjection that once made Nazareth a wonder and a joy to the angels.

CHAPTER XXX

In the Gospel record of the three days' loss (St. Luke ii, 41-51) there is a verse which is very consoling for the writer of this book. It is the forty-fourth verse of St. Luke's account and it reads: "And thinking that he was in the company, they came a day's journey, and sought him among their kinsfolk and acquaintances." Taking this in conjunction with the beautiful episode of the wedding feast in Cana as recorded by St. John (St. John ii), we can regard the idea of an isolated existence for Jesus as completely disposed of. Obviously, Mary's Child paid occasional visits to His relatives and friends and these visits were as often returned. They would also range from casual calls, calls on business, to regular family parties. It was St. John and not the writer of these lines who put a wedding feast on the list of engagements for Jesus and His mother.

The consoling feature alluded to is this, that if we are so well authorised to include such normal social contacts in even the hidden life of the Incarnate Word, we may assume them as characterising the early years of His immaculate, yet completely human, mother.

In this chapter we would concentrate our attention on the wedding feast which took place at Cana of Galilee. The most momentous truths are contained therein if we resist the temptation to mere superficial interpretation.

In this event we see in what we may call tabloid form the fruit of thirty years of Mary's intimacy with her Son and her God. Let us think back a bit. From the very moment of her Immaculate Conception Mary loved God perfectly and knew, moreover, that she was loved by Him with all the love that even a God could lavish on any mere creature. Moreover, owing to her unclouded intellect she never experienced the necessity of making an act of trust in God's love when appearances seemed to be against it. Such a necessity was very palpable in the case of Job.

Because, judged by human standards, his disasters did not seem the expression of a love which, claiming to be omnipotent, could have prevented them all. Mary always understood the Divine action, in so far as she could never even doubt the motivation of perfect love. This continued to be true after the Incarnation. For instance, it never even occurred to Mary to question the laborious flight into Egypt. Now to this perfect confidence was added a new practical assurance. For at every second she was made blissfully conscious of the reality of her divine maternity. Obviously, as a fact, it was real for her—as real as Gabriel, as real as the virginal birth, as real as a living Infant at her breast. But what time increasingly told her was how really the Incarnate Word accepted His condition, and especially her mothering of Him. Legends of the saints love to picture even new-born infants as doing something out of the ordinary. This little babe will bless itself as its first conscious act, that one will not partake of nourishment on days of abstinence! What is quite certain is that when there is question of the Divine Babe, it will be Mary who must wrap Him up in swaddling clothes and lay Him in a Manger (St. Luke ii, 7). What passivity! There is certainly no valid grounds for denying that this is what happened all along the line. Mary realised that her God was in very truth her Babe. This motherhood was no sinecure. It had to be exercised in all the situations where motherhood is ever exercised. Of course, all that we said about Mary's own infancy must be said over again only with an infinite degree of truth and significance. Mary was only an infant who was immaculate with all the practical results of this rare privilege. This Infant is the Second Divine Person. Surely even celestial lips could not hope to express just how lovable this Child was. And He was Mary's very own. During the early months and even years Mary had, so to speak, the monopoly of all this utter loveliness which was the Divine Child. What must it have been when He was one, was two, was four? As we said about Mary, there is a most intensely interesting and amiable period of childhood. If ever Heaven was on earth it was in that little home of Nazareth. He grows bigger, becomes older. "And Jesus advanced in wisdom and age, and grace with God and men " (St. Luke ii, 52).

Now He can talk with Mary. And always is He the perfect Son. Think what this may mean in even an ordinary household—a loving child lavishing respect and affection on parents, anticipating every desire, helping in all ways consonant with a young frame and mind. It does not happen too often. But when it is found it is a beautiful sight. There is certainly no valid grounds for denying that this is what happened. But we are dealing with a young Boy whose personality is that of the Word, not loving but love, not thoughtful but subsistent goodness, dealing not with a good mother but with the best mother even God could create. How Mary must have become used to the ingenuities of His love! Not that there were any prodigies as yet. But of this we are certain, that just as Jesus received everything which He had a right to expect from His mother, so Mary received everything which it was the duty of the best of sons to supply—He who had framed the Fourth Commandment.

Nor need we be disturbed by the interlude of the loss. That derives almost all its poignancy from its isolated nature. It is obvious that never before had Mary or Joseph to wonder where Jesus was or what He was about. And in any case the inspired narrative assures us that once Jesus had read His parents this painful lesson of His paramount business, He resumed the sweet life which had lasted up to then, resumed it until he would go forth with His face towards a green hill. " And He went down with them, and came to Nazareth, and was subject to them " (St. Luke ii, 51).

Now we maintain that all the sweetness and fragrance of those filial years are now revealed for us in a single phrase. " The mother of Jesus saith to Him, they have no wine " (St. John ii, 3). These are surely the words of a mother who has had long experience of the best of sons! They contain an exquisite appreciation of a Divine Heart. There is a similar depth of knowledge and confidence exhibited in the words of two sisters who had also intimate experience of this Heart. St. John tells us of it in connection with the illness of Lazarus: " His sisters therefore sent to Him, saying, Lord, behold, he whom Thou lovest is sick " (St. John ii, 3). If ever love has its nuances it is in these two phrases: " They have no wine " and " He whom Thou lovest is sick." Beautifully does St. Augustine comment on the latter: *" Non amas et deseris "*—" Yours is not a love that forsakes." If Mary and Martha had so learned Christ from the sweet intimacies of Bethany, what of her who had literally possessed Him as son from Gabriel's message until now? And in both cases the note of calm certitude was more than fulfilled by the event—wine bubbling in the water-pots, and a brother snatched from the grave.

"They have no wine." Here is a mother who, ever since her Child could speak and act had her slightest word obeyed, nay, her unspoken desires anticipated. Not that life in Nazareth had been a tissue of miracles. This very episode at Cana denies that. But in everything where a Son's love and a Son's power could please a mother, Mary had all her wills done by Jesus. How could it be otherwise? Her heart beat as one with the Will of the Heavenly Father, and " I do always the things which please Him." We have seen that Mary was taught by experience to exercise her motherhood to the full and leave miracles to God. These latter came when there was need of them but they came wholly from God and unasked by Mary. The best example is when she allowed St. Joseph to feel a perplexity which a word from her could have removed. But now there is a deeper note in her appeal. And it is an axiom that if God inspires a great request it is precisely because He wants to grant it.

It is His very spirit of which Mary is full that prompts her words: " They have no wine." It is necessary to share in that same spirit if we want to understand even Mary, much less Jesus. And the reformers never betrayed their interior bankruptcy as when they chose to misunderstand Cana. How they love to quote his answer: " Woman, what is that to Me and to thee? My hour is not yet come " (St. John ii, 4). Poor minds devoid of light, poor hearts empty of love. Can they not remember that it is God who speaks? It is no decadent descendant of poor humans, Saxon or otherwise, in whose mouth the word " woman " might really betray humanity's treason to the very concept. This is the God who made man and woman from the beginning. This is He from whose Divine and Eternal Mind the concept of womanhood was created. And He is addressing the one person who deserves the title in the full purity of its divine meaning. Let us remember that when He calls her " woman " once again as she stands beside a tree, bearing in truth the Fruit of Life.

The inspired words are heaping up mystery and significance. " My hour is not yet come." These are the words of eternal truth. Therefore if they mean anything they must mean just this. There will be no wine. Mary's request is refused. Even to an ordinary petitioner under such circumstances two courses are open, either to renew her request or to be resigned to the refusal. This is no ordinary petitioner. This is no importunate woman who cannot understand a plain no. Watch the reaction of the wisest of virgins to her Son's apparent refusal. " His mother saith to the waiters: ' Whatsoever He shall say to you, do ye ' " (St. John ii, 5). To the lover of Mary and to the defender of her great prerogative as " suppliant omnipotence " this narrative of Cana's feast is sheer joy. When choosing the heading of the present chapter we were strongly tempted to make it " Our Lady of Miracles." For to our mind Cana exemplifies perfectly what has happened so often since, especially at Mary's shrines. There is always the implicit statement of God Himself: " My hour is not yet come." It is written for all to see and for the poor victims to feel in gnawing cancer, diseased bones, eyes which see not and ears which do not hear. " My hour is not yet come." But the single all-embracing eternal decree must be conceived by our little minds as made up of decree within decree. And the Eternal God of Truth has sworn by His own verity to answer prayer. That is to say, He has solemnly promised to grant certain things if His children ask in the right way. Far more certain is it that He has engaged Himself by every bond of truth and filial love to grant whatsoever his mother asks. For at Nazareth, at Bethlehem, at Cana or now in Heaven she only asks, she can only ask what He inspires her to request. Therefore, secure Mary's intercession and immediately His hour has come. Oh, ask the cured at Lourdes about the thrill of that moment when tissue and bone and eye and ear proclaim that His hour has verily come. For Mary has spoken.

Poor, poor separated brethren. How have you failed to see all this. You do not like the new-fangled titles we give our mother, for instance, Our Lady of Good Counsel. When did she begin to have a right to that? Ask the waiters of Cana and they will tell you that they never received better or more fruitful counsel in all their lives than on that day when a queenly woman with calm assurance in her serene eyes, turned from a plain " no " and said: " Whatsoever He shall say, do ye."

Those who have been taught to underrate Mary maintain that in the Catholic scheme of things she gets in between the soul and God. That is what any ordinary human is at least capable of. Witness all heresiarchs, witness an Eighth Henry, an Elizabeth, a John Knox. But it is perhaps the only thing that Mary cannot do. Can the moon obscure the sun? " Beautiful as the moon"—Mary can give only one advice. She gave it at Cana. She will ever give it. "Whatsoever He shall say to you, do ye."

We wonder was there ever a greater crime committed, not only against God but against humanity, than the rending of Christ's seamless Robe of Truth at the Reformation? We say against humanity, for what has been its result? To-day, if ever, the wine is failing. The wine of faith in God, of fraternal love, the wine of all the sanctities, marriage, family life, the sacredness of life in its rise or in its decline. And through the various forms of the Protean lie which is Protestantism, poor humans are even prevented from addressing their tearful requests to the mediator with the Mediator—Our Lady of Cana.

CHAPTER XXXI

OUR LADY OF THE MAGNIFICAT

" My soul doth magnify the Lord " (St. Luke i, 46)

THE heart of Mary was the most grateful heart which ever beat in human breast. We must remember also for our consolation that it was in a completely human breast that it did beat. The shoreless unfathomable ocean of divine love was for ever pouring into the Heart of Mary's Son by virtue of the Hypostatic Union. But with Mary it was the heart of a human person. It is true that in her gratitude met no obstacles. Her clarity of mind enabled her duly to appraise all the motives while her perfect will went out with all its magnificent *élan* in ever-increasing acts of thanksgiving. Nevertheless, as in all other ways except her unique privilege she is one of us. We can follow in her paths even if it be at such a distance.

As regards appraisal of motive, Mary had the great advantage of the earliest possible capacity. How early is a matter upon which the ascetic writers differ. Certain it is that conscious, deliberate human acts began with Mary before they ever began with the greatest of human prodigies of early genius.

Let us consider for a moment this question of assessing motives for gratitude. At first sight we do not seem to be claiming very much for Mary when we say that from the earliest possible beginning she did valuate such motives, and perfectly. It is quite otherwise with ourselves. In fact we can hardly realise just how otherwise it is. But our present reflections may help us. We consider the instinct of gratitude as being a most normal element in human make-up. If now and then an individual be met with who is lacking in it or even devoid of it he is an exception and a type very repugnant to his fellows. Well, that is an extreme case. And, of course, as a one-eyed man is king among the blind, so as compared with our defective ingrate we are all very grateful and quite naturally so. But perhaps this is not an adequate standard. Our friend of the one

176

eye soon loses his pre-eminence when he is surrounded by those who possess integral vision. Is our gratitude so adequate, so spontaneous, so perfectly answering to gifts bestowed? Perhaps we may still say "Yes" to all these questions if we confine ourselves to human benefactions and the gratitude they evoke. But what of Divine? We think a study of Mary's gratitude will give us a humbler estimate of our own as well as a desire to imitate her better. And, thank God, Mary is imitable.

Her first great advantage was that clarity of mind which made her immediately alert to a Divine favour and perfectly aware of its extent. With many of us perhaps one of the kind functions of Purgatory will be to make us see almost for the first time and give us the opportunity of distilling gratitude from expiatory pain. For as we go along through the Divine favours of which Mary was conscious, we must become aware at the same time that we share many of them with her. But we are so obtuse. In what way was Mary aware of these favours? We do not claim for her the precise flashing intuition of the pure spirit. Mary was body and soul—thank God for it. But by virtue of the practical results of her Immaculate Conception her thought processes, though after the human mode, were not second in exactitude to the angelic intuitions. And there was no delay on the road such as our little minds experience. In Mary, there could not be any resting in self, any complacency which is always ready to ambush human endowments. She clearly saw herself possessed of certain wonderful gifts in every department of her being. She as quickly recognised their Divine source and from her pure heart flashed gratitude, fullest, warmest, most intense. "Because He hath regarded the humility of His handmaid." The first Divine gift of which Mary was conscious was God's eternal love of her. "I have loved thee with an everlasting love." Here begins our own heart-searching. If we succeeded in assessing this one fact we would possess such a source of loving gratitude as would make our lives one conscious response to the everlasting love. We grade our human friends. Such a one is an old friend. This is always an assured title to affection and esteem. Even with the oldest and truest friend we have there was a beginning of friendship. For many years of their lives our very parents had no knowledge of us, or of each other. It is not so with the Eternal God. He is an Eternal now. In an Eternal now He loves. We know and esteem people because they exist. They only exist because God knows them in that

N

eternal knowledge which is also love. Creatures of a day, we make multiplied decisions on a Tuesday which were not even contemplated by us on the day before. It cannot be so with the Eternal. Every existing creature testifies by its very existence that it has been the object of eternal knowledge and love. That is true for you and me. That is true for all the men and women who cross our path. Yet how we have forgotten it for ourselves as well as for them. Such a one is uninteresting! Interesting enough to have been thought of by God for all eternity! Interesting enough to have been drawn from the realm of possible beings and put there before you to slight and snub and depreciate!

Mary knew that she was the object of God's eternal love, and from that knowledge alone there blazed forth a very furnace of loving gratitude. "My soul does magnify the Lord."

It would never be possible for Mary to make God wait a little or long—for her return of love. How heroic it is of us to turn to God, to that God whose turning has ever been to us.

Although God is infinitely simple—pure act, as the theologians say—our finite and very puny minds find it necessary to divide up that act, as it were. We speak of His attributes as if they were all distinct one from another, whereas they are like so many facets of the one essential truth. In the same manner of speaking, thus adapted to our human minds we distinguish decree within decree, although in the Divine Essence there is but one. So within the eternal love of God for her Mary recognises her predestination to her Immaculate Conception. Speaking to her little protégée at Lourdes, Mary said: "I am the Immaculate Conception." But that is the assumed Mary speaking, who not only sees all that is needful about herself and creatures in the Divine Essence, and who is not at a loss for human language to clothe what she sees, whereas we are dealing with the little Jewish maiden for whom even the Annunciation was years ahead. We do not claim for her that she ever directly analysed her unique endowment, not to speak of giving it a name, but she was conscious of it in a way which we shall try to explain. May we utilise a little example? Suppose that a person possessed of a perfectly sound organic heart lived his life surrounded by those who all suffered more or less from cardiac disease. Such a person need not necessarily know the science of medicine or its jargon. In fact they need not even advert to their healthy condition at all. But very soon such a one would come to see that they were very different from their fellows. They would never be breathless, never lightly or unduly fatigued, never victims of any painful paroxysm. Now that is a fair picture of what Mary experienced. From the earliest moments of her conscious deliberate life she found her nature ever directed to God and to virtue. Never would she experience that twilight land of moral action where the *primo primi*—or first impulses—are found. And in corrupt nature those first impulses have generally to be corrected. All Mary's first impulses were perfect, and in their further development led to further perfection. Very probably Mary accepted all this as normal, until she noticed others. We do not think that her parents would have provided her with too palpable a proof of original sin. But, as we pointed out, there must have been others. And if we gladly believe that a very special Providence reduced the corruption in Mary's entourage to a minimum we still feel convinced that she had sufficient social contacts to realise that there was something wrong with the world which was not wrong with her. Then would take place the inevitable reaction—intense gratitude to God. In this field, too, of the recognition of God's preventive graces we are notoriously slack. The Immaculate Conception is Mary's unique privilege. But it seems to us that there is no soul which has not caught some reflection of its bright radiance in a weakness or a series of weaknesses which God has not even permitted to vitiate our spiritual lives. Many of us have never known what it might be to struggle from the darkness of heresy into the white light of truth. From our lives have been simply removed all those agonies of mind and practical obstacles which barred many a soul's progress to the truth. Here is a field for gratitude. But do we not leave it fallow? It is the same with a whole variety of temptations and occasions which have never even been allowed to beset our path. This truth is at the root of that sincere cry of the Poverello when he saw a poor criminal on his way to execution. " There goes Francis but for the grace of God." We are so far from these dispositions that we do not even understand them. Mary would not be slow to notice the practical conse-quences of her immune nature. She would see sickness round her and pain of mind. But she would not experience these. And all the time her gratitude would be increasing in intensity. A grateful person is a happy person. Such a one always finds more subjects for gratitude than for complaint and so they are always serene themselves and have the power to communicate their serenity to others.

Mary would be grateful not only for her moral perfection but for all her gifts of soul and mind and body. She would not take her supernature for granted. Neither would she regard her natural endowments as altogether due to her. On the contrary, she had a perfect grasp of the correlative ideas of Creator and creature. She knew she was nothing in herself. Yet there she was in all the perfection of her immaculate being. She never forgot, as we so easily do, that each moment of continued being is the continued act of creation. Already Mary had entered into the truth enunciated by the Preface of Holy Mass—we ought to render thanks always and in every place. For her creation and conservation had never lost their first initial thrill. Sometimes even among the poor children of Adam one is found to stumble on this truth. For such a one life opens up unlimited vistas of joy. They exult in their being and in its exercise with an ever fresh enthusiasm and hilarity. For them language no longer lists such a word as blasé or boring or monotonous. That is the language of creatures who have forgotten God's gifts, forgotten His eternal love, His free choice of them as rational creatures. Surely it is a triumph of hell to make a man so forgetful. Chesterton was not made in this mould. He had recaptured real *joie de vivre* with the faith which told him of God and of himself. Can we imagine how Mary must have exulted in all her gifts?

Perhaps a very good approach to some realisation of Mary's gratitude for natural endowments will be—paradoxically—a consideration of our own remissness in this matter. We read, whether in the holy Gospel or contemporary records, such as, for instance, those dealing with Lourdes, of the miraculous recovery of sight by one hitherto blind. Far though we may be from the scene of the Divine favour, the miracle arouses our interest. We can enter into the feelings of the privileged recipient of the gift of sight. Very often it will be a restoration of sight rudely destroyed by some accident. The peculiar joy will then be that of one who has seen God's sunlight and for whom merciless darkness had of a day shut out its brightness. How such a one will feel an altogether new pleasure in everything which presents itself to its gaze. There will be nothing uninteresting, nothing drab. In fact, such words will have dropped out of such a one's vocabulary as being impious, blasphemous almost, ungrateful. For one who as in the Gospel records was blind from birth, the gift of sight will be tantamount to the first creation of the universe at least for those new eyes. What almost infantine wonder, what fresh joy and what unceasing drawing on those ever living sources of jubilant happiness. It would be similar in the case of restored hearing. The object of such a miracle would come near, if anyone, to hearing the music of the spheres. All the sounds which permeate creation would give joy to those newly opened ears. The sough of wind through rustling trees, the chirping of crickets, the melody of the birds, the lowing of kine, but above all the voices of their fellow-men, all would be a glorious symphony of Divine music, wherein the score revealed ever new harmonies. It would be the same with any other physical restoration worked by the finger of God, crippled limbs straightened giving new liberty of movement, organic defects removed yielding place to joyous health. Oh, when we read of these things and they have happened ever since Christ performed them Himself, we are never surprised that the favoured ones are delirious with joy, that they leap and skip like children and wish the whole world to know their bliss. But what is wrong with us? What strange palsy is on our hearts? For what these people now see, what they now hear, what is in the range of their capacities now, we have ever seen, we have ever heard, we can now do what we have always done. But we are not hilarious. We do not leap and skip with sheer exultancy of blissful well-being. What is wrong with us? Has God less claim on our gratitude if he has given us sight as soon as He gave us eyes, if He has endowed us from the beginning with perfect soundness of sense and faculty and limb? We with-hold our gratitude. And it is at every successive moment that we withhold it, for at every moment God's gifts are pouring in upon us deluging our being. At every moment we are reborn, re-created. And, shameful negative of the Church's invitation in the Preface of Holy Mass, it is always and everywhere that we are ungrateful.

Now let us turn to Mary. From the very first moment of her deliberate conscious life she knew that God was all and that she was nothing. She knew that like any creature she was but a capacity for receiving Divine favours. But she saw that capacity enlarged almost infinitely and filled to over-flowing with the good, good wine of heavenly favours. Here is the setting and the source of perfect gratitude. The setting in Mary's clear vision of her own nothingness, the source in the gifts which flowed into that great native nothingness. So with

Our Lady there could not even be the slightest temptation to regard herself as a source. That is an ever-present danger with us. Mary's eyes were ever directed towards the Giver of all good gifts and that is why the light of gratitude shines so brightly in them. In Mary her perfectly correct attitude to God and to His gifts became a source of increased gratitude at every second —" Always and in every place." When we read the momentous words which begin the Book of Genesis. " In the beginning God created. . . ." we are misled by the past tense of the verb. We read about that event as of any occurrence in profane history. " Created," it took place once, so long ago. This is all wrong. When we read these words we are present here and now at their verification. For creation goes on, as God goes on. Mary saw it precisely thus. She was like an unspoiled child receiving caress after caress, with gift after gift pouring into her lap from loving hands. And always is the young face upturned with loving gratitude. " My soul doth magnify the Lord." As the panorama of all visible things ever unrolled before her eyes gratitude mounted at every moment. This is as it should be. We talk of the difficulty of prayer and above all of sustained prayer. The Creator did not seem to think He was imposing a strain when He said: " You ought always to pray and never to faint." Certainly if one function of prayer is to give thanks we have at our disposal as many stimuli of gratitude as we have proper objects acting upon the senses. The light which envelops us with its nurturing rays is a fresh gift at every successive moment. Can our gratitude languish? The beautiful sights which we see at every moment, mountains with their purple shadows, clouds iridescent with the light of dawn or of the setting sun, green fields and golden cornlands and the mighty deep, all these things are His gifts to the eye which He has framed to see them. Mary saw these things, not in a listless way but with gratitude ever alert. She saw also her fellow rational beings, the men, women and children of her environment, each one a living record of eternal love. And Mary was glad to see them as God was glad to create them. She saw the smile of recognition which so often lit up a friend's face. She saw love, such love on the countenances of her own parents. And her gratitude increased and ever increased. It was so with the exercise of all her senses and faculties. For the gifts that flowed in on her eyes, for the gifts that came in hearing's wake; for intellect and memory and imagination; for her perfection of physical being she was grateful and ever more grateful. So far Mary's gratitude has been in perfect proportion to her knowledge touching God's action in her. But this knowledge itself was incomplete as it did not as yet cover the motive of the Divine benefactions. In other words, Mary had not as yet glimpsed the destiny which will explain both herself and her endowments.

We have seen enough to realise that even at this stage her gratitude almost infinitely outmeasured ours, even for gifts which we share with her, such as our very existence, our rational nature, too, with its marvellous apparatus of sense and faculty. But Gabriel had not yet come. Well may our minds tremble and fail before the contemplation of what that gratitude became when Gabriel had said all and Mary understood all. She had appraised the love eternal which had given her being every second of her existence, had made her more and more aware of the singular endowments of that being. Now in a flash she is conscious of the primal Divine decree in her regard in the light of which her special privileges were bestowed. What did she see? Just this; that by an utterly gratuitous movement of love God had chosen her out of all women and preferably to all possible women to be the mother of His Only Begotten. And Mary knew that God's Son must Himself be God. So there flashed upon her mind the revealed truth promulgated so many centuries later by the Council of Ephesus—that she was called to be the Theotokos, Deipara, Mother of God. What new motives of gratitude were furnished by this knowledge? Remember that not all the holiest ones of Israel had yearned for the Promised One as this Virgin. Now she hears that He has come. And the Messias is her very God. Nay, He is her very Son. Already she had been grateful for the special light from on high which had traced out for her so long before any one else the dedicated path of absolute chastity. Now life stirs within her womb, and her virginity is intact, nay infinitely enhanced.

For God's sake she had accepted a condition considered as a reproach by the very best of Israel's women. Now her virginity has borne the eagerly sought for Flower—the Desired of the Peoples.

Endowed as she was for her mission of Divine maternity, Mary sees, nevertheless, by her side at God's behest the noblest, most chaste, most loving of Israel's sons—even Joseph.

Need we go through everything? The multiplied interventions of Providence exercised on behalf of Joseph and Mary and the Divine Child. And if to see the human things and folks she saw, if to hear the sounds of life as it surged round her made Mary grateful, what are we to say of the gratitude which welled up in her immaculate heart at the sight of Him—when He came —and the blessed sound of His voice? We could not assess the gratitude which was Mary's at her conception and what it had become fourteen years later. We are more helpless still before the magnitude of it as it was enclosed in that virgin breast beneath which another heart was already beating. It went much further. But further we will not dare to follow it. We will be content to tarry with the grateful virgin of the fiat, the Divine mother of the Word made Flesh, Our Lady of the Magnificat.

CHAPTER XXXII

MOTHER OF FAIR LOVE

IT is when treating of Mary's love for God that spiritual writers are most likely to succumb to the language of hyperbole and exclamation. However, in accordance with the avowed object of these pages we shall endeavour to show that even here Mary is imitable, not indeed in the intensity or degree of her love but in her human manner of loving.

First of all, it is helpful and even necessary to clarify our ideas on the very concept of love. There is a world so loved by God that for its salvation He delivered up His Only-Begotten Son. And there is a world for which that same Son would not pray. "I pray not for the world." Let us not imagine that this second world thus shut out from the prayer of the Redeemer is reprobated because composed of men who are sinners. "I did not come to call the just, but the sinners to penance." But there are sinners who love their sin, who identify themselves with it and, loving it to the end, die therein. Of such is the wicked world which has not Christ because it will not have Him. This world has ever lived its perverse life since corruption provoked the first Deluge. It lives all round us to-day and always it provokes a Deluge—number one and two and. . . .

It is not shy and retiring going about its wickedness in a shamefaced manner. It is, on the contrary, brazen, and noisy and assertive with a code of its own and a language of its own. It does not always bother to coin new words, but uses the very language of God's friends but in a perverted sense. So often does it prate of love that it claims that it alone understands the term. In its sacred name it commits its crimes. Its literature prostitutes it on every page. Its talkies blare it forth in picture and sound. And its music weaves jungle rhythms around the theme. Yet the truth is that the wicked world has no right to utter the holy word, for it knows not its meaning. When it tries to say Heaven it really spells out Hell.

185

If ever there was a creature who knew what love signified it was Mary. She did not gaze on it from afar in reverent salutation. She was herself immersed in it. She possessed it in her mind and heart. And of a day she sweetly imprisoned love in her virginal womb. She cradled the Living Love in her arms. To her, therefore, may we well go to find out its meaning, to find out how she loved, how ourselves to love.

In the first place, a principle guided all Mary's judgments, thus ensuring the dominion of Divine love in her heart. It was this. Mary made both herself and all creatures relative to God and not *vice versa*. It may shock us to think that we could ever do otherwise. Yet what is the source of so many speculative doubts which assail our love for God? For instance, when contemplating His eternity the mind almost grows dizzy and even recoils from the idea. Why is this? Because we are making ourselves the starting-point. We begin with the creature of a little day and try to advance to the notion of the Eternal now. Our process should be just the other way round. Eternity is not relative to time, but time to eternity. It is only God's eternity which even explains and renders possible all derived temporal being, including my own. In a similar fashion we bring God's Providence to judgment before the little bar of created events. Such a calamity takes place. Can God be omnipotent who did not prevent it, all-wise who did not forestall it, all-loving who let it be? Thus we judge God by our own limited vision. Rather starting from His infinite attributes, should we say, because He is omnipotent this permission of His must issue for the best, all-wise, therefore, no miscalculations need here be feared. All-loving, too, therefore, in spite of appearance, the best interests of all are being served. How quick we are to call an event or creature evil? We forget that a thing is bad only relatively. For instance, it is a relative evil that bodies and homes should be shattered by bombs. But it is good that natural laws should operate when put in motion by free wills. If we are so foolish as to have the wrong angle on these matters our love of God will be always challenged.

Mary ever enjoyed the perfectly correct orientation towards God and that without any mental struggle. In her life everything was relative to Him and, therefore, everything ministered to love and tranquillity. Gabriel's message, St. Joseph's worry, Bethlehem journey, the goodwill of friends, the malice of foes, all events only increased the love in Mary's heart and the peace

which enveloped her. We are not so. Mary was not dependent on creatures for motivation of Divine love. She had an
all-sufficient motive in God Himself. She knew that before the
world was, God existed in the Unity of His essence and the
Trinity of His persons. In this Triune God she recognised the
uncreated love which is so amiable in itself and which alone
makes creatures amiable. Mary saw God as Creator, stamping
all things with the royal seal of His own nature, namely, love.
She saw in love the divine law according to which creatures
stand or fall. They exist because they are loved. They exist
to love. Love is positive. It is diffusive of itself. It is these
two things, because it springs from God, the Subsistent Being,
who alone is, who creates and conserves His work by the continued outpouring of His gifts. Love means good creaturehood.
It means being just what God wants one to be. It means the
law of nature and particularly for Mary it meant the Decalogue.
For her those Commandments were radiant signposts to love.
And already she had reduced them to the one Commandment
and that other one which is like to the former. It would be
unthinkable that Mary should not love a creature which owed
its very existence to God's eternal love. Nor could she confuse
men's sin with men. The defects only emphasised God's primal
plan and indicated the very road to restoration thereof.

Mary could not be betrayed into that smug complacency which
considers its love as a heroic largesse to those on whom it is
bestowed. Just as it is God's nature to love and He finds His
felicity therein, so our power to love is the most Divine power
we possess. To be even able to love is His gift. If we
abdicate this Divine right even in the smallest instance we do
ourselves a greater injury than all the world can do us. How
far are we from this outlook when we even court such occasions
as lessen our esteem for others? We make our set. We allow
a favoured few to bask in the sun of our affection. Even those
privileged ones must be careful. Let them offend, we withdraw
our love. Is not this the record of all the coldness which marks
our dealings with others? Our love is guided by anything but
principle. It waxes and wanes like the moon, enkindled by a
smile and extinguished by a frown. What fools we are. This
power to love is the Divine gift within us. It may be, it must
be exercised on all creatures. In God's own case it was His
love which created, it is His love which ever creates anew by
conservation. God could not give up His power to love. See

how magnificently this is proved by the failure of man's treason to kill God's love for the race. Came sin, came the redemption. That is God's way, ever to love. All His Commandments and Counsels if read aright are injunctions to love as He loves, in order to be happy in loving even as He. Hell is primarily the place where love is utterly impossible. For all these reasons Mary's love never suffers diminution but increases divinely with every moment of her being.

Three great stages may be marked in her love. The first of these marks a beginning so conditioned that we cannot even guess at the degree of initial love in her. Her love was great in her immaculate coming. Her love was greater and grander still in His coming. And it received almost a fresh creation in His going. We will review these several periods in more detail. What was the degree and intensity of Mary's first act of love in her Immaculate Conception? Whatever it was it had a nine months' increase when Joachim and Anne first laid their eyes on their little girl—and God's. Mary's birthdays came and went. Not to her could the reproach be made that she could discern the face of the sky without reading the deeper signs. The face of the sky she could, indeed, read, but far more visible to her inward eye was the lovely countenance of the Creator hidden behind His handiwork yet revealed and gladly revealed to the heart which loves. There were no scales on those clear eyes. No mist eddied through and round that mind untouched by the primal fall. Those senses, those faculties were keyed up to the highest pitch of perfection and efficiency. She will see the invisible things of Him from the things which He had made.

Mary read aright the handwriting of God in creation manifesting to her that " which is known of God " (Romans i, 19). In the world's contingency she saw the eternity of God. Saw His power, too, in herself and in every creature. Already full of His spirit, she will have first the lessons He will afterwards teach with the human mouth of her fashioning. She will see the blowing lilies and will read His solicitude in their sheen and delicacy and utter loveliness. And as the birds made the air alive with their chirping and their curvings, she will adore the ever-opening hand of the Great Provider. In the mighty sea or inland lake she will see His omnipotence, and His delicacy in the dew drop trembling on a blade of grass. The sun beating down on her dark young head will tell her in mute language of nurturing heat of a love big enough to whiten harvests for chosen people and for thankless gentiles alike. The fruit-bringing rains will say the same thing by their kind, kind drops. But so far, even for Mary, He is still the invisible God. He is revealing Himself through creatures which are yet distinct from Him. She hears the rustle of His garments as He passes by in wondrous symbols of created beauty. She sees the traces of His Divine footprints and hurries along in their scented track. And then Gabriel came—and went.

He is still invisible. But how audible now. As audible as heart beats in union with another heart. What will these nine months do with Mary's love? We are not left without indications. There was that journey in haste over the Judean hills with its aftermath of a salutation and a wondrous cleansing. Mary's love for God was never for a moment divorced from love of neighbour. For childhood's span it would be filial love for Joachim and Anne with all the perfection of duties faithfully accomplished. And these would be the duties of any child in any home. Now it is the solacing of her cousin in woman's trying hours.

Then came Bethlehem. Now He is visible to her, clothed in the lineament of her own flesh and blood. She sees her God before her. Always has she loved Him as most perfect of creatures her great Creator. Always has her heart loved Him alone as peerless maid her Divine spouse. Now she is to love Him with a mother's love. Her heart has been fashioned for this. When she looks into these Baby eyes she is met by the gaze of the Second Person. And she does not die, because for this has she been given life. What will it be as He grows up? The joy of the Eternal Father, the glory and delight of the Angelic hosts—this Word by whom and for whom all creation yearns is Mary's Child. And he is no dream Child, but a dear winsome boy with all Heaven in His eyes and those eyes all for Mary. What will her love be like on the morrow of each wondrous day spent in His utter possession? This love will gather strength and intensity from every circumstance. It will be stimulated by the very dangers which seem to threaten to rob her of Him. Dear the Babe in Bethlehem, but even dearer the little evacuee in Egypt. Then followed the peace of Nazareth and all the sacred intimacies of home. But His hour came to go and His going swelled her love into a Divine crescendo of yearning. Came the hour of sacrifice. All mothers know how love thrives and grows on the failing breath of a dying child. What height, then, did Mary's love reach when she stood beneath His cross? *Stabat Mater.*

Mary is the mother of fair love. But she is no less the mother of a love which is stronger than death. Never did she so prove herself the strong lover as when she cradled the dead, wounded Body in her lap—and loved each one of us who had done that to Him. If Christianity is opposed to anything it is to the spirit of resentment. And if there is one way more than another wherein we play false to our Christianity it is by our daily and hourly yielding to resentment. Cannot we see how Christ was enjoining happiness on us when He told us to requite hate by love? This is to love as God loves, it is to recognise our royal power of loving and to cling to our Divine prerogative. It is to imitate the Son and the mother where they are most alike. For behold, our sins dug those wounds in His hands and feet and side. And yet these wounds are the enduring source of our perfect trust. We know, too, that we can count on her undying love. For she has held His inert body in her mother's arms—not now warm and clinging as in His first coming, but cold and lifeless through the going we had fashioned for Him. She knows by heart all the livid scars we inflicted on Him. But she is a queen. And love is her kingdom. Never will she step down from her regal throne. We cost Him that. Therefore, we must be saved. That is the Divine logic of heart and head. It is the logic of her who is the mother of a love which is fair, of a love which is stronger than death and hell.

There is a third stage in Our Lady's love, and it has special significance for us all. When she accepted the motherhood of Christ, it was of the whole Christ head and members that she accepted it. He was her Only-Begotten. We know that if we know anything. Yet He is called her First-Born. This is quite correct, because He is the First-Born of many brethren and we are His brothers.

As we have already remarked, it is not easy to show gradation in a love like Mary's. It is like viewing a magnificent mountain range where although its highest peaks are hidden in the clouds, its lowest altitudes are too high for our adequate appraisal. No one can see where the plain gradually ascended. All that can be done is to at least point out the greater ascensions when height swept upwards to still greater heights.

Undoubtedly Our Lady's love for humankind received a new ratification as it were, almost a new creation in those blessed words of the Dying Saviour: " Woman, behold thy Son " (St. John xix, 26). When will we realise that the words of Christ are the words of God? They are the words of the Word. They are the words of Him whose first fiat brought into being from nothing angels and the universe and men. To remember this central truth is to listen with awe as that first fiat is uttered. At this moment we see its fruit in all the being which surges round our being. With awe, too, we hear that Divine voice raised over a little bread and wine. We know who speaks and what He said. So we bow low before his upraised Body and Blood in the mystic Calvary of Holy Mass. We hear His words uttered over a Simon Barjona, over eleven others as frail as He. And we know where Peter dwells to-day and where those are who rule with Him—bishops and priests of His Church. And now we hear His donation to us, in the person of St. John, of His greatest treasure on earth. Then did Mary enter solemnly into her motherhood of us—of His members for all time?

The aspect of the Mystical Body which we wish to stress here is the love which It elicits from Mary's heart. Although the doctrine is so full and rich that it is not exhausted by even Papal pens, it is nevertheless a simple doctrine, leaving no doubt whatsoever about its implications. We have only to view it in the light of our own body and members. We are not even tempted to postulate any division in these. We are one person. All our faculties and senses and members work as one unit in perfect co-ordination. The well-being of one member diffuses pleasure through the whole person. What is more significant for our purpose, the suffering of one is the suffering of all. If we have some pain or defect we do not think of treating it roughly. In fact, such a sore spot receives a special measure of protective treatment. The last thing we ever wish to contemplate is amputation. Cure is always the objective with its resultant good to the whole body. The human race has gone so far as largely to forget not merely its unity in Christ but even its natural human solidarity. That was one of the crimes inflicted on the race by the 16th century Reformers. Its baneful results were immediate but were not felt by all at the same time or in the same measure. And so the great apostate nations could proceed on their course of bludgeoning their neighbours in the name of Empire building. These poor neighbours felt it. And the criminals were really bludgeoning themselves too. For we are one human family. Yet it is only now in this 20th century that they are finding out what they have done. For our present chaos is just a matter of an almost defunct person with its murderer beginning to realise that he is one with his victim.

Now, if anyone understood perfectly the implications of the Mystical Body it was Mary—and especially at that solemn moment when she heard His voice: " Woman, behold Thy Son." As the most enlightened member of that people to whom the words of God were entrusted, Mary knew best of all that humankind had solidarity with Adam. Her own unique privilege underlined that solidarity in its grand exception. But with even greater clarity she saw the race's oneness with the second Adam who was now nailed to the Tree of Death. She grasped as fully as created intellect could grasp the full import of the Divine words which made her the mother of men. Perhaps we have never come near even to grasping the effect of this truth on her love for us. For it means this, that Mary loves head and members with one love. Since that is true, how can any manifestation of her love for us cause us surprise? Does it not explain Cana and Lourdes and Fatima with their ever newer wine of miraculous benefaction? And since an enemy is always quickest to see where a wound may do most harm, can we be surprised that the characteristic note of all heresy is a denial of Mary's prerogative and an attempt to withdraw souls from her Maternal influence? May all such deluded souls give ear even now to a Voice which spoke just before It was temporarily stilled in death. It is not the voice of any priest or Pope. It is the voice of Him who made both, as He made all things that are. It is the voice of the dying Saviour. " Behold Thy mother " (St. John xix, 27).

CHAPTER XXXIII

It can come almost in the nature of a shock, and that after many years in the sanctuary, how a priest's life, his powers and his duties resemble Mary's life, what she did and what she was even created to do.

It is a moment of great grace for a priest when this comes home to him. It will startle him. But it will carry with it the conviction that unless Mary lives within him by her sweet dominion over soul and body, sense and faculty he will not be able worthily to exercise his priesthood. He will realise further that it is very much to the interests of the whole Christ that Mary should so succour him. And who can doubt her readiness to do so?

The history, recorded or not, of every priestly vocation has at its starting point a very definite Annunciation. There are pious people who have no hesitation in asking a priest quite bluntly how he got his vocation. Do they really expect a full and adequate answer? If they do they are rating very low the Divine wooing. The priest confronted by such a question belonged broadly to one of two classes of youngsters when young he was. He may have thought always of the priesthood and thought of nothing else. This is certainly found and it is a great grace. In such a case, with all due regard to totally different levels, such a born priest has caught a ray of her Immaculate Conception. Or, at least, like the as yet unborn Baptist, her voice has called him from his mother's womb. Oftener it will be somewhat different. A boy will spend many years without thinking of the priesthood. Then he will find that the priesthood attracts him. He will be a priest. What has happened? The Annunciation has happened. The great archangel has come and delivered his Divine message. Only it may have taken months in the giving. This parallel is not far-fetched. Already the youth has started on a road made fragrant by virgin feet. They were Mary's feet. For implicit in the choice of the priestly state was the choice of yet another—the royal road of virginal chastity. In Mary's case, too, that call came before Gabriel, long before him. " How can this be done. . . ?"

What a consolation it is for the young Levite to realise that in this big choice Mary goes before him, Mary stands beside him —unto the end.

And what is the priestly vocation? Is it not to bring forth Christ first in oneself and then for others? Who has a better right to the title of Christ-Bearer than the priest? And as in Mary's case the first price demanded for this Divine fruitfulness is voluntary and perpetual virginity. Mary heard the angel's message. It did not take long to deliver. The chosen soul hears it, too. But it may be given in many ways and over an indefinite period of time. In both cases, however, heaven awaits the oblation of a human will, endowed with sacred and inviolable freedom. The youth echoes Mary's fiat. And, although Bethlehem is not yet, the Christ springs to life in His elect one. There is a priest in the making. So far the parallel is as true as it is striking. But it is not until the anointed of the Lord stands for the first time at the altar that the analogy is complete. As we said already he may not realise it at his first Mass nor at his hundred and first. But if he is a man who ponders things in his heart it will come upon him in a burst of realisation. Let us think about it now.

Mary's life from her Immaculate Conception may be said to have moved towards the supreme moment of her fiat. It is true that at Bethlehem she found Him in her arms and thus rendered visible for herself and for us. Yet the Incarnation became an accomplished fact when Mary said to the Ambassador of God: " Behold the handmaid of the Lord. Be it done unto me according to Thy Word " (St. Luke i, 38). For this supreme moment with all it held of most enduring reality Mary had been prepared by what we may call in feeble language a triple predestination. There was her call to existence as a rational creature, her call to Immaculate Conception and her call to the Divine motherhood. This latter call was, of course, first in the Divine mind but posterior in execution to the other two. If the preceding pages have told anything they ought to have told even inadequately the stupendous graces and the magnificent practical sequel of these in the young girl who was Mary of Nazareth.

Back into the eternal years these graces and endowments had their roots. Every second of her existence from the very first second was a preparation for the fiat and what it brought. Precisely owing to her Immaculate Conception Mary was able to give the fullest co-operation to each successive grace. Progress and fruitage is the very law of grace and here was undiminished progress and a fruitage which the eyes of God could appraise as perfect. All that Mary brought to His coming.

The priest stands at the foot of the altar. " I will go unto the altar of God. . . ." Phrase follows phrase, bringing the priest nearer and nearer—to what?   Twenty minutes, nay a quarter of an hour separate him from that which followed Mary's fiat. For in that short time he will have accomplished Nazareth and Bethlehem in one Divine formula. Jesus Christ, True God and True Man, the virgin's Son is in his poor human hands, is before him in the new manger of the outspread corporal.

Surely it must be obvious to every priest that if he has shared Mary s function in giving the God-Man a new being and a new earthly habitation he must share also in her privileged dispositions. But this poor priest is a son of Adam. His soul and body felt at their first fusion the taint of original sin. From his earliest years he has been made to realise this fact even as a Paul of Tarsus realised it and groaned aloud in affliction of spirit. The priest has not been prepared for this hour by the removal of every taint and the infusion of every virtue. And yet by virtue of his priesthood he must give Christ to the world as Mary did. What can he do except to beg the immaculate virgin to live in him and to lend him her pure heart for the sake of her lamb.

Yes, in very truth, a priest may well be shocked and affrighted by the identity of his rôle with Mary's. Once the sacred words of consecration have been uttered He is there for his priest as He was there for her. What difference is there? It is true that the species conceal Him. But Mary did not see the divinity. She saw the humanity of a weak shivering babe. So the priest needs Mary's faith, that faith which elicited Elizabeth's praise. " And blessed art thou that has believed, because those things shall be accomplished that were spoken to thee by the Lord " (St. Luke i, 45). And in his case as in hers, that faith must show itself in deeds. How is the priest to look at the Eucharistic Saviour? How is he to handle Him? Oh, God, how necessary is Mary to him with her eyes of faith and purity and loving adoration. How necessary she is with her mother's hands which so reverently cradled Him and pressed Him to her virginal heart.

Surely there will never be occasion to chide a priest for brusqueness of gesture and for signs more mysterious than mystical. How necessary for the priest will be Mary's heart with all its love for her child. How gladly she recognised that her babe was no fleeting vision but a lovely enduring reality. Later on it will nearly kill her to lose Him for a space. With her heart beating in his priestly breast the priest will be anxious to keep Jesus as long as possible before him. Like the disciples of Emmaus he will say: " Abide with me, Lord." Far from him will be any indecent haste to conclude the Divine tryst and get back—to men and to himself.

How one with Mary he is when he has received Him into his heart in the Communion. That is true of all the faithful at that sublime moment. How true is it that the Church of the Blessed Eucharist is also the Church which knows and loves the immaculate virgin. Why, without her, those gifts of God would be almost cruel, just as the Divine motherhood without the Immaculate Conception would have been cruel to her. And when erring men rejected the Adorable Eucharistic Sacrifice and Gift they soon came to think that they had no need of her.

Like Mary, too, is the priest who must show Jesus to his people. He does this at the Elevation. He does this at Benediction. How it brings back that first showing to shepherds and to kings. Like her he must give Jesus to hungering souls. This he does at the Divine Banquet of the ever-spread Communion rail and this he does also when he gives to his people the living bread of true doctrine, the word of God, really God Himself. Mary must be in the priest's heart to lend him also her blessed lips. Just as Mary was always the Mother of God, in all her thoughts, words and actions, so a priest may never, not for a second, lay aside his priestly character and office. He will not be always acting ministerially but always he will be a priest, set apart to give Jesus to souls, always to give Him and in all. This can be accomplished only if Mary lives in the priest. Then his every word will be hers and souls will bless him even as Elizabeth blessed her. " And it came to pass that, when Elizabeth heard the salutation of Mary, the infant leaped in her womb. And Elizabeth was filled with the Holy Ghost. And she cried out with a loud voice, and said: ' Blessed art thou among women, and blessed is the fruit of thy womb. And whence is this to me, that the mother of my Lord should come to me. For behold as soon as the voice of thy salutation sounded in my ears the infant in my womb leaped for joy ' " (St. Luke i, 41, 44). Priests may not realise the power with which their office invests their every word and gesture. If Mary lives in them they will see stupendous proof of this power. They will say what to them is simple and almost casual, yet the Christ life will be born in souls at their words, or will gain an increase. They will be the medium through which the Holy Spirit will seize on the soul and bodies of their hearers and thus in ever broadening rings the ocean of grace will extend at the priestly words. The faithful themselves are not slow to make the priest realise that he is the natural mediator between them and God. They will come to him looking for exhibitions of love and wisdom and power which the poor priest will know are not in him—not in him but in Christ through Mary. Cana is always in progress. Since the Second Person espoused the sacred humanity all life is the Divine Marriage Feast at which Jesus is present and at which His mother is present, too. If she is in the priest she will use his consecrated lips to say over and over again: " They have no wine." And His hour will never come until she has spoken. Oh, well for the people who possess priests full of the Spirit of Mary. For them the red wine of grace never ceases to flow until it becomes that torrent of glory which gladdens the House of God.

Although Mary herself never forgave sins, she gave to humanity the Saviour whose authentic rôle was to " Save His people from their sins " (St. Matthew i, 21). Therefore, the priest will need her in his ministerial office in the Sacrament of Penance. Not only will it be his happy privilege to absolve in the name of Jesus but it will be his duty to help souls to avoid sins and grow in virtue. Look into these two duties and see their real significance. No sooner was Jesus born than His life was menaced by the evil Herod. But Herod was the incarnate instrument of impure sin—his own sins and the impurities of all men. If Christ were again passing in our midst there would be a million Herods on His track—though their names might be very modern—God grant not our own. At any rate, Mary saved Jesus from Herod and saved Him from every enemy until He chose Himself to die. That is also the function of the priest. His it is by example and exhortation to stem the tide of sin and lessen it as much as possible, in a word, to save the Saviour, to lessen the Passion of Christ. Only Mary in the priest is adequate for this. Because the poor priest has Herod and Pilate and Judas lurking in his own bosom. But Mary is immaculate and she will help the priest against the corruption without and within.   And the Christ Child will again slumber in peace, as once in Egypt.

The priest must help souls to practise virtue.   But Christ has said that those who do His will are His father and mother and kin.   He has said the doing of the Father's will is His very meat. So the priest must mother Christ and minister to His growth in His Mystical Body.   Mary alone knows how to do both perfectly—for she was created thereto.

Since Mary is so necessary for the priest in order to bring forth, nourish and give Christ to others, we cannot doubt that she is more than anxious to be all this to the anointed of her Son. She will do it all because she loves the Eternal Father, and she knows His will touching His priests—that they should go forth and bear much fruit and that their fruit should remain.

CHAPTER XXXIV

FAIR AS THE MOON

It was a feast of Our Blessed Lady. It was a major feast too, though we cannot recall which one. The time was either the late fall or even mid-winter. And it was about 4 o'clock in the morning. Owing to the time of the year, it could have been pitch dark. As it was, however, everything was bathed in the pure mellow light of a beautiful moon. Its rays poured down on the figure of Mary in a Grotto, making even the statue look supremely lovely. For the soft light removed the hard lines of stone even as a brow is smoothed serene by a caressing hand. Quite spontaneously came to heart and lips the inspired words of the song of songs. "Fair as the Moon." Indeed, it was the only adequate sentiment. But it seemed adequate at that moment.

Even for those few minutes it seemed to us that we had come nearer to understanding the significance of the words as applied to Mary: "Fair as the moon." For that night, if ever, a fair moon rode in the skies, the light it shed on this planet was perfect in its kind. Every object stood out in bold relief under its rays. You could read a book. You could walk here or there as freely as if the noonday sun lighted your path. And yet there was such a soft quality about the light. You could gaze up at the bright orb without having to lower your gaze. And this was the moon and not the sun. As its myriad attendants it had the glittering stars. Not one of these twinkling lights suffered eclipse from the major luminary. We have said that this was the moon and not the sun. We are not wholly correct. For was not this the light of the sun tempered to our eyes and answering our needs when the surrounding darkness threatened? The dawn would come as comes each dawn. And the moon and the stars abide. But they are caught up into and absorbed in the great light from which their light is enkindled. "As the morning rising . . . and fair as the moon"—how beautifully and how truly has the Spirit of God limned her loveliness!

What, above all, struck us that night was the fact that the moon not only reflects the light of the sun, but that it does so in a way which renders that light most serviceable to us and most congenial to our weakness. Then it was that in a flash we saw the utter nonsense of the assertion that Mary gets between us and God. At any rate, she is as much an obstacle to us as is the moon which in a sense gets between us and the sun. Praise be to the Creator of all for such a beneficial mediation!

In this chapter we will try and reflect on Mary's rôle as creature to Creator.

Creation is a concept which few people ever try to fathom. We must be of that few here and now. We find the universe all round us and we find ourselves in the universe. If we do not go so far as to make ourselves the centre of all reality we come very near to regarding creation as the only reality there is. The fact is quite otherwise. It is a fact enshrined in the message that God gave Moses of old. "I am who am." There is the stupendous truth. God alone is. The totality of being in its fullest signification can be predicated of God alone. He alone is. He alone is necessary, is self-sufficient. Everything outside of God, the universe, we ourselves, are creatures. That is to say, we came into being at His word and it is only in virtue of His continued fiat that we continue in being. This is true not only of our essential being but of all the forms which that being takes. One form is growth. That is all from God. All the potentialities of being are likewise His creation. So that it is with the created mind that the so-called wise men study creation and discover more and more of its potentialities, that is to say, more and more of the created modes dormant in creation. So, electricity is a creature; speed is also a creature. Finally, all the resources of energy locked up in the atom are creatures, as is the atom itself. Why have we forgotten all this? To remember it is to be always more and more pene-trated with adoration, with gratitude, with love. Why has scientific progress marked a corresponding falling away from God? If this perverse attitude has robbed the Creator of that glory due to Him from His rational creatures, it has not less deprived them of a source of boundless happiness. Because when we keep in mind that God is giving existence to all things and energising them we recognise ourselves as witnesses of

Creation, not as a tale too often told but as a living pageant of exultant being springing into existence before our very eyes and passing by in its multiform wonder and loveliness. With this view, which is the true one, to exist would be to be happy. Every fresh moment of existence would spell greater interest, greater gratitude. Very particularly would we be filled with the most intense respect for all creatures of no matter what grade. We would recognise in the little insect dancing in the sunlight a being thought of by God from all eternity, brought deliberately from the realms of possibility into that of reality, chosen freely in preference to countless other possible beings and here and now drawing still upon the Divine omnipotence for all the little expressions of its nature. Viewing further the hierarchy of created things, we would come to appreciate the free choice which has made us rational creatures, capable of understanding and of willing freely. Man has actually replaced all these truths by their opposites. And one of the swiftest punishments has been that he no longer derives joy from creation, he has no longer the secret of the creature's dignity and so he maltreats the lower forms and as our age knows to its cost, maltreats his fellow-man.

In the sphere of religion the Protestant revolt was marked by a removal of all the primal truths which were the very charter of existence. If God creates and conserves all things, it is hardly likely that He will let men make and break at their caprice the system of giving due honour to God, which is organised religion. Yet is there any more dominant note in the whole discord of heresy? It is from the beginning to the end a series of, I am of opinion, or I cannot see, or perhaps with some pretence of humility, Martin Luther holds or John Wesley maintains. But has God said anything on the matter? If He has said any word, then it will be the last word. And the only legitimate function for any human in any age will be to echo God and say again and very reverently exactly what God has said, no more and no less.

To remember the great fact of creation with all its implications would save us from the mental attitude of incredulity which makes us unworthy of the Divine interventions. For realising God's action in all and at all times we would be always ready for any manifestation of it which God chose to give. On the other hand, we would not be so avid of signs and wonders, for we would know that a miracle is only a speeding-up—or from another point of view a slowing-down—of creation designed to force our attention for the things which occur constantly are apt to lose their value in our eyes. For instance, as a doctor of the Church says, the multiplication of the loaves and fishes recorded in the Gospel was a great miracle and evoked the grateful admiration of those for whom it was worked. Yet is it a greater work or more stupendous than the sustenance of the whole human race since the beginning by the recurring harvests given by the Divine provider?

God has many thoughts and they are all good in themselves, and very good for us. Man makes one contribution of his very own. It is sin. God is not the author of that. But since man cannot create, this contribution of his is in the nature of a defect. It is, in fact, nothing. God sees its malice and its deformity. But we cannot see sin. We do see something which we mix with sin. In fact, only too often we transfer to this thing the opprobrium and abusive language which really has reference to sin as such. We refer to that which is the result of sin and its just punishment even in the natural order—defect, deformity, pain. These things are not sin. They are only comparative evils. And as such they are used by the just God. They are used by the merciful God, too, because if we will have it so, they are medicinal, not vindictive, and enable us to atone for our sins and free ourselves from them. That is why God could say in the Old Testament: "Is there evil in the city which I have not made?" But most definitely God has not made sin. From all this it follows that everything in the universe which has a positive existence is God's creation. We have laboured all this in order to bring home to the reader the astounding truth so often forgotten that everything in the realm of mind or matter is in existence through God's creative act and continues in it through the permanence of that Divine fiat. So wherever we look at things or at men we see only the Divine action. How, then, can anything come between us and God? We know that this can happen. The very fact of sin testifies to its possibility. But the perversion lies not in the created object but in the free will of the rational agent. As we said, if creation had been remembered, heresy would never have dared to raise its ugly head, with its arrogating to creatures views and persuasions and rights. And it is in their attitude to Our Blessed Lady that non-Catholics have brought their forgetfulness of God's creative action to its highest pitch of criminal folly.

We have said that God has many thoughts and that they are all supremely good. In the very record of creation God emphasised this truth several times by the refrain: " And God saw that they were good." But He has one supreme thought. It is a thought of Himself embracing all His infinite perfections. This thought of God is His word, His Son, whom He eternally begets in His bosom by the Divine intellect. This is the Word of whom St. John writes: " All things were made by Him; and without Him was made nothing that was made " (St. John i, 3). Consequently, the dignity of each creature lies in its relation to this Word.

Now, with reverence, let us follow the thoughts of God as He thinks them and as they body forth in created reality before our eyes. Remember that we have contributed nothing to them. They are God's thoughts and the more wholly they are and remain His the less right have we to do anything except admire and appraise.

God had a thought. In our language we call it womanhood. In our era we have come to think that woman is relative only to man. Womanhood is God's thought. It is a thought of beauty and strength and fruitfulness. It is a thought of mental endowments and physical structure, holy and designed for God's designs.

God had a further thought of virginity, where that exquisite model of womanhood should be for God alone and for no man. He thought again and this time it is motherhood. A thought surpassing fair in which womanhood is fruitful through God's plan involving man. Then in His omnipotence and love God had a thought combining those two thoughts—virginity and motherhood. Has God the right to think such a thought? In the arms of that virgin, now a mother without man's co-operation, God places a child. It is His Word made Flesh. God has no fairer created thought than that child and that mother. And it is the Flesh and Blood Mary of Nazareth with the Flesh and Blood Jesus—Son of the Eternal God and Son of the virgin.

In Mary God has shown us His thought of utter kindness; of a gentleness that perhaps we would not even have connected with omnipotence. She is God's thought of solicitude—" they have no wine;" God's thought of fortitude—the suffering mother.

In a word, Mary represents all the beautiful thoughts of God other than His uncreated thought—His Word. So is she like

the moon only reflecting the light of the uncreated sun. And
that light through her is tempered to our eyes. No longer the
omnipotence which affrights but the omnipotence which creates
a Mary in order to woo our frightened hearts; no longer the
white justice which sears our stained souls but the merciful
mother—God's living thought of clemency. Mary then is like
the moon. But she is also unlike it. And here is where the
heretics stumbled. The moon is inanimate. It reflects light
because it cannot help doing so. Mary, on the contrary, is a
Divine thought of supreme free will, conscious of its freedom,
conscious of what God asks and giving all that God asks always
and perfectly. "Behold the handmaid of the Lord, be it done
to me according to Thy Word." Now, let us ask our separated
brethren; what does God reward or punish in His creatures?
It is not precisely the due submission of a free will or that free
will's revolt? Why are the angels confirmed in glory, and why
do hell and its prisoners exist? Are we not following in God's
own Divine footsteps when we regulate even our puny honour
so? You have never made the mistake with regard to your
human heroes, real or imaginary, which you have made touching
God's masterpiece. You place your military heroes on plinths
and plaques but her you have banished from your hearts. Mary
is God's most beautiful thought after Christ. Moreover, she is
wholly His. Never has she introduced that personal contribution, that jarring note of sin. She is God's thought of perfect
unsullied holiness. No longer, indeed, the blinding light of
uncreated sanctity but perfect holiness shining forth in flesh and
blood. In a word, she is what God always said she was—when
He thought of her and made her—what He told His Church
she was, what she, echoing God, told her little protégée, Bernadette: She is "the Immaculate Conception."

CHAPTER XXXV

OUR LADY OF THE CHURCH

" Thou alone hast overcome all heresies in the whole world."

THESE are strong words of praise addressed to any one creature. Yet the Church addresses them to Mary. It is all the more remarkable when we remember that even the greatest doctors of the Church were raised up to combat this or that heresy. For none of them was it claimed that they had overthrown all. Indeed, some of the very heresiarchs became such because they became over-obsessed with one truth. It was true. But they took it out of its context. Elaborated it in isolation. Made a cancer of it. Yet Mary is said to have overcome all heresies in the whole world, and single-handed. We think that she owes this unique power to the fact that she is the mother of the whole Christ—head and members—of His Mystical Body as of His historic Body. We will show, please God, in this chapter how this identity of head and members issuing in the Mystical Body or the Catholic Church provides at every turn a simple yet adequate refutation of all heresy everywhere. Now we could not have the Mystical Body if we had not first the historic Christ— the Head. And Mary gave Him to us. In mothering Him she mothered also His members and it is in this glorious fact that we must seek the reason of the Church's unique praise. " Thou alone hast overcome all heresies in the whole world." The best refutation of any lie is the living truth. It is best for two reasons. It does not satisfy itself with showing up the liar, but in showing him the truth it provides him with salvation from the falsehood which was strangling him. If he is sincere he will embrace the truth and live. If he will not do so it is because he loves his lie. The ancient verdict is again verified that darkness has been preferred to light. It is best, because it is the adequate refutation. Merely verbal contradiction may only stir up obstinacy, may even itself be partly motivated by pride. Truth is a living thing. It warms and gladdens. When we confer it we are benefactors. Truth which does all this proceeds from love. It presupposes love and it finds a ready audience in a loving heart. It is always the heart which is in error, not the head. For the intellect has the true as its proper object. But the heart sends up a smoke barrage. Then the poor intellect receives dictation. The fool sayeth in his heart, there is no God. See, that judgment pertained to the intellect. And the intellect could never have sanctioned it. But the heart wants things which make God an awkward truth. So the heart usurps the functions of the head. "There is no God."

A lie is a negation, a dead thing. The truth is pulsing with life, is positive, constructive, fruitful. Since the human heart can never love a lie when seen as such, we harness the innate function of the will when we lead it first to love and then to embrace the truth. For all those reasons controversy is most often fruitless. Now no man will embrace an abstraction. Nay, more, he will hug his dear lie more closely to himself if he thinks it has more reality than the abstraction. What an injury we do the truth when we present it thus, as if it were a disembodied theory! The most telling testimony to the rôle of the heart in practical judgments lies in this. Where our ordinary interests are clear, that is to say in practically all life outside of dogma or official religion, no man makes a false judgment because no man wants to. There are many things a man will not say in his heart. He will not say, for instance, that two and two make five or three. And if he did say it, no inquisition would be more ruthless or more speedy in action than the whole body of men with whom such a one had business relations. If he persisted in saying it, if moreover, he decided to form a new mathematical group holding to the new theory, he would be given unlimited leisure to meditate on his scheme in a cell— possibly padded. No fool would say in his heart, it does not matter much what platform I get in on, all trains travel in the same direction. No, that would be another candidate for the big house.

But all these arguments are used in the religious field. And companies of unlimited liability have been formed on their basis. The heart has said its say and the light of intellect has been blacked out. Why is there not a similar reaction on behalf of the general public? Because the heart of the man in the street has told him a lie, too. It has said: "Such comprehensive liberty of thought does not hurt me. So let them carry on."

Doesn't it hurt you, old man? Your number one war and your number two, and the one that looks as if it were coming? It seems to have hurt Hiroshima. And it may be Manchester to-morrow, or New York or some noble city on the Volga. "For the wrath of God is revealed from Heaven against all ungodliness and injustice of those men that detain the truth of God in injustice. Because that which is known of God is manifest in them. For God had manifested it unto them. For the invisible things of Him from the creation of the world are clearly seen, being understood by the things that are made, His eternal power also, and divinity. So that they are inexcusable. Because that, when they knew God they have not glorified Him as God, or given thanks, but became vain in their thoughts, and their foolish heart was darkened " (Romans i, 18-21). What a terrible indictment. See the gradation so plainly asserted by the Spirit of Truth. Truth was manifest to men. Truth in the warm nurturing form of creatures, surrounded by a universe which was obviously designed in power and wisdom and, above all, in kindness. St. Paul does not say, poor wretches they knew no better. On the contrary, he says: " They are inexcusable." And he is talking of the pre-Christian world which, at any rate, had not seen and heard Christ. He was not talking to our era which has turned its back on the fullness of Divine Light. What would he say to us? In ordinary life gratitude is so normally elicited and expressed. Thank you for a mere duty information, thank you for a commercial service. But for being, and life— no thank you. Then the inevitable happens. The heart has played the traitor. The folly is its, not the head's. " And their foolish heart was darkened."

St. Paul! Where did you get all this wisdom? Or do you ever remember a gentleman named Saul and a little mission which was his on the old Damascus road? " And Saul, as yet breathing out threatenings and slaughter against the disciples of the Lord, went to the high priest, and asked of him letters to Damascus, to the synagogues, that if he found any men and women of this way, he might bring them bound to Jerusalem. And as he went on his journey, it came to pass that he drew nigh to Damascus, and suddenly a light from Heaven shined round about him. And falling on the ground, he heard a voice saying to him, Saul, Saul, why persecutest thou Me? Who said, Who art Thou, Lord? And He, I am Jesus whom thou persecutest. It is hard for thee to kick against the goad. And he, trembling and astonished, said, Lord, what wilt Thou have me to do? And the Lord said to him, Arise and go into the city, and there it shall be told thee what thou must do. . . ." (Acts ix, 1-7).

An infidel was thrown from his horse. He rose from the ground a believer. What will this Saul yet be? We, the descendants of the Gentiles, know what he became for himself—and for us. Later on in his life Paul will beseech prayers for himself lest, having preached to others, he himself should be a castaway. This fear was a valid one, rooted in St. Paul's knowledge of his own personal frailty. But this much we can say. If, apart from God's grace, Paul could have become a great sinner, he would have had to do violence to himself to become again an unbeliever, and infinitely more violence to become any sort of a heretic. For on that road to old Damascus he had seen precisely that true, warm and living vision of the Church, which is the sufficient and adequate answer to heresy in all or any of its protean forms. He had seen that vision which is precisely the one missed by all those outside the communion of the Church. He had seen the living, breathing truth of the Mystical Body.

Watch the sacred text. The Holy Ghost gives to the prospective victims of Saul's wrath their proper title, "Disciples of the Lord." Then, speaking from the myopic angle of those outside He speaks in terms familiarly in use by heresy ever since. Saul went to the high priest. But this is a self-styled high priest. The old law has passed into the new. The priesthood, too, has been translated. This, then, is an impostor. Not all the vestments of the Holy City can commission him. It has always been an easy thing to call oneself archbishop of this and that, and easy, too, to furnish oneself with all the external regalia of office. But if the Most High spurns, who can stand? Saul may go to that high priest. Paul will never return to him.

"If he found any men and women of this way"—how plain it is that the Vision has not yet burst upon him. This, too, is familiar jargon. Men speak of their convictions, their persuasions. As if religion was a man-made thing taking on all the forms of subjective vagary. Even the external universe exhibits a design. Not even profane science would be possible if subjectivism ruled in material things. But it may rule in the domain of man's relations to his Creator! Dare it? It was a great thing and a wonderful thing that a Man who had been nailed to a Cross and consigned to a tomb should thus speak to Saul. Yet if Saul had heard no other words than "I am Jesus," the revolution in his soul would have been dangerously incomplete. In fact he might have been convinced that to him was vouchsafed the only complete revelation of the Son of God. It was the phrase which followed that made Paul what he never ceased to be: "I am Jesus whom thou persecutest." What a jumble of people was conjured up in Saul's mind by those telling words! That little servant girl, that apostle of His who claimed to speak for His Master, all those persecuted ones, different in rank and endowment yet united in faith in a Person. No high-brow savants, no ignorant fanatic bigots, just every class of mind yielding itself to love, not to a phrase, not to an interpretation, but to a Person. And now on Saul's astonished ears the vital truth falls. The Person and His disciples are One Person. Yes, it was the Mystical Body which Saul met on that road of grace. Each Saul of to-day is so because he is blind to It. If he glimpses It, a Paul he must become, or closing his eyes to the light thunder on his way adown the road of life, persecuting the First Born of many brethren. We would wish to help all our separated brethren to see this true vision of the Church as Christ's Mystical Body. For we are convinced that for them, as for Saul, the only road to truth is the Damascus road. Is it not the way Christ chooses for recognition of His Truth? He has told us that unless we become as little children we cannot enter the Kingdom of Heaven. We must receive this Kingdom as a little child. Now put a normal child before as big a crowd as you wish and ask that child to pick out its own mother. Will the child measure height, will it interrogate several likely candidates? Oh, what utter nonsense! The child already knows its mother. Heart speaks to heart. And the heart keeps the head right, notice that. In a flash the child has thrown itself into the arms of that one and only person who has ever mothered it.

In order to help non-Catholics towards this grand recognition we would first of all like to clarify their ideas of just how we Catholics regard them. Here is our outlook. We divide heresy into formal and material. The first is a deliberate choice of false doctrine. It is not for us to judge any man, but it is difficult to exculpate the heresiarchs from this sinful choice. Generally they were men of sufficient learning. They at least could have consulted the identity disks. They were therefore formal heretics. They were of the class to which the apostle of love forbids believers to say, "God speed you." But it is quite otherwise

with the bulk of their followers in the course of time. Few, if
any of these, have made a deliberate choice of their sect. Through
no fault of their own they were born into it. Once again a
distinction must be made. Ministers of heresy may too often be
in bad faith. They are educated. They ought to be able to read
the signs. Either they just refuse—implicitly—to do any thinking on the matter and just throw themselves into their work,
such as it is, or they see the Vision approaching and turn aside.
For the Vision might be very awkward. It did change everything for Saul. As we said, he had no longer an *entrée* into the
high sacerdotal coterie. He only had Christ. But happily the
greater number of ordinary non-Catholic rank and file are in
good faith. That is to say, they sincerely believe in their way.
Only it just is not " the Way "—" I am the Way."

We address ourselves to such, and feel that we can disclaim all
desire to offend honest conviction. Only by showing them the
Vision we hope to convict their honesty. And, please God, more
dear members will unite themselves to the Mystical Body which
at present they do not know, may even deride and deny. " I am
Jesus whom thou persecutest," and you thought it was only a
Pacelli, or a Stepinac, or just plain Father Murphy or plainer
Mrs. Mulligan and her papist brood. Whatever our separated
brethren see, think they see, or even appear to see, it is not the
Vision which made the scales fall from Saul's eyes. And in
reality when they do not see this Vision they see nothing. At
any rate, whatever half-glimpses of the truth are vouchsafed to
them are designed by the God of Truth to lead them to the
Vision Splendid. This Vision is nothing less than the whole
Christ, head and members. It is Christ and His Mystical Body.
It is the Church. Apart from this authentic and integral Vision
there is only hallucination. There may be a twilight wherein
the shadows of falsehood are receding, where the dark mists of
error may be lifting. Then is it that men are seen as trees walking. Everything is blurred. But praised be God for it, blurred
truth is better than a brilliantly etched lie, and focus and perspec-
tive will come in God's own time. Our attitude to those erring
ones must be always animated by the hope that it is so with
them and that they will see. We must help them towards the
Vision.

That the proper conception of the Church is precisely what
is lacking to non-Catholics comes home to us by a fact to which
experience attests. Let us take it that a group comprised of

Catholics and the denominations is engaged in friendly conversation. If the members of such a group meet often enough and are friendly enough, religious topics are bound to crop up. Then, if we look for it, we will notice a significant fact and it is this. It will be possible to speak on many religious subjects without it appearing that there is any cleavage in opinion amongst the speakers. There is no doubt that friendly non-Catholics love such a situation and fondly believe that Christianity is more truly expressed in such than in those dogmas which set up rival camps. Let the talk be about God. We appear to be one. To safeguard unity even on the Deity we won't discuss the Adorable Trinity, because Mr. So-and-so is a Unitarian. Generally speaking, we have, or appear to have, the same concept of Christ, His Identity and His Mission. Sin will be vituperated by all present. But now watch. Let the simple phrase " the Church " be uttered. There is a challenge in that word. And if we want to keep our party happy over their teacups and cigarettes we must not probe that idea too far. For an empty room would have to result, if sincerity was maintained. For each person present realises in his heart that all are divided in their concept of this vital phrase, " the Church."

Let us try to see what it must mean for each in the company. For the ultra-high Anglican its first meaning must be their own communion. For their claim is something like this. There was always, and there will always be, the authentic Church of Christ. For vague reasons of history the great British people objected to certain practical effects of dogma in national life, and in the life of great nationals. So they protested. Many, too many, went too far in their righteous anger and walked out of the Ark. But they built one themselves on the model from which the abandoned Ark deviated. Time marched on. The empire established its greatness without any interference from pretentious prelates. The great nationals got all the wives they wanted and died, nevertheless, in the course of time. Tempers cooled down and, as always happens, vision ceased to be so distorted. At a considerably recent date many of the descendants of the sulkers realised that there could be only one Ark—the old one. So without as much as by your leave they all made for the trusty old vessel. But would you believe it, the pilot would not let them in. Said their visas were all wrong. However, they did not worry. They just kept on saying, " We belong." But even a slogan like that, all sung together, won't be proof against the deluge. So in our company, when the High Anglican speaks of the Ark, of the Church, he is speaking about a very safe dwelling to which he really does not belong. And the Catholics know that he does not. What may our Presbyterian and Methodist friends mean by " the Church "? Before we venture our opinion we want more than anything to assure these good people that we do not wish to wound their feelings. Only truth, with the charity inseparable from it, can both illuminate and heal. We count among our friends some non-Catholic ministers of religion. Among our kith and kin we possess dear ones belonging to these communions. Therefore we are in a position to recognise both their sincerity and their zeal. So true is this, that there is only this personal striving to take the place of any formal ecclesiastical background. What is this latter for them? The two denominations mentioned above agree in their general opposition to Roman Catholicism, and to episcopal institution. Apart from these negative views there is a vague atmosphere of select synodal gatherings where the preacher's voice may even be of feminine timbre. There may be, and there often is, the suggestion of a very pious and faithful home-life where some of the ancient sanctities are honoured in a most evangelical manner. All this it may be, but all this is not the Vision. It is not the Church.

Let us try to see through St. Paul's cleansed eyes and behold the Church as she is in all truth, the Church presented to his startled gaze long ago when to his stammering query came the Divine response: " I am Jesus whom thou persecutest " (Acts ix, 15). It was the Church of 1 A.D. It is the Church of 1950. And when time ceases and the One Christ, head and members, reigns for ever in Heaven, it will again be the Vision of St. Paul—only at Home and in glory. The doctrine of the Mystical Body may be briefly expressed as follows. The Church is the whole Christ. Now Christ is already in Heaven, but in His members, that is, in His Mystical Body He is still on earth. It is not our object to make this a strictly scientific treatise. But we would point out that by the word " mystical " is indicated that the Body in question is not the physical Body of the historic Christ, which is in glory at the Father's right hand. Nevertheless, " mystical " does not mean " make-believe." Holy and learned divines from the very first ages down to our own day have expended all their spiritual gifts and mental endowments in the explanation and elaboration of the doctrine. The reigning Holy Father, the 12th Pius, has made it the object of an Encyclical. Those who have access to all this literature will not need our poor words. But for sincere non-Catholics and for the humble faithful we venture to assert that although these learned writers have embellished the Vision with a wealth of scientific phraseology and brilliant exposition they have seen no more than Paul saw on that Damascus road. What did he see? or rather what did he hear, for " Fides ex auditu "—Faith is from hearing.

When we come from the nebulous ideas of the Church entertained by the sectaries to the clear-cut Vision of St. Paul we bid an eternal adieu to vagueness.

There is, first of all, light. And it is from Heaven. That is to say, it is no longer the faint and quickly extinguished sparks which may be struck from the poor flint of the human intellect as such. No longer are we lulled into a mental torpor by vacuities and inanities, by opinions and personal viewpoints. What Saul heard was not a confused murmur of many voices—Luther and Wycliffe and Huss and Knox and Wesley—but a voice. " Saul, Saul, why persecutest thou Me?" This voice was directed not to the world conscience or the British honesty or the Teutonic superman—but to Saul. And then the answer: " Who said, who art Thou, Lord?" And He: " I am Jesus whom thou persecutest." No vagueness here. Saul knew the historic Jesus. He could put his hands on the official acts of His trial and execution. Up to that moment He was for Saul just " one Jesus deceased " whom a crowd of pious lunatics affirmed to be alive (Acts xxv, 19). Stephen had been one of them. And Saul had seen his end—and had seen it gladly. " And the witnesses laid down their garments at the feet of a young man whose name was Saul. . . . And Saul was consenting to his death " (Acts vii, 57-59). And right now he was hot-foot on the track of others of the brood. Oh, Saul knew whom he was after. They were all so individual, so flesh and blood. When they were stabbed or stoned, red blood gushed forth and real pain twisted real features. And now: " I am Jesus whom thou persecutest."

As long as time lasts persecution will be an infallible signpost pointing to the Mystical Body, to Christ's one and only Church. How can it be otherwise if Saul heard aright? " I am Jesus. . . ." During His historic life He was above all the persecuted One. He was persecuted unto death. But Christ the Head dieth no more. Persecution cannot reach Him any longer. But that was as true for the Head, on that Damascus road, as it is true to-day. Christ was at His Father's right hand, where Stephen had seen Him, " But he, being full of the Holy Ghost, looking up steadfastly to Heaven, saw the glory of God, and Jesus standing on the right hand of God. . . ." (Acts vii, 55). Yet—" I am Jesus whom thou persecutest." See the vision of truth bursting on Saul. The faithful were identified with Jesus. They were His Body, not His real Body in Heaven but his Mystical Body on earth, not the glorified Body inaccessible to suffering, but His Mystical Body still open to persecution and persecuted always because it is His. It must be so. If Christ thus identified Himself with those who believe in Him, never can He, never will He lose this identity. That was the whole Christ in Paul's day. That is the whole Christ in ours. And God be praised for it, the identity disk is in order. When has the Roman Apostolic Church ceased to be persecuted? When have the sects ever suffered it? Nay, in their very birth, or rather abortion, they were the persecutors. Tyburn tree has only that tale to tell. It is the glorious dirge of every mountain and glen of our own dear land. If, almost by accident, the sectaries suffer at anybody's hands, it is phenomenal, not normal. If they will talk of bloody Mary, she was an episode. But persecution is not episodic in the Church's life, and it is not episodic in the life of the Roman Church. If the State ever victimised non-conformists, it was because they would not embrace the heresy in the State's fullest acceptance of it. But they are not persecuted because of their religious tenets qua religious but qua anti-Cæsar. They are not persecuted as the Mystical Body. Not of any of these, nor of all of them does Christ say: " I am Jesus whom thou persecutest."

It is indeed so obvious that the Mystical Body suffers persecution because it is His Body. It was obvious in Saul's day and is not less so in our own. For look. Who were Saul's prospective victims? Slaves, young men and women, children even and old people. If there were a soldier or two, even a commissioned officer, if there were a member of the priestly caste, or a matron of blood, or a wealthy person, these were the exception—" Not many noble." And who were the persecutors? All the power of the Roman Empire. The might of that empire whose legions marched in every land was hurled against those weak ones. Against them was pitted the organised strength of sacerdotal Jewry, now friends with Cæsar over the Galilean's Corpse. It was always so. When England was in its glory it hurled itself

against defenceless priests and nuns, against poor yokels and
tender youth. It is so to-day. Mighty Russia can find no better
fodder for her juggernaut wheels than priests and nuns. Men
without a weapon in their hands are hated and feared and persecuted and slain by those who possess the armaments of the
world. Why is this? Because these persecutors are animated
by a spirit which recognises who those weaklings are. As of old,
he feels constrained to cry aloud: " I know who Thou art, the
Holy One of God." And they incite their dupes to throw themselves upon them—nay, upon Christ. And time also discloses
the correctness of their instinct. For when men have forgotten
a Nero or a Domitian, an Elizabeth, a Cromwell, a Tito or a
Stalin, they remember for ever a Philomena, or a Margaret
Clitheroe, an Oliver Plunket and a Stepinac. " I am Jesus
whom thou persecutest."

Even though persecution is a constant and characteristic noble
note of the Mystical Body it is not the only one. It was the note
brought into play there and then by Him who was the subject
of the Vision. But what the Vision had stressed principally was
the moral union between Christ and His members, and it had
stressed that in terms of an identification. The significance of
this was never again lost on St. Paul. There will be no
reformer so obsessed by the unique mediatorship of Christ as
Paul was truly gripped by it. Nevertheless the inspired Apostle
will also hold in his illuminated mind that other truth which
they lost and even spurned, the actual contribution of the
Mystical Body, that is, the contribution to redemptive grace and
to its diffusion of such humble people as Saul was then pursuing.
Paul will be second to none in recognising the all-sufficiency of
Christ's Sacrifice. But it will be this same Paul who will boldly
say that we must fill up what is wanting in the sufferings of
Christ. For Paul had seen the Vision and heard the Voice.

Since Jesus affirmed identity between Himself as Head and
His faithful as members, not only must this identity for ever
endure—for Christ is not divided—but it must issue in a repetition on earth of all the mysteries accomplished once by the
historic Christ. It is not in suffering alone that these mysteries
will be reproduced. Since this is, it is quite clear that there must
be some vehicle of expression, so to speak, some way of rendering visible, of externating this constant stream of Divine life
whereby the Head lives again in His members. Suffering is
quite sufficiently externated and the world, which is Christ's

enemy, has never been at a loss to provide the vehicle of expression—in rack and rope and scaffold and concentration camp. But the Mystical Body must surely have its own divinely sanctioned way of portraying the life of Christ ever active in her. It certainly has, and that way is the Sacred Liturgy. Here let us say with finality that the body claiming to be Christ's Church and disclaiming a liturgy thereby proves that it is counterfeit. Such an institution can only be man-made. It was not in its name that the Voice addressed Saul, making him Paul. Those High Church bodies which have tried to recapture the liturgy are no less shams than those who deny its value. They are condemned by the Christ-affirmed identity of Head and members. Christ was thus one and whole on that day of Vision. He was not less so in the 16th century. But as in His mortal days men left Him and walked no more with Him—also because of His Body—so men left Him at the Protestant revolt. Only on that occasion they severed themselves from His Mystic Body. Then they experienced what all severed branches must experience. They dried up and withered, and decayed. To pile grape clusters and greenery over these dead branches in the 20th century cannot make them live. Only it does prove that there is a fruitful Vine somewhere. And they may be grafted in again. God make it so for those poor souls.

Not only do the sects fail to see how their disclaiming of liturgy is a disclaiming of oneness with Christ, but even when they recognise its need they no longer realise why. For them the Vision has faded out. For instance, a non-Catholic chaplain in the recent war—a Methodist, we think—stressed it as his conviction rising out of his war experiences that the denominations should go in for more ritual. His motive is quite clearly to clothe with some form of suggestiveness the ministrations which appear too empty and futile in themselves. They appear so, because they are so. This is not the soul animating Catholic ritual. Here we have forms, not arbitrary but crystallised, externating the real pulsing life flowing from the Head into the members. These forms are dramatic in the extreme. The writer owns to have been most exceptionally impressed by the Holy Saturday liturgy in his own monastic church. He had participated in these ceremonies for many years, never without being impressed but never so impressed as on the most recent Holy Saturday ('48). During the Holy Week you are made realise in every possible way that once more Christ has turned

His Face to Jerusalem. And the Church's invitation to her children to participate in His liturgy is an effective acceptance of the Apostle Thomas' cry: "Let us go up and die with Him." The arrangement of the Divine Office, its form and its content, the psalm tone for the triduum. Tenebræ, everything breathes Calvary. And on Good Friday we again die mystically with the Saviour. Then is the Tomb victorious. For the first part of Holy Saturday's liturgy death still reigns. And then with the flash of the Resurrection everything changes. Music, vestment, everything. Christ rises again before our eyes. The liturgy makes us see Him do so. Above all, this is no make-believe. This is no stage upon which hallucinations are produced to be dispelled by the hoot of a passing auto.

The Paschal grace floods our souls. How could it be otherwise? And we His members rise with Him to a new life, the harbinger of the one that will never pass. Oh, poor, yet most dear separated brethren, give up your make-believe which starves your souls and be again engrafted on your Head and ours.

If the Vision, according to Saul, meant anything it must mean this. That Christ has never ceased to be in our world, and that in a very real sense. We have not yet come to His unique Eucharistic Presence. Even apart from that august sacrament He is in the world, covering all space and time through His Mystic Body, that is, His Church. This, then, is the only adequate conception of the Church. It is our Divine Head, and His members on earth, His Mystical Body. How far is this conception from the sectarian views? And lest they take refuge in vagueness and say that this particular sect is the whole Christ we are given a tessera of challenge. Show us the authentic activities of the Head in your members. If you retort that these activities, being all-sufficient, are completed once and for all, then we challenge you with Saul's Vision. True, Christ our Head dieth now no more, but in His members Christ suffereth still, still dies, still rises again in grace and glory. "I am Jesus whom thou persecutest."

But what of the other authentic redemptive acts of Christ? Self-sufficient again, yes, we admit, but capable of reproduction in His members even as His Passion is. Where is the Calvary for the sectaries, where the Supper Room and the Divine Banquet? Where are the chosen ones who speak in His Name, where is Peter the Rock? Where is the giving of the Spirit and where the forgiveness of sins? For these were ministerial acts of Christ flowing from His Messianic office. And if He is always sufferer, He is still more truly always Saviour.

The Holy Mass, as celebrated in the Roman Catholic Apostolic Church, is the only rite which even claims to be a reproduction of the One Redemptive Act.   But strange it would be if the suffering which led up to the Atonement should still be reproduced and not the very atonement.   It is no sign of the influx of a Redemptive Head into members the meaningless service of the Protestant Supper.   Had you been present in the Supper Room and seen Christ take bread in His Venerable Hands and bless and break . . . and then go from Protestant temple to Protestant temple you would be reminded of nothing.   No Emmaus these!   But go into the humblest Catholic church when Holy Mass is in progress, or go into St. Peter's at Rome and you will know what Cleophas and his companions meant when they told the assembled eleven, "How they knew Him in the breaking of bread" (St. Mark xxiv, 35).   It is not without significance that it is the visionary of the Damascus road who was chosen by the Holy Spirit to underline the Synoptics' account of the Living Gift.

"For I have received of the Lord that which also I delivered unto you, that the Lord Jesus, the same night in which He was betrayed, took bread and, giving thanks, broke, and said: 'Take ye, and eat: this is my body, which shall be delivered for you: this do for the commemoration of Me.' In like manner also the chalice, after He had supped, saying: 'This chalice is the new testament in My blood: this do ye, as often as you shall drink, for the commemoration of Me.   For as often as you shall eat this bread, and drink the chalice, you shall shew the death, of the Lord, until He come.   Therefore, whosoever shall eat this bread, or drink the chalice of the Lord unworthily, shall be guilty of the body and of the blood of the Lord'" (St. Paul i, Cor. xi, 23-27).

Certain it is that the historic Christ made a great and unique promise as recorded in St. John, Chapter VI.   He allowed disciples to leave Him rather than retract the literal meaning of His words.   To those who remained, to those who ever remain He has fulfilled that promise in the Eucharist Gift. Where is that bread distributed in His Mystical Body? Can we see the Christ of St. Paul's vision in the pale and empty ceremony of the Protestant communion?   It is true that the piety and good will of those concerned do invest the act with some meaning.

But by their Church's avowed profession it is not what Divine lips said it was at the Last Supper which was also the first. Was it for this ceremony devoid of all substance that the Great Creator of life's staff and of the heartening wine chose just these two elements with all their obvious suggestion of reality and nourishment?   Was all the tantalising discourse of St. John's sixth chapter but the prelude of a rite which merely commemorates?   The people whose starved souls are content perforce with ritual silences and cenotaphs may accept it thus.   But the men who walked away from Christ's hard saying were more incredulous if you will, but also of more logical build.   And Christ the Son of God let them go, as He will always let free wills go their chosen path, though a word from Him would have explained all.   And that word He said.   But it was not a word of softening down pointing to the reformers' empty symbols, but a word of terrible asseveration: "Amen, amen, I say unto you: except you eat the flesh of the Son of Man, and drink His blood, you shall not have life in you" (St. John vi, 54). Where then is the banquet spread which claims to give us His Flesh and His Blood?   Where is the Divine Love Feast ever in progress?   Go into any Catholic Church at the hour of Sacrifice and you will hear once more the Voice of the Head and you will see the living members approaching the Holy Table—"There shall the eagles also be gathered together. . . ."

Many thronged around Christ during His earthly life.   And He called all, welcomed all, repulsed none.   Yet in a very special manner He called twelve.   So special was His call to them that it ranks as one of His official Messianic acts.   The Baptist was a great solitary, a voice proclaiming Another and leading all to that other.   With Christ it is quite different.   One cannot even conceive Him without the circle of His chosen apostles.   Not arbitrary was their number.   For when one dropped out the sacred text calls them "The Eleven"—suggesting obviously that they should be twelve.   And Matthias made them twelve again.   To these chosen ones Christ gave a special training.   To them He committed great power, even His own Divine Commission.   "As the Father has sent Me so do I send you."

Christ lives to-day in His Mystic Body.   Where are the twelve? Is there a church which claims to be His while denying the historic Episcopate?   Is there a church which dared to deny and then to resurrect?   And if we seek for the twelve can these be apart from their head?   In what communion is Peter claimed

and Peter's fellow-Bishops? There is the Church shown to Saul
long ago. But Christ is to-day, yesterday and the same forever.
"And thou shalt call His Name Jesus. For He shall
save His people from their sins" (St. Matthew i, 21). Thus did
an angel of the Lord designate what may fairly be regarded as
the Chief Messianic mission of Christ. For no adequate reparation could be made to the outraged Majesty of God unless Christ
both identified Himself with humanity and cleansed this latter
from sin, original and actual. He has done both. He has done
so not merely radically by His atoning sacrifice but also ministerially by declaring sins forgiven in the individual. Blessed
indeed were the ears of that paralytic which heard the Divine
words of absolution: "Son, thy sins are forgiven thee" (St.
Mark ii, 5). But sin abounds to-day and we are sinners. Where
is Christ's voice heard in absolving mercy to-day? Where is
there heard that crisp and clear declaration of pardon for the
individual? For it was by no vague stirring up of hope in a
general amnesty that Christ preluded His corporal cure of the
man crippled in body and soul alike. The Church which claims
and exercises sacramental confession and absolution is the Mystic
Body: "I am Jesus."

When Jesus wished to present His credentials as the Divine
Envoy He answered the messengers sent by John thus: "Go
and relate to John what you have heard and seen; the blind see,
the lame walk, the dead rise again, to the poor the Gospel is
preached" (St. Luke vii, 22). If Jesus is so one with His
members that He suffers in them, can we imagine that the
Mystical Body will have pain alone without the prodigies?
No, indeed. If a communion can point to no miracles
if, in fact, it decries such, it stands self-condemned. Where is
the Church of the miracles? Where is the Church which
possesses a Lourdes, which dares to demand miracles of its
members alleged to be saints? Wherever it is, it is one with its
Head. It is the Mystical Body. And all know well both where
that Church is and where it is not.

When sin had once disrupted the beautiful God-designed
relation of man and woman, increased abuses in the matter
made it always a burning question agitating the minds of men.
Surely it would be brought to Jesus Christ for solving. It was.
And He solved it for all time. He did not make it the subject
of a long and subtle discussion in which all human psychology
is brought forward in argument. His answer was not based on

neurosis or incompatibility of temperament or race or clime. No, indeed, in a short utterance worthy of His Divinity He brought back marriage to its Divine origin. "And there came to Him the Pharisees tempting Him, saying: Is it lawful for a man to put away his wife for every cause? Who, answering, said to them: Have ye not read, that He who made man from the beginning, made them male and female? And he said: For this cause shall a man leave father and mother, and shall cleave to his wife, and they two shall be in one flesh. Therefore, now they are not two, but one flesh. What, therefore, God hath joined together let no man put asunder" (Acts. St. Matthew xix, 3-6). There lies the Divine Charter of holy marriage? From those Divine Words have germinated and must ever germinate all the beautiful sanctities of homes and fruitful progeny. Unlike our barren savants Christ not only laid down the law clearly and without subterfuge, but also instituted a sacrament giving grace to married people. He alone could and did change the water of unaided human nature into the rich wine of super-natural grace, which act of omnipotent love was plainly insinuated by Christ's first miracle at the wedding feast of Cana.

But the relations of the sexes still remain the subject of men's enquiry. They bring it to Cæsar. They bring it to their passions. When they bring it to Christ He makes the self-same answer. Where is that Blessed Voice to be heard to-day? Is it in that assembly which, speaking hypothetically about this Divine matter, has opened the door to a deluge of abuse and birth pre-vention? Is it at Cæsar's forum where bonds are severed and homes destroyed by the sweep of a pen? Not so did Jesus speak. Not so does He ever speak Head and members in His Mystical Body of the Church. So the attitude towards marriage is an infallible signpost pointing to the Church of Christ, the Church shown to Saul.

If Jesus thus ennobled holy marriage He invited to the higher state of absolute chastity. "He that can take, let him take it" (St. Matthew xix, 12). He will never cease to issue the same invitation. To His members He offers countless opportunities of living the life of the counsels. His Church blooms and blossoms with every variety of institution offering the higher life. In His Church the religious state must be in existence and in honour. Where it is so, there is Christ's Mystical Body, there is His Church, there He Himself. He is truth itself. He is the faithful God. Never can He contradict Himself. It could not be He who would crush out the state founded on and by His very counsels. Could it be He who, in the 16th century, demolished the holy houses raised up by Him in the first? Could He honour His religious in the first and slay them in the 16th, in the 20th? And if moved by some spirit of shame the children build the sepulchres of those whom their father slew, they only prove thereby that they are in very truth their children. They may materially build up the ruins of stately abbeys, may materially restore a prescribed ritual, but nothing that they thus do can incorporate them into that Body whose members their fathers have slain. Nay, they are themselves the slain members.

Jesus came also to pray. He was the great prayer *par excellence*. In His earthly life He prayed as Head. He never ceases to pray in His members. Where is the Church claiming and honouring an official prayer which ascends to the eternal Father echoing Christ's prayer by day, echoing His prayer by night. " He was all night in the prayer of God." Where is to be found the institution of the Divine Office? Where is the Church capable of asking chosen members to dedicate their whole lives to the demands of public prayer? Where is the Church whose living members use still the holy prayer forms inspired by the Holy Spirit? Wherever it is, there is the Mystical Body, the Church of Christ, there is Christ Himself praying without cessation in His members. And where it is not, Christ is not. It is no prayer of His which must have the imprimatur of Cæsar, of which the formulæ may be vetoed or retrenched or increased by vote of unbeliever no less than believer. It is no prayer of Christ's which can be left to even the piety or improvisation of individual men. It is not Christ who prayeth thus.

The chief argument employed by the alleged reformers, namely, that error had obscured the true Church, is shattered by the doctrine of the Mystical Body as contained in Saul's Vision. For the Jesus of that Vision was an integral Jesus, Head and members. This whole Christ must preserve His identity in every age. He is ever in the world. And so we have only to look at Him in every century, only to hearken to Him, in order to recognise His Church and to possess the whole truth. See the way for little ones. Even a fool—if the head alone be weak—cannot err therein. There is no need of scientific lore, where a soul has cost the life blood of God.

How could the contention of the reformers have ever been made, had they remembered what Saul had heard? For they say that up to the 16th century truth had been so overlaid by error, so obscured, so lost even, that the very lineaments of Christ could no longer be recognised. It took forsooth the clear eyes of an Eighth Henry or a Luther, of a Calvin or a John Knox, to wipe that Divine countenance and restore it to men's sight. Strange Veronicas these! But what does Christ plainly state His Church to be in His utterance to Saul? Is it not the members of Christ living with their Head's life? Then is the contention of the reformers blasphemous. A living person is always one with himself. Let them not say that it was the members who lost their Head. That cannot happen to a living person. Or if it in any degree happens, the person remains integral, the severed members die. And Christ is the living God. So it has never been a matter of the turn of a text or so-called higher criticism. Even in the Old Law the Living God spoke to His people before His words were recorded in any book. The end of the law is Christ, not the revised version, not even the Vulgate.

Always and in every place the Whole Christ lives and has ever lived. Always the members have known the Mind of their Head on all the vital truths, Divine Identity, Episcopate and priesthood, Atonement and application thereof through Holy Mass, the sacraments. Let them not say the Church did not thus in the first century. For Christ and His Church are one and do ever the same thing, yesterday, to-day and forever.

With Jesus there was never yea and nay, but Divine affirmation. "I testify what I see." In His members He speaks the same language of Divine assurance. In them He speaks as One having authority. They see with His eyes and speak with His voice. Where there is the note of compromise, of soft comprehensive treason wherein is silenced dogma in order to promote a false fraternity, there Christ speaketh not.

Above all, Jesus is ever the Son of Mary, He is not less her Son in His members. The voice which is raised against the mother, which rails at her prerogatives, which denies to her any real influx on the life of the Mystical Body is not the voice of the Son who is the best of sons since He is God—who framed the Fourth Commandment. What kind of monster would that be whereof the head and members had not the same mother— and mothering? Jesus is ever mothered by Mary. She never ceases to lavish on His members the maternal services she lavished on their Head. She conceived Him in her womb through the Spirit's overshadowing, resulting on her free accept-

ance in faith of the Divine embassy. In His members she con-
ceives Him still. She brought Him forth at Bethlehem and then
mothered Him, nurtured Him, saved Him, the Saviour, from
His foes until the hour of sacrifice struck. And then she immo-
lated Him in union with His own immolation. Corredemptrix
in every truth. She ever brings Him forth in His members and
does all over again for Him in them. Her prayer with that of
His chosen ones hastened the coming of the promised Paraclete,
and where she is are all the gifts and fruits of the Spirit, nay, the
Spirit Himself, who has never ceased to possess her wholly.
Ever is Mary in the midst of the Mystic Body obtaining for it
and conserving in it the holy Spirit of truth. Where she is not, is
darkness, and lies and death. Where is the Church which
recognises, and gladly recognises, this position of God's mother?
Where is the Church to which God has revealed Mary's unique
privilege? There is Christ's Mystic Body. There is Jesus, as
ever, with Mary. Truly have His holy ones cried out of her in
benediction: "Thou alone hast overcome all heresies in the
whole earth." For in mothering Jesus she has mothered His
Mystical Body. And in mothering it she has given the lie to all
heresies and to all possible heresies.

Have we not the obligation of loving those erring ones, those
other sheep of Christ which must be brought to Him so that
there may be but one fold and one Shepherd? But have we not
also the duty to hate all the error which has wreaked such ill
upon them and to cry out to heresy, " J'accuse "?

Since the Church is Jesus Christ, Head and members, it
follows that any other Church is a lie and a sham. Actually
heretics do not know Christ at all, despite all their unctuous
sayings. Whatever may be true in these latter, whatever
semblance of piety seems to be attached to them is but the
memory, ever dimmer and dimmer, of the True Vision to which
their poor eyes were blinded. There is no Protestant theology.
For Protestantism is nothing. Of course, even a caricature owes
its verisimilitude to the reality parodied.

Heresy, therefore, has done an untold injury to Christ and
continues to do so. For if it may not break a bone of His Sacred
Body it has torn His living members from Him. Almost more
than any other factor heresy is responsible for our present world
catastrophe, and for all impending evils. For when it dismem-
bered Christ it made of those poor torn members dead things.
For centuries it has deprived whole masses of men of sacrifice

and priesthood, of sacraments of pardon and peace, of guaranteed truth, of union with the Head which alone would bring union between the members. Deprived of their supernatural nourishment, man has become the animal which two recent world wars have shown him to be. The pardon and peace denied has been sought from psychoanalysts and psychiatrists. Truth has been banished from their minds and so their hearts must perforce have darkness issuing in every foul thing, in the quenching of life at its source, at the extinction of life before its bourne.

Perhaps heresy's foulest crime is this, that it has taken from broken bankrupt humanity the one plank of salvation leading to the Saviour.

The wine has failed long since. There lie the huge waterpots of natural incapacity. But it is forbidden to cast even a glance of anguished pleading towards that loving maternal figure standing beside, as ever she stands beside, the Divine Saviour. Heresy has caused the wine to fail. But it renders impossible the miracle of Cana.

How long, oh Lord. How long!

CHAPTER XXXVI

WE would take the liberty of giving to one of the recorded utterances of Our Lady a completely new meaning. When she found her Son in the Temple after the harrowing experience of His loss she said to Him: "Son, why hast Thou done so to us . . .?" (St. Luke ii, 4, 8). We will put that question once more on those maternal lips, but this time we may read heavenly joy upon the countenance which in the first instance was shadowed by one of her keenest dolours. This time we ask, through Mary herself, why God conferred upon her the unique privilege of Immaculate Conception. Of course, we think that we already know. And we do—but perhaps not as completely and adequately as our needs demand. Obviously the first and radical reason for all God's works outside Himself is His own glory. But our little minds must probe further if they are to possess more than a vague concept. God made Mary immaculate for the sake of His Only-begotten Son. She was the Eternal Father's gift to the Incarnate Word. We cannot be surprised at the magnitude of the gift when we reflect on the love which the Father bears to His Son. So far as it was possible for a creature, Mary was to be worthy of Jesus. The first relation she was to have to Him in His created nature was that of mother. It followed, therefore, that she was to be the best possible mother God could create for His Only-begotten. In the course of these pages we have tried to show some vision of the perfection that this involved in every sphere of Mary's being. We can say, therefore, that God made her immaculate, not only because He would not present as mother to His Son a creature stained with that very thing which was the essential enemy of God—and therefore of Christ—but also because a vitiated nature could not have risen to the exigencies of the Divine motherhood. The unique privilege, therefore, was in view of the mother's need no less than the Son's rights.

It was given, we repeat, in view of Jesus. But who is Jesus?

As we have already seen, He is the whole Christ, Head and members, as He Himself proclaimed Himself to be to the erring Saul. The Immaculate Conception is God's gift to the members, as to the Head. It is His gift to us. The purpose of this chapter will be to show that this gift has practical consequences for us as it had for Mary herself.

Twice in St. Matthew's Gospel, and again in St. Mark, very strong words of Our Lord are recorded. " And if thy right eye scandalise thee, pluck it out and cast it from thee. For it is expedient for thee that one of thy members should perish, rather than thy whole body be cast into hell. And if thy right hand scandalise thee cut it off, and cast it from thee; for it is expedient for thee that one of thy members should perish, rather than that thy whole body go into hell " (St. Mat. v, 29-30). For our purpose it is a significant fact that the context of these Divine words is where Jesus is condemning internal sins, that is, precisely those sins which bubble up as it were from corrupt nature. In the eighteenth chapter of this same Gospel Jesus repeats His warning and recommendation, adding this time the foot to the members which might call for spiritual amputation. This time the setting is the peculiarly touching one where Christ showed at once His love for children and little ones, and His corresponding hatred of anything which could injure their fair innocence. " Woe to the world because of scandals " (St. Mat. xviii, 7). St. Mark recounts the same scene and the same terrible words.

It is always an awe-inspiring thing to listen to the words of the God-man. But there is something divinely compelling in words where the Incarnate God emphasises His clear meaning by repeated phrases. He does so in this case, as He did so in the matter of His Eucharistic promise.

It is true that spiritual writers generally confine the full application of Our Lord's words to occasions of sin which are proximate. If such an occasion by virtue of place or person or thing seems as dear and as necessary to us as a member of our body, it must be plucked out or cut off without mercy. That meaning has always been plain to sincere Christians. And many a great and grand destiny, sometimes culminating in the honours of canonisation has been built on a man's honest assessing of his personal frailty. Might we not say that it was the pledge and all it meant of heroic effort which changed Matt Talbot from

R

what he was, to what he became—to what, please God, he may yet become?

But we hold that the words have a much wider application. And we will see that wide and very personal application if we ask ourselves this question: "Is there anyone in the whole human race who, looking Our Lord in the eyes, can say: No sense of mine, no faculty, no member scandalises me?" Should we be so foolish as to say these words with our eyes on His, very, very quickly would we have to lower them in confusion. And Jesus would not have to say a word. Our hearts would say it for Him.

But one there was who could say it to Him—Mary Immaculate. Has He not said: "By the fruit the tree is known" (St. Mat. xii, 33). And has He not catalogued in sad precision the things that proceed from the corrupt human heart? (St. Mat. xv, 19). But He had made her pure heart a celestial fountain of all sweetness. He was the very first to quench His love-thirst at this unsullied fount. But it is for us, too, and how we need it!

Is not that precisely what her Immaculate Conception meant in practical result, as we have tried to show? Each sense and faculty and member perfect radically and in operation, because preserved immune from the original blight. But now let us gladly make our admission. Our eyes are a scandal to us. How often are they lit by the baneful gleam of bitterness, envy, and darker and more sombre shadows? Our ears lend themselves so readily to the lying voices of the fiends, with their domestic accomplices, ambition and self-love. What are our hands but bungling members, able indeed to cut and wound and even slay but so seldom stretched out to help, so inefficient in well-doing. With our feet we are experts in racing away from grace down the slippery incline of our passions. How dark is our intellect, how badly served by memory and imagination. How prone to evil is our will and using its native strength to shout out " No " to God and His grace. Surely we will gladly admit to Our Divine Lord that we are just such as He said should pluck out and cut off members. We will go further. In His Divine unselfishness He spoke of these members being a scandal to us or to others. But are they not first a stumbling block to Himself? Is it not first over His dead Body—in her lap—that we must cross to eternal perdition? It is at this point that the remedy becomes clear. We must get rid of each sense and faculty and

member. We must divest ourselves of ourselves. But we cannot
live at all thus maimed. It is not so He wishes us to live. Cannot we see it? Why has she that perfect soul and that perfect
body? For Him, we saw. For us, no less. And so to our
surprise we see a scriptural and, therefore, a very, very old basis
for the devotion which seems to sum up all devotion to Mary in
these our days. In fact it is called " true devotion " and is connected with its great expounder, St. Grignon Marie de Montfort. But may we not claim that this rôle was to expound what
had been insinuated and recommended by the Divine Saviour
Himself?

To realise this scriptural background is to remove the last
prejudices against the slavery of Mary. These objections were
due to almost all the false notions of Mary's rôle in relation to
God. Fair as the moon! They allowed themselves to think
that they even could be preoccupied with Mary—as if she was
even capable of concentrating hearts on herself. They objected
to the notion slavery, because they had not realised that we
abdicate from the tottering stool of human corruption in order
to enter into the divine heritage of the queen of angels.

By thus yielding ourselves to Mary's gentle sway we allow
her to use her prerogatives for us. And this is supremely
pleasant for this most unselfish of creatures. Moreover, she is
only too conscious that in queening it over us she is safeguarding
the Christ-life within us, saving Him again from Herod and
Pilate and Judas. But we must beware of a delusion in the
practice of this true devotion. God has never and will never
force a free will. Heaven and Hell alike testify to that. Consequently, no verbal consecration can in itself make us Mary's
slaves. We must will to be such. In practice this means that
we must study her heart, her mind, and think, speak and act
in conformity with her thought, speech and action as her mind
shows it to be. May we hope that these humble pages may give
some faint and fleeting glimpses of that purest of hearts in its
workings. We may borrow the spirit of one of the liturgical
prayers and, addressing our queen, say to her: " Compel even
our rebel will to follow thine."

Well will it be for Jesus when we live by Mary's life. Well
will it be for His Mystical Body. If we are wholly hers she
will seize upon our very thought and word and deed to increase
His sway over souls. Her slavery will save us from being a

stumbling-block to ourselves, to the little ones of Christ and to the Divine Child Himself.

"Son, why hast Thou done so to us?" And pointing to His elect, gathered together at last in the abode of peace and joy, Jesus will reply: "For My own sake, mother mine, for yours, and for all these." May we be amongst that blessed number!

CHAPTER XXXVII

ASSUMPTA EST

MARY is a thought of God. So are the angels. And so are we. The angels are such lovely thoughts of His that He has kept them in His Heaven from the first. As for us, we are born as ugly caricatures of His first design for us, and when baptism brought restoration, all our lives are a striving not to blur His image overmuch, not to obliterate it even. And love had to invent a merciful purgatory where the alloy is melted out and the Divine Refiner sees Himself again in a soul. Only then can He say, " Come."

Mary is God's thought. She is not as the angels. And thank God for it, she is not like us—at least in the things which are least like God's Plan for us. Of course, as we saw in the matter of the Divine decrees, there is really only one decree. For God is infinitely simple. So also is His thought of angel or of man a complete thought. In it there can be no development, no advance from little to big, from good to better. And this Divine attribute shone out in the angelic creation. For when He called them into being they stood before Him in integral nature, as they now are and shall ever be. That is why even the fallen angels trail such greatness after them. It is a greatness for evil, yes, but a greatness for all that. Great in their immortality, great in their volition, in their intelligences too, great in their refusal which has blasted all their being and gifts. Thank God for it, we were not essentially great enough to say a mighty " No " to God and say it for ever. With poor Eve it was a halting, hesitant rebellion—munch after munch of the forbidden fruit. God made us small enough to find a way of saving us. We would not have liked to start off as an archangel!

In humankind, therefore, we can see the development of God's design—even though the plan is already fully drawn. We can see the house a-building. We will see now the building of another ark—the Ark of the Covenant.

God had a thought. It was a soul. It was a soul reflecting

as perfectly as creature could the Infinite Holiness of the Most
High. And He united this peerless soul to a worthy body.
Mary has begun to be. She now lives and breathes who will
one day reveal her identity to a Pyrenean maid.

"I am the Immaculate Conception." God's loveliest created
thought has become visible to us. It is a thought of womanhood as God first thought it. A soul unsullied united with a
beautiful body. Oh, let us tread reverently on this holy ground
where all is of God, all from God. There is here none of that
defilement which a wicked world had piled up around the sacred
creation which is womanhood. Here, around this cradle the
angel hosts keep watch and ward. There the massed legions of
the Seraphim, their flaming love leaping higher as they gaze on
Him and, seeing Him, see also her. The Cherubim are here.
And their illumination from the light of His Countenance becomes more radiant still as they see in Him the Masterpiece of
His creative wisdom. All the choirs are here and Heaven is
vibrant with their adoring cry: "Blessed is God, and holy in
all His works." Aye, of a truth, holy in this His newest
work—the immaculate one.

Yes, this is God's first and last and best and only thought
of womanhood. A fair body perfectly fitted for wifehood and
wifehood's crown—gift of progeny. This is the woman who will
be a helpmate to man. To all men, to a man—but first to a
Man who will be also God. This soul, this body is made for
God. Never was there a woman made for anyone less. This
thought of God is not clothed with the supernal splendours. No,
indeed, rather is she a little bundle of exquisite babyhood. She
is the Immaculate Conception. Yes. But with dark baby eyes
looking out of a little infant face. Hands, too, she has with
little flesh and blood fingers that open and clench as is the way
with baby hands. Not yet may she tread earth's firm floor with
baby feet. But feet she has—and there is no crescent moon
beneath them yet—just cradling clothes.

And God's thought grows. The baby becomes a toddling
child. And childhood blossoms into beauty of girlhood. How
God can think beautiful thoughts. The little one sleeps and eats
and plays. Sleep refreshed that little body which must of a day
give a body to the Holy One of God. Food will build up that
little frame and give it ever newer health and strength for the
weaving of His humanity. This is God's thought in peerless
mind and flawless will, in perfection of every sense and faculty.

And then came Gabriel. And then He came. Oh, how God's thought is overwhelming us with its majesty and wisdom and love. That silent holy night shed its starlight over David's City. And now we see God's thought of womanhood crowned —a Child in her arms. This is God's thought of motherhood. But she is His mother and therefore is she maid. Beautiful Divine thought of virginity.

And now her eyes will gaze into His. He who feedeth amongst the lilies will look back into her eyes and see only what He yearns to see—immaculate innocence.

Now those arms will enfold Him and press Him to her immaculate heart. Always were they round Him in spirit, but now so real, so warm, so loving. And a woman He made her for this, that she should give Him birth and suckle Him. Always has she given Him the sweet food of His Will accomplished, but now the liquid richness of her virginal breasts filled from Heaven for Heaven's King. From her and through her He has taken the humanity which made suffering possible for Him. From His very entrance into her chaste womb suffering had found Him, and His pain was also hers. Clothed in vulnerable flesh and blood—her flesh and blood—He had become the target of sin and of its human agents. The Heavens of Heaven could not contain Him, yet now in His human nature He was so small, so impotent, so utterly unable to protect Himself. And Herod and all Herod's men were on His track. But it was for this that the Father had given Him such a mother. So on her bosom He slept as the Egyptian frontiers and safety were sought and reached. Then God's thought became one of home in little Nazareth with those years of most loving intimacy. How He came to love her footfall, to hear the sound of her voice. Once His Father's business brought Him forth. And her love was in the winepress. But He had returned. How grateful He was to His Heavenly Father for that immaculate privilege of hers which made her a sinless being whose will was ever one with that of the Father. And so Jesus yielded her obedience in all, not as He would of a day obey even Cæsar and Cæsar's minions, but gladly, as eating the bread of His Father's Will, which was also hers. But He went forth again. And this time He will not return. The baby feet which stumbled in her footsteps in Egypt and Nazareth, which as the feet of a child and of a youth were never far from her, are now nailed to a Cross. He cannot come to her. But she will come to Him. Yes, if it is almost shyly and covertly that she will suggest a miracle at Cana, it is not shyly or covertly that she proclaims her motherhood of Him who dies on the tree of infamy—aye, infamy though ours.

And if all the time God's thought was one of beauty now it is seen as strong with the strength of the Most High. For it is of a mother who stands beneath her Son's Cross, of a mother who is of one mind and heart with Him in His immolation of Himself—in His immolation of her with Him.

It is the Divine thought of a God-Man who redeems and of a woman, His mother, who redeems with Him—Co-Redemptrix.

Having given all to us and for us, had Jesus aught else to give? He had the greatest of all His treasures, His mother. And He gave her to us. Only then was it safe for us that He should go. Jesus is dead. But Mary lives. God's thought still bodies forth in her. Now it is the mighty Lover who, with her murdered Child clasped to her bosom, draws thither, too, the guilty heads of those who have slain Him and crushed her heart. She cannot forget those dying words: " Mother, behold thy Son."

Then He rises from the dead. And although the inspired writers do not mention it we have no doubt that He appeared to her first—as to her He had first come in that quiet prayerful room long ago. Comes His Admirable Ascension. Mary, too, must gaze heavenwards with fondest yearning!

God's thought is now filling in even for our poor vision. Now is she Mary of the Supper Room, Mary of the Apostles, Our Lady of the Church. Through her intercession is hastened the coming of the Paraclete. Now He overshadows that upper room as He once overshadowed her. Christ is born again in His Mystic Body.

Now God's thought takes on a homing note. She is at Ephesus with the virgin disciple. And from the Father's Right Hand the Son looks down. Oh, Son of God, why look down on earth? Are you not happy with your myriad angel hosts?

Aye, He loves His angels. But he did not choose one of them to mother Him, He chose her. And she is still down there. If God loves all that He has made surely must He love the dear humanity of her by which she bore Him, nurtured Him, suffered with Him. That humanity of hers enabled her to be His mother. Can He forget the embrace of those dear arms, the hands which clothed His infancy, which guided His first steps? Can he forget the love-light which shone in His mother's eyes, the sweet cadence of her voice as she called Him—my Son?

Is He unmindful now of her protecting love which saved Him from His enemies until the hour of Sacrifice had come?

Mary's is God's thought. And He loves this thought of His. Loves it in all its sweet humanity. Never will He allow it to see corruption. Abyss calleth to abyss. The Infinite love of the Incarnate Word is answered by the created flame leaping from the immaculate heart. He cannot wait any longer. " Come, my love, my dove, my beautiful one."

He cannot wait. The Church knows, and one day will proclaim that He did not.

Assumpta est Maria!

EPILOGUE

Before this book had become even a year old, the wish expressed in its concluding lines has been gloriously verified by the Solemn Dogmatic Definition of Our Lady's Assumption. For that we are overjoyed, quite apart from the book and the unwitting prophecy.

If *Fair as the Moon* has in any measure succeeded in focussing attention on what the endowment of Immaculate Conception has meant in terms of the living breathing Mary, it cannot but gratify both author and readers, that what the great Definition has said in the last analysis, is that all that peerless beauty of sense and faculty, of soul and body—in a word—the whole Mary, Soul and Body, was assumed into Heaven.

THE END

PRINTED BY CAHILL & CO., LTD., PARKGATE PRINTING WORKS, DUBLIN.